Harmonies of
Heaven and Earth

B. Picart dir.

AMPHION BÂTIT LES MURS DE THEBES AU SON DE SA LYRE .   ‖Amphion, erbauwet Thebe, unter angenehmen Seyten spiele .

Amphion builds the walls of Thebes by the Music of his Lyre .‖Amphion, bouwt de Muuren van Thebe ondert speelen op de Lier .

Harmonies of Heaven and Earth

The Spiritual Dimension of Music from Antiquity to the Avant-Garde

Joscelyn Godwin

THAMES AND HUDSON

For Janet

Frontispiece: Amphion builds the walls of
Thebes by the music of his lyre, engraving after
B. Picart from *Jardin des Muses*, 1733.

Parts of this book have appeared in *TEMENOS*, no. 6,
and in *The American Theosophist*, vol. 73, no. 5.

Printed and bound in Great Britain by The Bath Press

Contents

Preface and acknowledgments

This book is the keystone of a project in Speculative Music which began with my paper 'The Revival of Speculative Music', given at the American Musicological Society's meeting in Denver, November, 1980. This paper, subsequently published in *The Musical Quarterly*, and (in German) in *Musiktherapeutische Umschau*, dealt largely with the German-speaking domain. In my collection of essays by Marius Schneider, Rudolf Haase and Hans Erhard Lauer, entitled *Cosmic Music: Three Musical Keys to the Interpretation of Reality* (Lindisfarne Press, 1987), this revival speaks for itself. Next, a two-part article in *TEMENOS*, nos. 4 and 5 (London, 1984), 'The Golden Chain of Orpheus: an Introduction to Musical Esotericism in the West,' outlined the main contributions to this musical branch of the Perennial Tradition, from ancient Greece to the nineteenth century. Some sixty of these sources, in turn, speak for themselves in my anthology *Music, Mysticism and Magic* (Routledge and Kegan Paul, 1986). As much again remains ready for eventual publication: it is the source-material for Part III of the present book.

Harmonies of Heaven and Earth also collects the thoughts of others, some well known, others never before mentioned in English. But rather than proceeding chronologically, it moves through successive layers of a universe which may broadly be called Hermetic. The book is organized in three Parts. Part I discusses the theory and nature of music and its effects over the different levels of a scale of being which includes ourselves and stretches from the stones beneath our feet to the Empyrean Heaven. Part II returns to earth to treat the human dimension of music as it concerns the composer and listener, its moral and religious implications, and its relation to the hidden currents of history. Part III follows, in a chain of linked sections, with the speculative attempts to integrate music with mystical and esoteric theories of the universe: the shifting harmonies of the planets in their courses, and the correspondences of the seven notes of the diatonic scale, the twelve of the chromatic scale, and the unlimited range of harmonics. Part III contains material difficult to find elsewhere, but it is at times rather technical, and not all readers will want to attempt it, nor need they.

Preface and Acknowledgments

This is a personal contribution to the current revival of Speculative Music, for which none of my sources should be held responsible. Neither should those many people who have helped me in various ways, whom I gratefully acknowledge here. Their assistance has ranged from a well placed word to the laborious reading of drafts. Some of them have also gone on wild-goose chases on my behalf, for which I am no less grateful. It is therefore a pleasure to recognize my friends and correspondents John Allitt, Stephen Arnold, Milton Babbitt, Christopher Bamford, Todd Barton, Janet and Colin Bord, Alastair Boyd, David Britt, Elliott Carter, Keith Critchlow, Frank Denyer, Anne Doueihi, Antoine Faivre, David Fideler, Joel Funk, Ailene Goodman, Penelope Gouk, James Haar, Jonathan Harvey, Jackson Hill, David Hykes, Emma Kirkby, Charles Krigbaum, Robert Lawlor, Siegmund Levarie, Cathy Lowne, Shimon Malin, Victor Mansfield, Thomas Mathiesen, Caitlín and John Matthews, Charles Mauzy, Albert Mayr, Ernest McClain, Adam McLean, Michael McMullin, John Michell, Barry Millington, Dexter Morrill, Richard Nicholson, Marco Pallis, Alison Peden, Jill Purce, Kathleen Raine, Luis Robledo, Anthony Rooley, Amnon Shiloah, Robert Stewart, Hildemarie Streich, Colin Timms, Gary Urton, Jeffrey Wollock, Richard Wedgewood, Arthur Wenk, and Basil Wilby. At Colgate University I thank the Research Council for paying typing expenses, my typists Marilyn Jones and Patricia Ryan, and David Everett of the University Library. Finally I mention four people who might have enjoyed this book, but did not live to see the degree to which it is indebted to them: the late Paul Brunton, Anthony Damiani, Albert Seay, and Perkin (D.P.) Walker. What to me is merely speculation, to them is certainty.

PART I

ASCENDING PARNASSUS

CHAPTER ONE

The Marvellous Effects of Music

Amphion and Zethos, twin sons of Zeus and Antiope, were, like many heroes, raised in secrecy to avoid the malevolent forces that sought to destroy them in their infancy. While they were growing up among the herdsmen on Mount Cithaeron, Amphion was favoured by Hermes with the gift of a lyre. Zethos, the more practical brother, taunted him for his devotion to the instrument, which seemed to prevent him from doing anything useful. But later, when the twins had conquered Thebes and were occupied in fortifying the city, it was Amphion's turn to smile. The music of that lyre caused the stones to slide effortlessly into place, while Zethos toiled to shift them with his own brawn. Thus the walls of Seven-Gated Thebes were raised through the power of music.[1]

The myth of Amphion has always been a favourite of writers on music's extraordinary powers. With Orpheus, melting the heart of Pluto with his song, and Arion, summoning his dolphin-rescuer, Amphion completes the mythological trinity of figures who stand like guardian spirits at the head of many an older treatise. Once their stories were simply told, without comment. Later there were attempts to find psychological or symbolic explanations for their apparently incredible feats. Now perhaps the time has come to see them in a new light: for commonly held opinions of music, not to mention stones, are in need of revision.

To dismiss this or any myth as fiction or folly is not to deserve the name of interpreter. Even a materialist must try to find a meaning adequate to the reverence which has always been paid to myths; a core of truth to justify the thousands of years of retelling which no mere fiction can support. Perhaps the best a rationalist could do with the Amphion myth would be to regard it as a folk-memory of the Cyclopean period whose enormous stone monuments are scattered all round the Eastern Mediterranean. Amphion might then have been some prehistoric engineer, possessed of the mathematical knowledge which undergirds all ancient music theory and is one of the legendary gifts of Hermes to mankind. Such a one would have known of techniques and calculations that would make his stone-moving feasible, but the levers, counterweights, and adjustment of inclined planes would have been mysteries to his workmen and onlookers, well deserving the name of 'natural magic' that technology would bear until the modern era. And if this archaic engineer also knew of the helpful effect that rhythmical movement and work-songs can have on a group of labourers, the picture is complete: Amphion was not singing incantations but chanties.

The supernaturalist, on the other hand, will be quite willing to take the myth literally as witness to long-forgotten techniques of prehistoric civilizations. A medieval Arab writer, Masoudi (d. 957), reported a no less extraordinary procedure for the building of the three Pyramids of Gizeh:

Leaves of papyrus, or paper, inscribed with certain characters, were placed under the stones prepared in the quarries; and upon being struck, the blocks were moved at each time the distance of a bowshot (about 150 cubits), and so by degrees arrived at the Pyramids.[2]

And the American Edgar Cayce (1877–1945), who gave his readings of the past in a state of unconscious trance, described the Great Pyramid as

erected by the application of those universal laws and forces of nature which cause iron to float. By the same laws, gravity may be overcome, or neutralized, and stone made to float in air. The Pyramid was thus built by levitation, *abetted by song and chanting* [my italics], much in the same manner in which the Druids of England set up their huge stones at a later period.[3]

Some time before Cayce, A.P. Sinnett had also described these structures as having been built by 'the power of modifying the force we call gravity',[4] while his fellow Theosophist H.P. Blavatsky, referring specifically to the role of sound in such enterprises, went so far as to remark that 'Sound may be produced of such a nature that the pyramid of Cheops would be raised in the air.'[5] And for evidence that this power, like any other, can destroy as well as it can build, we have only to recall the Fall of Jericho, as described in Joshua 6.

Amphion's myth seems to have preserved a record of something on which occultists, at least, are in approximate agreement: the existence in ancient times of secret forces which mankind has now lost. Music, or at least sound, appears to have had some part to play in this.

One of the obsessions of the Renaissance (taking the period in its broadest sense, up to 1700) was the question of ancient or modern superiority in the fine arts, in literature, music, and even in technology. Are we as good as they? – that is the theme of the Battle between the Ancients and the Moderns. If we are not, the human race has declined, as the Ancients always said it had done through its succession of Gold, Silver, Bronze, and Iron Ages. If on the other hand we moderns are superior, then there is hope for a future of unstinted progress, not to mention cause for self-congratulation.

Before this battle was decisively won (at least in the vulgar mind), reverence for antiquity inclined people of the highest rationality to believe myths such as Amphion's. Father Marin Mersenne (1588–1648), for instance, the friend of René Descartes and enemy of all magicians, saw in the old stories of music's power an analogy with the demonstrable power of an organ pipe to set in motion a massive paving-stone, so that one can feel it rattle.[6] He and other Renaissance savants thought that such effects might well have been possible on a larger scale. But in the cold light of modern mechanics, we come no nearer to the truth of the myth through analogies such as this one, or the power of a voice to shatter a glass, the moving of a straw on a sympathetically vibrated lute-string, and other favourite instances of Renaissance theorists. Since they all depend on the normal behaviour of matter under the influence of air waves, the energy received cannot possibly exceed the energy expended. Even in the case of the glass, or of a bridge shaken loose by soldiers marching in step, the disproportionate result is brought about by an accumulation of energy over a period of time. The myths and visions, on the other hand, involve a real disparity between the physical energy expended by singing or playing, and that received through several tons of moving stones. If they have any meaning beyond the reductionist explanation, it is only to be found by taking the plunge into a magical world where unfamiliar laws hold sway: where the most intractable of materials renounce their nature and follow the dictates of some higher order of things, conveyed through sound.

No matter what happened or did not happen at the building of Troy or the raising of the Pyramids, the insight at the core of the Amphion myth is this: that Nature is ultimately responsible not to the common-sensible laws of cause and effect which seem to rule the material world (stones are heavy, hence difficult to move, etc.), but to transcendent principles which have a perpetual existence in a higher order of being. Whoever knows these, as is sometimes granted to Man, can bypass the habits of material nature as one might appeal to a high court over the honest but mistaken decision of a simple policeman. Zethos represents the man – let us say Newtonian man – who is content to abide by the manifest laws of matter. Amphion has seen beyond and learned, as the modern physicists are learning, that the very existence of a self-contained material world is an illusion. It is only an apparent state of universal energy, or perhaps purely of consciousness, and the laws by which it comes forth are musical or harmonic laws. We can scarcely forget that certain manipulations made at this 'immaterial' level can bring about effects so far in excess of the initial impulse that all earthly life now stands in danger of destruction, through the diabolical application of forces that may, long ago, have been tamed to useful ends.

Perhaps Amphion's art was a kind of alchemy of sound, bearing the same relation to everyday mechanics as alchemy does to chemistry. Here again, the rationalist may take it or leave it: but alchemy should be taken seriously in this context, since its principle of reducing an element to its indeterminate first matter, prior to reconstructing it in a nobler form, has its exact parallel in the primal function granted to sound by several schools of esoteric philosophy. One of the most explicit of these is the school of Hindu philosophy known as Sāṁkhya, which analyses minutely how the universe emerges into consciousness. Sound as viewed by the Sāṁkhya is not merely one of five senses – the one caused by air-vibrations – but rather is the parent of all senses. The element to which it corresponds is not air but aether (akaṣa), that all-permeating fifth element ('hence quintessence') out of which the other four have condensed and into which they may be returned. Prior to all perception and to all objects of perception, according to the Sāṁkhya, there must arise the sense of selfhood or principle of individuation (ahaṁkāra). This in itself is 'absolutely homogeneous, inert and devoid of all characters except quantum or mass. With the co-operation of *rajas* [the expansive principle] it is transformed into subtle matter, vibratory, radiant and instinct with energy, and the *tanmātras* [subtle essences] of sound, touch, colour, taste and smell arise.'[7]

These subtle essences are the parents both of the five gross elements (respectively aether, air, fire, water and earth) and of the senses that perceive them. Sound and aether are thus the very first manifestations of objective consciousness – not the first in time, necessarily, but the first in the hierarchy of being. Stones, made largely from the element of earth, could not even exist if aether had not congealed to the degree necessary to form them. He who works with sound is therefore manipulating the source of all we touch and see, taste and smell. But just as the alchemists say, 'Our Mercury is not the common Mercury,' so this sound is not the common sound. That is nothing but a fluttering of the air felt by the eardrums. This primal, etheric sound is perceived in the meaning that may be conveyed to the receptive mind – or, in exceptional cases, the receptive stone.

But it is not necessary to be so philosophical in order to recognize the existence of an unheard music all around us, even permeating our own bodies. All matter is perpetually in a state of vibration. The fact that a certain range of vibrations affects our sense of hearing as sound deafens us, for better or worse, to the immensely wider range of vibrations which we cannot hear. A group investigating megalithic stone circles in Britain,[8] notably the Rollright Stones in Oxfordshire, has found that the stones actually give off ultrasonic vibrations of extraordinary strength, varying in regular patterns according to the time of day, phase of the moon, and season of the year. The professional chemist Don Robins who is in charge of this research has been brought to the conclusion that the matter of the stones and the geometry of their placement transduces the microwave energy coming from the sun, amplifying it to a very high level and giving it off in regular pulses. Applying his methods to a modern stone circle, built according to the ancient principles, Robins says that he found the ultrasonic energy so high that it damaged his instruments.

How did the Ancients detect this energy, and, if they were aware of it, what did they do with it? Robins is too cautious to speculate, restricting his programme to measurement and observation. But when one learns that scientists today are experimenting with ultrasonic vibrations to dissolve kidney-stones, and to levitate and isolate cancerous cells in the blood, it does seem that perhaps something is being rediscovered rather than freshly invented, needless to say under different conditions from those that prevailed both in Man and Nature even as recently as four thousand years ago. Deeds such as Amphion's are more laborious today because the solidification of the world has gone too far. The German Romantic writer Novalis (1772–1801) was one of the first of the modern age to recognize that the world itself must have altered significantly since mythical or even archaic times. In his philosophical novel *Heinrich von Ofterdingen* he writes:

In olden times the whole of nature must have been more alive and conscious than it is today. Impressions which the beasts scarcely seem to notice nowadays, only being perceived and enjoyed by humans, would in those days move even lifeless bodies; and so it was possible for ingenious men to do things and produce phenomena which we now consider altogether incredible and fabulous. Thus it was in very ancient times, in the lands which are now Greece, so travellers say who have heard these tales told there even today by the peasant folk. There were bards then who were able to apply the strange sounds of their marvellous instruments in such a way as to waken the secret life of the forests, the spirits hidden in the tree-trunks; they could revive the dead seeds in barren wastelands so that gardens would blossom forth; they tamed terrible beasts and induced savage men to become civilized and orderly; they imbued them with gentle dispositions and taught them peaceful pursuits; they could transform raging torrents into still waters, and transport even the dead stones in regular dancing motion. At the same time they were soothsayers and priests, lawgivers and healers; the higher beings themselves were drawn down by their magical arts, and instructed them in the secrets of the future, the proportions and natural structures of all things, and revealed to them the inner virtues and healing powers of numbers, plants and all creatures. It was then, so the story goes, that the manifold tones and wonderful sympathies and orderliness came into a nature which before had been completely wild, disorderly and hostile. It is seldom that any of these traces survive to this day as a memorial to those benefactors, for either their art or that tender sensitivity of Nature has been lost.[9]

There is no compelling reason, after all, to believe that the physical world as we know it is in its only possible state, particularly if it is granted a value contingent on the spiritual, rather than an absolute value in itself. The more subtle and uncongealed its substance, the more susceptible it will be to the formative forces of sound. The modern Swiss scientist, artist, and physician Hans Jenny has demonstrated exactly this.[10] Under laboratory conditions he has photographed the effects that tone has on smoke, fluid, and the finest granular substances such as lycopodium powder: it forms them into beautiful and orderly shapes, extraordinarily similar to those of Nature, both organic and inorganic. Jenny brings to his researches a sensitivity to the cosmos as a living entity, and calls his new science 'Cymatics' (from Greek *kyma*, wave), dedicated to the study of creative vibration on every level from the molecule to the galaxy. He is uncovering hidden laws which, if Novalis' surmise is right, were once evident to all.

One element of the far-ranging myth of Orpheus also concerns this power of music over the Kingdoms of Nature. Some say that Orpheus' lyre was the gift of Apollo, and his instructors the Muses; others that his teacher was the lyre's original inventor, Hermes. All ancient authors agree that his powers were miraculous: he could move stones and trees, charm beasts, and even receive obeisance from the 'mountain tops that freeze'. At his music 'Mount Ismaros saw the foliage on her trees grow stiff and her forests course up and down her sides' (Martianus Capella).[11] The claims advanced on Orpheus' behalf are so extravagant that even Classical commentators tended to interpret them tropologically, suggesting that the 'stones' and 'trees' concerned were the breasts and hearts of men as dense as rocks and as dumb as vegetables. But the vegetable kingdom is not so dumb, and it certainly is not deaf. In another place the fifth-century poet Martianus Capella introduces us to Apollo's Grove at Cirrha, near Delphi, where 'a sweet music arose from the trees, a melody arising from their contact as the breeze whispered through them'.[12] The highest, middle, and lowest branches produced, he says, the basic intervals of octave, fifth, fourth, and whole-tone, thus pouring forth, 'with melodious harmony, the whole music and song of the gods.' The Jesuit polymath Athanasius Kircher (1602–80) accepted this idea, as he did so many ancient musical myths, saying that the wind in pine-trees does actually have this effect if the trees themselves are of suitably proportionate heights.[13] But he went further with the observation that some plants are harmoniously proportioned in themselves. He cites in particular the equisetum (horsetail) as having its nodes spaced exactly as the divisions of the monochord, in the proportions 1:2:3:4. . . One of Kircher's pupils actually made an instrument from a giant cane with fifteen subdivisions, and found that Nature had provided the requisite proportions for perfect intonation over two octaves. The details of construction are not given, but I presume that he cut its sections up and blew them like a panpipe or Syrinx: another mythological instrument.

Taking advantage of Nature's wisdom in another way – and perhaps influenced by the medical thought of Paracelsus, for whom every healing plant embodied the influence of a particular star – Giovanni Battista Porta wrote in 1558 that diseases could be cured by music if played on instruments made from the stalks or wood of plants having the appropriate curative properties.[14] Lymphatics might be relieved by piping on the stalk of the hellebore, as they are by ingesting that herb; people might be sexually stimulated by flutes made of the aphrodisiac satyrion, and so on. It is a bizarre concept, but fully in accord with the idea of a nature imbued with the 'wonderful sympathies and orderliness' to which Novalis refers.

Wood is of course the resonant substance *par excellence* and the primary material of most musical instruments: the viol and violin families, the lute, the harp, harpsichord, piano, and all the woodwinds, to name only the Western ones. It is remarkable that in so many of these the resonator is of wood while the actual sound-generator is of animal origin. The bowed instruments work through the friction of horsehair on 'catgut' strings (actually sheep's guts). On the plucked instruments the fingers usually touch the gut strings directly, while the medieval psaltery and lute were played with feathers. Quills, or occasionally leather plectra, pluck the strings of the harpsichord; leather or wool (felt) covered hammers hit those of the piano. Drums and tambourines have heads of skin, and the wooden cornetto a horn or ivory mouthpiece. Marius Schneider (1903–82), the Alsatian musicologist and ethnologist who will appear several times in this book, has observed that in the cultures where music is still used as a magical force, the making of an instrument always involves the sacrifice of a living being.[15] That being's soul then becomes part of the instrument, and in the tones that come forth from it the 'singing dead' who are ever present with us make themselves heard. Certainly it seems that the more highly refined animal substances are necessary to obtain the fullest range of musical vibrations, while the best vessels for receiving and amplifying these are provided by the vegetable kingdom (wood or gourds). It is appropriate, then, that the Greek philosophers used the word for wood, *hyle*, to denote the material substratum of the universe, passive to all the formative forces which may well be looked upon as vibratory or musical in nature. The ultimate symbol of this is the figure of Christ, the Creative Logos, crucified upon the wooden Cross, its four beams representing among other things the four elements that make up the material world.[16] The metaphysical poet George Herbert (1593–1633), contemplating this, wrote in his poem *Easter*:

> The crosse taught all wood to resound his name,
> Who bore the same.
> His stretched sinews taught all strings, what key
> Is best to celebrate this most high day.

Since Herbert was still part of the late Renaissance intellectual movement which accepted the doctrine of correspondences, the parallel between the Crucified and a stringed instrument is no mere poetic conceit but the representation of a true harmony or resonance between different levels of the cosmos. The doctrine of correspondences, which has its first foundation in the Hermetic axiom 'As above, so below', regards these likenesses not as chance or whim but as the very texture of a cosmos which without them would lapse (as it has for some people today) into meaninglessness.

The mythical powers of Orpheus' music over growing things might, in the same context, be interpreted as his knowledge of those laws of correspondence, those harmonic laws that lie behind and govern all of Nature. This would be fully consonant with the tradition of Orpheus as sage and theologian, not merely musician, and of music as the all embracing science of things both natural and divine.

A more literal interpretation comes to mind, however, when one reads of the many experiments made with growing plants and audible, not intellectual music in Peter Tompkins and Christopher Bird's *The Secret Life of Plants*.[17] These authors have collected an impressive body of evidence that plants flourish when certain music or even single tones are played in their vicinity. They describe experiments in India, Canada, and the USA which find that plants have germinated and sprouted fast, or produced more crop, in the presence of sounds as various as Indian ragas broadcast by loudspeaker over rice paddies, *Rhapsody in Blue* played all day and all night, continuous loud tones of certain high pitches or of no particular pitch, and an electric tuning-fork played for half an hour at dawn. On the other hand, the note F played for eight hours a day, or random noise, has been known to retard or even kill the plants subjected to it. Obviously one cannot generalize from the scattered evidence of uncoordinated researchers, except to say that plants apparently thrive under conditions that would drive a person crazy.

Tompkins and Bird describe something more interesting and provocative in the work of Dorothy Retallack,[18] who subjected plants experimentally to various types of music, judging their response not only from their general state of health but from the degree to which they leaned towards or

18

away from the loudspeaker that was broadcasting the music. Retallack's experiments, carried out in 1968–1971 at Temple Buell College in Colorado, brought her national fame, or notoriety, as the case may be. She found the following scale of responses:

Most favourable

Plants incline towards sound source	⎧ Indian sitar music ⎫ ⎨ Western classical music, 18th and 19th centuries ⎬ ⎩ 'La Paloma' played on strings; Jazz (Armstrong, Ellington) ⎭
Plants indifferent to sound source	⎰ Silence; Country and Western music; ⎱ String quartets by Schoenberg, Berg, Webern
Plants incline away from sound source	⎰ 'La Paloma' played on steel drums ⎱ Percussive and 'hard rock' pop music

Least favourable

The responses to the Retallack experiments were predictably emotional. People are very defensive about their musical tastes, and to see them rated high or low by the impartial plant-critics made some complacent, others angry. The excitement generated by the media prompted some experts (though certainly not expert in this kind of study) to dismiss angrily the whole concept of plants' sensitivity to music as just another bit of amateur pseudo-science. The *New York Times* remarked that the academicians found the whole thing an excruciating embarrassment, and by now it has been conveniently forgotten.

As Tompkins and Bird point out, it is usually not theoretical scientists but practical ones, such as engineers, who become interested in such phenomena, being free from the baggage of accepted dogmas as to what can or cannot happen. And of course no devoted gardener needs any statistics to prove that plants have feelings.

The third mythical exponent of music's remarkable powers over the lower worlds was Arion, the dolphin-charmer of Lesbos. No one has told the story more beautifully than Novalis, following immediately on the passage already cited from *Heinrich von Ofterdingen*.

In these times once it happened that one of those wonder-working poets, or rather composers – since music and poetry can actually be as one, and perhaps really belong together like mouth and ear, the mouth being only a mobile and responsive ear – one of these composers wished to voyage across the sea to a foreign land. He was rich in beautiful jewels and other valuable objects which had been given him as rewards. He found a ship at the port, and the people seemed willing to take him to his destination for the fare agreed upon. But the beauty and elegance of his treasures soon aroused their covetousness to such a degree that they plotted to throw him in the sea and then divide his property among them. So when they reached the open sea they fell on him and told him he must die, because they had determined to throw him overboard. With the greatest composure he bade them spare his life, offered them his treasures as ransom and prophesized that the worst of misfortunes would befall them if they should go through with their plan. But neither plea nor threat could move them, for they feared now that he would reveal their crime if he lived. When he saw them so determined, he asked if they would at least allow him to play his swan-song before the end, and then with his polished wooden lyre to leap into the sea before them, of his own free will. They knew well that if they heard his magic song their hearts would melt and they would be seized with remorse; so while allowing him his last request they took care during his song to stop their own ears tightly so that they would hear none of it and hold to their resolve. And so it was. The singer voiced a wonderfully rousing song: the whole ship resonated with him, the waves joined in, sun and stars appeared together in the sky, and out of the green waters leaped dancing shoals of fish and sea monsters. The sailors stood angrily apart with their ears stopped and waited impatiently for the song to be over. Soon it was finished. Then the singer, his face radiant, sprang into the dark abyss with his miraculous lyre in his hand. Scarcely had he touched the shining waves when there rose beneath him the broad back of a grateful monster, and speedily it swam away with the astonished singer. After a short time it reached the coast to which he had wished to go, and set him down gently in the reeds. The bard sang a song of joy to his rescuer and went on his way with thanksgiving. But after a while he returned once more to the shore of the sea and in melting notes he mourned the lost treasures which were so dear to him as mementos of happier hours and as tokens of love and gratitude. And as he sang, suddenly his old friend came splashing out of the sea again, and let fall the stolen treasures from its jaws on to the sand. The sailors, after the singer's leap, had straightaway begun to divide their legacy; but fell to quarrelling over the portions and ended with a murderous fight which cost most of them their lives. The few who survived could not manage the ship alone, and it soon came to shore where it broke up and sank. It was all they could do to save their own lives and reach dry land with their hands empty and their clothes in rags. And so the grateful sea-beast found the treasures at the bottom of the sea and restored them to the hands of their rightful owner.

Novalis does not name Arion, nor mention, as does every ancient source from Herodotus[19] onwards, that the sea-monster was a dolphin, of all animals the one whose intelligence seems to be closest to that of man. Other classical authors have written of the dolphin's fondness for humans, especially children. Pliny the Elder tells a tale of a boy whom a dolphin used to carry each day to school in a town along the coast; the late Greek poet Oppian of another who would summon his dolphin friend by name, play with it, embrace it, and ride far out to sea on its back.[20] In the past it was customary to dismiss Arion in the same breath as Amphion (and often to confuse the two), but nowadays such stories begin to seem more plausible again. Dolphins, both wild and in captivity, have shown themselves both highly intelligent and unusually sympathetic to man, being eager to play with humans without any of the normal animal motives of reward or domestic dependence. They seem to play as man's equals, which in brain size they certainly are, however differently they may apply their brains. In recent times they have been known to save the lives of swimmers in distress, nudging them toward the shallows. In several parts of the world individual dolphins have become familiars, like the female in Oporoni, New Zealand, who in 1955–56 was adopted by the village because she was so friendly to the local children. Like the dolphins of legend, she too would take them for rides, which is something that no untamed and untrained horse, let alone any wild animal, would do.[21]

But what makes dolphins, and the Cetacea in general, especially interesting is their musicality. Their hearing is exceptionally acute, extending far beyond the human audible frequency range to pitches as high as 180,000 Hz (the adult human limit is about 18,000 Hz, over three octaves lower). Since sound travels well in water, propagating with a speed four times as fast as on land, it is quite wrong to think of the ocean as silent, or of its inhabitants as mute as aquarium fish. Dark it certainly is; and for this reason the toothed whales (sperm whale, killer whale, dolphins, and porpoises) do their hunting as bats do, by sonar or echo-sounding. The sperm whale hunts giant squids and octopi in the perpetual night of oceans 3,000 feet deep. The vast 'melon' of its head is apparently an echo-locating organ which gives it directional information superior to that of any current human device, and from which it can tell the distance, shape, size, species, and some say the intentions of other animals. Dolphins, whose sonar has been more thoroughly investigated, use a highly refined vocal mechanism of clicks and whistles, produced internally by recycling rather than expelling air, which is capable of imitating human words and is potentially so loud that it is thought they may use it to stun or kill the fish they feed on.[22] Normally the dolphin sends out periodic sonic and supersonic clicks in bursts of up to 800 per second. Their echoes bring all the spatial information the dolphin needs; animals in captivity do not mind being blindfolded by experimenters, but they will never allow their melon-foreheads to be covered, for this is apparently where the information is received.

It is difficult to imagine such a mode of perception, and one can only guess at the acoustical elements that carry the messages, but according to all accepted definitions the animal's experience must be a musical one. If the dolphin is in motion, the echo will be heard with the pitch-change characteristic of a Doppler effect (as with the siren of a fast-moving ambulance: the pitch is heard to rise as it approaches, and fall as it leaves). All distances will be perceived as different rhythmic intervals. An echo heard as the next sound is emitted will give rise to beats or to a chord. One's imagination may supply other intriguing features. They prove that the dolphin's world must be literally shaped by sound, as ours is by sight. It is therefore not at all surprising that these animals should be attracted to our music, as we are to birdsong. One modern observer actually reports that 'woodwind music, gently played, attracts dolphins to swim around a sail boat stationary or slowly moving at sea, where the waves are quiet and there is no engine to suppress the notes. They seem to listen with enjoyment and certainly are very curious at first, poking their heads out of the water to stare at the source.'[23]

It is the other suborder of Cetacea, however, who are the real performing musicians. These are the giant, toothless baleen whales who feed by straining the water through their whalebone moustaches. Many people have heard the recordings of the humpback whale which have been an inspiration to composers (George Crumb, Paul Winter) and conservationists alike. These songs, unlike the dolphin's clicks and whistles, sound really musical to the human ear. They are long and sustained, far-ranging, wandering melodies, strangely punctuated with noises, and full of the eerie resonance of the underwater world. The humpback whales have been separated for untold ages into the Atlantic and Pacific groups, yet the songs of the two regions still have some phrases in common. But the most surprising thing is that in each ocean all the humpbacks sing a different song each year. The same song has been found on the same date at places 750 miles apart. How do they learn it? What does it mean as it resounds through the depths, sometimes audible at the incredible distance of 100 miles? Do the songs perhaps embody the true meaning of whale-life, to which survival is merely a means? One cannot help wishing to believe that other animals than man also live for aesthetic, relational, or intellectual values.

In view of all this it is fitting that the dolphin – the only cetacean common in the Mediterranean – should have been sacred to Apollo. The god himself took this form in order to compel a Cretan ship to sail to the place of his oracular temple at Delphi, where the sailors were appointed servitors of his cult and bidden to worship him as 'dolphin-like' (*Delphinios*).[24] And it is also appropriate, considering the importance we are going to see given to music in the journeys of the soul, that in late antique imagery dolphins should be the vehicles by which souls cross over Ocean and voyage to the

Fortunate Isles: a symbolic meaning to which the myth of Arion is also susceptible, in every detail (even those added by Novalis).

Certain legends of the effects of music on animals became commonplace in ancient, medieval and renaissance writings. Martianus Capella, a favourite source for later writers, includes in his *Marriage of Philology with Mercury* a long speech by Harmonia – an 'omnium gatherum' of our subject-matter – in which she mentions the charming of stags by shepherds' pipes, the clattering sounds that cause fish to stop swimming in the stagnant pools of Alexandria, the strains of the cithara that attract Hyperborean swans, and the Indian elephants and cobras that can be restrained by music, the latter bursting asunder from the effect.[25] Such a tradition was also current in the medieval Islamic world, especially with regard to the use of songs to encourage camels to work. In his essay on music the famous philosopher A.H. Al-Ghazālī[26] repeats a popular story of a man who visited a desert encampment and found there a black slave in fetters, and every camel lying dead save one. The owner explained that the slave had sung the driving-song in so fine a voice that he had made the camels perform a three-days' journey in one night, after which they had died of exhaustion. The guest longed to hear the voice. 'Then when the morning came he commanded that he should sing to a camel that it might draw water from a well there. And when he lifted up his voice and that camel heard it, he ran wild and broke his tether and I fell on my face.'

Athanasius Kircher[27] tells from his own experience of the luring of swordfish by music, which he witnessed on a journey to Sicily in May 1638. The fishermen attracted their prey by sounding bells and singing a certain song – no other would do – whereupon the swordfish came close enough to be harpooned. Kircher says that he was at first of the opinion that the song was an incantation that brought about the desired result through the agency of demons. But after thinking it over, he decided that there was a natural explanation which he preferred to the superstitious one. He knew from experience that all sound is propagated spherically from its source, and that as it meets various obstacles most of them will not respond, but some may be set in sympathetic motion. So he surmises that, just as in the experiment of two lutes, or of the loose paving-stone rattled by a certain organ note, perhaps certain animals respond to specific sounds because something in their 'animal spirits or phantasy' (explained below, pp. 25–26) vibrates in sympathetic mode. In some cases, he says, this occurs across a whole species: all bears, for example, love to hear the flute. In others it is specific to the individual, as in the proper names we give to dogs, horses, and other domestic animals. Kircher has even heard tell of a dolphin named Simon and a manatee named Martin who would always come when called. Why, then, should not the Sicilian fishermen have discovered the exact sounds to which all swordfish are, as it were, attuned, and to which they automatically respond?

Even Kircher's own pupil, Caspar Schott, found this theory a bit far-fetched.[28] But in general Kircher's explanation of the power of music by way of the sympathetic vibration of 'animal spirits', or of some equally intangible substance, is typical of nearly all the pre-modern accounts of the matter. It presupposes the existence of a subtle aether, already explained above as posited by the Sāṃkhya school, which is a fundamental assumption alike of ancient Greek, Oriental and Renaissance natural philosophies. In order for this aether to be acceptable in the light of modern science, it must be distinguished (as we do by its spelling) from the universal ether accepted by physicists until the end of the nineteenth century, and of course from the chemical substance of the same name. Esoteric philosophy relates the aether more to states of consciousness than to states of matter, while allowing that in some way it may be the bridge between the two.

In the *Confessio Fraternitatis R. C.* of 1615, one of the anonymous manifestos of the 'Fraternity of the Rosy Cross', there is a list of marvels that are promised to mankind through the Rosicrucian Philosophy. Among these is the following:

Whosoever can sing with the voice or play on an instrument so as to attract not the rocks of Amphion, but pearls and gemstones; not the beasts of Orpheus, but the spirit; not Pluto from Tartarus, but the mighty princes of the world: he shall enter the Brotherhood.[29]

The English physician and theosopher Robert Fludd (1574–1637) was moved to support this manifesto with a defence of the unknown Fraternity against its detractors. In his *Tractatus Apologeticus* of 1617, while treating this particular claim, he gives a revealing account of the Hermetic world view within which such things could actually come to pass. The Sun or Apollo, he says, showers down each year the 'notes and harmonious sounds of his lyre into the aethereal matter concealed in earth and sea'. These 'tones' remain concealed in creatures, as fire lies hidden in wood, whence whoever can strike a light or apply another fire can bring it forth. In the same way, he who knows 'the true Phoebic tones' of objects can bring them into sensible action and draw them to himself. Observing that pearls and precious stones are especially full of this aethereal nature, Fludd suggests that if one could produce 'a unison of celestial harmony in note and voice, there might occur that consonance, by virtue of the middle or airy spirit, by which the bodies of pearls and gems would be moved.'[30] In a telling parallel, he says that it is no more impossible for a wise man to move with his harmony this essential substance which has descended from the aethereal heaven into lower bodies, than it is for the soul to move the body of an animal.[31]

Few words have been burdened with more different shades of meaning than the English *spirit*, the French *esprit*, and their parent the Latin *spiritus*. They can mean anything from the Third Person of the Trinity to the volatile fumes that emanate from brandy. In particular, they have been used in two distinct ways by writers belonging to the Western esoteric tradition. Recently, under the influence of Theosophy, Spirit tends to mean the most divine part of Man, equivalent to the Greek *Nous* or Higher Intellect, hence superior to its companions Soul and Body. The other meaning, which prevails in earlier texts, is of something far lower on the scale of being that is neither body nor soul but in some way unites them. It is this meaning that concerns us here, and for which I retain the Latin term *spiritus* or use the plural 'spirits'.

The recognition that a subtle or aetheric essence is involved in human vitality, emotion and perception is almost universal. The Hindus know it as *prana*. In the Chinese Taoist treatise on spiritual alchemy, *The Secret of the Golden Flower*, it is a light that circulates through the body. Its acceptance in the West was due at first to the authority of Galen, the second-century physician whose works were canonical to both the Christian and Islamic Middle Ages. Although *spiritus* is generally regarded as invisible, the mystical philosopher Ibn Sina (Avicenna) described it as a luminous substance, varying in quantity and quality from one person to another.[32] At the beginning of the Scientific Revolution, it received a new lease of life through its unquestioning adoption by Francis Bacon, an example that was followed as often as not well into the eighteenth century. After that time it lost its medical respectability but recurred in less orthodox quarters under such guises as Mesmer's Animal Magnetism, Baron Reichenbach's Odic Force, Bulwer-Lytton's Vril, Wilhelm Reich's Orgone. People today who see auras, either unaided or through Kilner screens, are probably perceiving it.

One of the most enthusiastic writers on *spiritus* and music was the Renaissance Platonist Marsilio Ficino (1433–99).[33] His book *De vita coelitus comparanda*[34] is a treatise on how to preserve oneself in good condition through the proper conduct of physical and mental life: something of which he says scholars must be particularly careful, since they lead a sedentary existence, are prone to melancholy, and are always using up their *spiritus* through the exercise of the imagination. One of the best ways of improving the *spiritus*, according to Ficino, is through music. This is because the medium of sound, air, is the most similar to it in substance. He describes part of its operations as follows: 'Musical sound by the movement of the air moves the body: by purified air it excites the aerial *spiritus* which is the bond of body and soul: by emotion it affects the senses and at the same time the soul.'[35]

But how exactly does this excitation work? The composer and theorist Agostino Steffani (1653–1728), a late musical Ficinian, wrote in 1695 of how on hearing the interval of the octave one feels a dilation of the *spiritus*, and a little less so with the perfect fifth and other consonances. Dissonant intervals, on the other hand, constrain the *spiritus*, and as they become harsher cause actual discomfort.[36] Earlier in the century Tommaso Campanella thought of the subjective effects of music on the *spiritus* in quite another way: low-pitched sounds bruise, condense, and thicken it, while high ones rarify and lacerate it. Consequently the most therapeutic music for him is the consonant combination of the two extremes.[37] But most writers are content to treat the effects in more general terms, sometimes glossing over the distinction between this subtle substance and the element of the air.

In the eighteenth century the whole understanding of perception was in a state of flux as earlier concepts were found wanting, yet no new discoveries served to take their place. The question was, how do the tones get from the ear to the perceiving soul? The philosopher Leibniz, in the 1690s, wrote that our 'animal spirits' (i.e the *spiritus*) respond to the sympathetic echo caused in us when we hear the air in regular motion,[38] this anticipating his famous definition of music as an 'occult numeration of the soul'. The musical theologian Johann-Michael Schmidt (1754) explained that although everything in the brain is astonishingly subtle and escapes observation, the tone-vibrations 'imprint the material surrounding the seat of the soul.'[39] For the physician Richard Browne (1729), as for Ficino, *spiritus* again acts as the link between music and Man, distributing its effects both to the body and the soul. The greater the secretion of the *spiritus*, the better the animal machine works, and the happier we feel – for 'there is a sympathy betwixt the Soul and the Animal spirits'.[40] Singing helps augment the *spiritus* by building up air-pressure in the lungs and speeding up the blood circulation.[41] Opium, too, 'makes the spirits flow in gentle undulations', but should not be over-used.[42] Browne goes on:

But of all the Exercises whatever, dancing to a well-played consort seems to be the most beneficial, for it does not only elevate the depress'd Motions of the Solids and Fluids . . . but at the same time is assisted by the mighty Power and Energy of Musick: for as the Harmony of Sounds, by means of the Organ of Hearing, communicates a sovereign Pleasure to the Intellectual Principle, and fills the Mind with gay enlivening Ideas, so by Sympathy it transmits its delightful Influences to the Body, adds new Life and Vigour to the whole Machine, and raises Sensation and Motion to their utmost degree of Perfection.[43]

Another English physician, Richard Brocklesbury (1722–97), was also concerned with how music affects the body, and concluded that it was through changes in the mind. But things did not seem so simple to him as to the cheerful Browne. He admits in a book of 1749 that in order to stay healthy and retard old age the spirits must be continually renewed, as they are exhausted by inordinate passions and pains.[44] The process can be helped by music, to the extent that modern musical cures can be claimed just as well as ancient ones. (He himself had cured a man, driven to hopeless depression by the loss of his two sons, by means of music.) How it actually happens we will never understand unless one day we 'have equally clear ideas of the properties commonly ascribed to spirit, as we can possibly have of those of material objects; yet the essences of both are equally involved in obscurity, and may probably remain eternally inexplicable to limited beings.'[45]

Brocklesbury has touched the subject to the quick: to think that *spiritus* really explains the mind-body connection is to assume that we know more than we do about either mind or body. One is in danger of needing an indefinite series of further links to explain the connections between soul and spirits, spirits and body, and so on.

Several of his contemporaries had given up altogether this search for missing links. The famous mathematician and amateur of music Leonard Euler (1708–83) believed in 1739 that there is no bridge between the body and the soul but the nerve-endings in the brain's *corpus callosum*.[46] Johann Wilhelm Albrecht (1734) ingeniously explained the effect of music on the body as happening quite independently of the ear, through the direct resonances of the body's own fibres, corresponding in tension and length to the tones.[47] What is remarkable about Brocklesbury is that he is not only a Ficinian but also a Berkeleian mentalist, hence able to make an epistemological leap and consider the whole process from the opposite direction to these other philosophers: all simple perceptions of mind, he says, are primarily caused by an impulse from within that is somehow impressed on the sense organs. These in turn convey images of external things to the sensitive part where the mind resides.[48] Brocklesbury appears to be describing some such process as this:

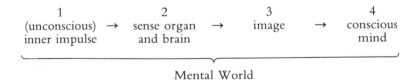

1		2		3		4
(unconscious)	→	sense organ	→	image	→	conscious
inner impulse		and brain				mind

Mental World

27

which is significantly different from the commonly imagined sequence:

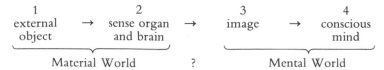

1		2		3		4
external object	→	sense organ and brain	→	image	→	conscious mind
Material World			?		Mental World	

Having started from the harmless idea of animal spirits and an intermediate, etheric world in which sound is properly at home, we have now plunged into deep waters indeed. Whence does this 'inner impulse' arise, and if it is within us, what is the object that we perceive? We must turn briefly from epistemology to metaphysics, for otherwise the whole subject of this book will be without a philosophical foundation.[49]

The Orient, at least, has long known that the subject-object or mind-body gap can indeed be bridged, but only by rising to the level at which both contraries retreat into relative unreality. That there is a primary consciousness in the innermost core of the individual, every traditional philosophy admits, and every mystic knows. It is here that experiences can take place which reverse the everyday state of subject-object consciousness. For instance, in the course of contemplating an object – perhaps a flower or an icon, or equally a piece of music – the person may dissolve into the thing seen or heard and for a while become identified with it, so that the object is experienced as indistinguishable from the subject. Or again, through practices such as self-observation, the subjective consciousness of the person may itself become objective to a further, impassive witness-self, from which vantage-point the spectacle of one's person acting and perceiving *vis-à-vis* a material world constitutes a unity. What is essential to this 'mentalistic' line of thought is that no independent objective world can possibly exist without the presence of consciousness: the two arise and fade together.

In Buddhist philosophy, the entire universe with all its beings is created anew and destroyed at each instant. For the Sufis, God's desire to know himself brings about his splitting into innumerable consciousnesses, each with its distinct variety of objective experience. The common ground between the two is the reduction of the body-mind dichotomy from an absolute to a relative status. Subject and object are like two faces of a coin which can never come together except through the gold upon which both are stamped, and which is the coin's reason for existence. As soon as the gold is coined from its molten shapelessness, it has to have two faces looking in opposite directions.

So in the present case one can say that the experience of music entails (a) an objective material world in which people play instruments, air and eardrums vibrate, electrical impulses act in the brain; and (b) a subjective world of musical emotions, images, and rational thoughts. But (b) is no more the result of (a) than it is the cause: the two simply arise together as twin aspects of a single event (Brocklesbury's 'inner impulse') whose reality is of a mental, not a material order, and inaccessible to physical science.

Neither brain nor *spiritus* is denied by this metaphysical view: they exist as parts of a mechanism for presenting the world-thought to consciousness. But that which actually becomes conscious is the soul, and it is here that music properly belongs. Here it works its effects of cause and cure. The 'Brethren of Purity' (Ikhwān al-Ṣafā'), a community of tenth-century Muslim encyclopedists, wrote that

The matter which is the subject of every art that is practised with the hands is composed of natural bodies, and its products are all physical forms, *except for the matter which is the subject of the musical art, which is entirely composed of spiritual substances which are the souls of the hearers*, their effects also being spiritual manifestations. In effect, melodies which are composed of notes and rhythms leave an impression on the soul similar to that made by the artisan's work on the material which is the substratum of his art.[50] [My italics.]

Music is able to make this direct impression on the soul because 'it is allied to us by nature' – the words with which Boethius (*c.* 480–524) opened his treatise on music and which were read by every university student of the Middle Ages and Renaissance. This similitude, however, has been interpreted differently at different times, and the form which it takes will depend on the particular philosophy of human nature which is assumed by the interpreter. For the Pythagoreans, by whom Boethius was largely influenced, both music and the soul share a basis in number. Music is demonstrably numerical, as experiments with the monochord had shown them. In the Pythagorean tradition the soul is also made from number because it reflects the structure of the World-Soul, whose mathematical formation is set out by the Pythagorean philosopher Timaeus in Plato's dialogue of that name. We will have more to say in later chapters about these cosmic and numerical dimensions of music. A theory such as Schopenhauer's also belongs in this context. Although this philosopher's ultimate realities were not, like the Pythagoreans', mathematical ones, his claim that music is the image and expression of the universal Will that is also the ground of our being[51] places the 'natural alliance' at a very deep level.

For music theorists of the eighteenth century, the similarity tended to be a more superficial one. Music was regarded as an imitative art, as surely as painting, its particular function being the imitation of emotional states and their reproduction, by some means or other, in the soul of the listener. The Romantics, being less mechanistic and more intent on the individual, placed the emphasis on the feelings of the composer himself, which being experienced by the listener made of music a language of personal communication in which soul speaks to soul. Later, the reduction of the human mind (one dare not call it soul) to a processor of information made it possible for music to be understood in terms of information-content alone, its emotional baggage being mere behavioural side-effects. Alternatively, if as in Marxism the human being is inconceivable apart from social relationships, music can be interpreted quite cogently as the bearer of social significances alone.

There are numerous legends that illustrate how music may affect people even against their will, forcing their souls into alignment with it. The classical instance most often repeated over the centuries is that of Pythagoras himself.[52] Walking out one night to contemplate the heavens, he came upon a young Sicilian who had been jilted by his woman and, incited by the Phrygian music of a nearby aulos-player, was preparing to set fire to her house. Instead of accosting the crazed youth, Pythagoras approached the musician and asked him to change his tune to a slow and solemn spondaic one. The youth, his emotions already in thrall to the music, responded instantly by calming down, and soon went home.

Another favourite variant of the same theme concerns a king, and shows that even the greatest of the earth can be ruled by the power of music. In the story of 'Alexander's Feast', as immortalized in the poem by John Dryden (later set by Handel), the famous Greek bard Timotheus was once performing at a banquet celebrating the victory of Alexander the Great over the Persians. As Timotheus sang of Zeus, king of the gods, Alexander seemed to the onlookers to become himself a god. When the bard turned to praise of Dionysus, everyone felt intoxicated and the king seemed ready to fight all his battles again then and there.

> The master saw the madness rise,
> His glowing cheeks, his ardent eyes;
> And, while he heaven and earth defied,
> Changed his hand, and checked his pride.
> He chose a mournful Muse
> Soft pity to infuse . . .

In the poem Timotheus brings Alexander and the banqueters in turn to pity for the vanquished Persians, to doting love, and finally to a rage for revenge, whereupon (like the Sicilian youth) they all go off to burn the Persian palace down. In the original account by Plutarch[53] which inspired Dryden, Alexander actually killed a man while under the influence, whereupon Timotheus (better late than never) changed his tune to instill sorrow and regret for the deed.

I do not know whether it was history, or merely historians, who repeated themselves in some similar instances. The sixteenth-century Danish chronicler Olaus Magnus[54] tells of King Eric of Denmark, who was curious to find out just how effective the music of his court minstrel could be. Overruling the musician's objections, he insisted on hearing music which took him through a series of intense emotions and insane delusions; according to an earlier account, the experiment cost the lives of four men. Two known musicians of historical times have been credited with similar powers. The lutenist Francesco di Milano (1497–1543) is reported[55] to have played an after-dinner fantasia that made the diners turn angry, melancholy, ravished, and ecstatic, thus showing that 'modern' music was just as powerful as ancient. Claude le Jeune (*c.* 1525–1600), composer and organist to Henry III of France, playing the organ at a wedding, is said to have so affected one of the courtiers that in the presence of the King he unforgivably drew his sword and swore he must fight with someone there and then, until Claude changed his tune.[56]

This kind of tale is not restricted to the West. The ruthless Sultan Murad IV, after the siege of Baghdad (1638), was preparing to massacre the Persians when his bloodthirstiness was appeased by a musician.[57] The Indian Emperor Akbar (1542–1605)[58] once insisted on hearing a raga (song-type) whose property is to create fire. Under protest, his musician obeyed, but as the song proceeded the unfortunate singer burst into flames which could not be extinguished even though he leapt into a river. Indian musicians are well acquainted with the application of music's power, for each raga has a particular character and an appropriate time for its performance. Sometimes a definite emotional effect is attributed to it, but the usual association is with times or seasons, so that the effects aimed at do not concern the transitory emotions but the alignment of the psyche to diurnal rhythms and to cosmic time. There is no particular emotion which one need habitually feel at noon, for instance, but the sun at zenith has certain effects on earthly life and mind which the raga serves to complement.

A similar purpose probably lay behind the plainsong chants of the Catholic liturgy which are ascribed to the various Offices or Hours – the eight services celebrated in the course of each day by monastic communities. No music is further from the moods of an Alexander, yet it is not unlikely that the anonymous chant composers had certain definite musical properties in mind as they set each part of the liturgy. Finally, under this heading, one must include the Vespers and Matins of the original Pythagorean community. In Iamblichus' words,

When they went to bed, they purified the reasoning power from the perturbations and noises to which it had been exposed during the day by certain odes and peculiar

31

songs, and by this means procured for themselves tranquil sleep, and few and good dreams. But when they rose from bed, they again liberated themselves from the torpor and heaviness of sleep by song of another kind.[59]

The Pythagorean practices were what we now call Music Therapy, understood in its broadest sense. Perhaps the earliest recorded instance of this science, or art (the modern division makes no sense here), is in the biblical chronicle of Saul and David (I Samuel 16.14–23). Saul was periodically tormented by an evil spirit, for which his servants recommended that a man be found skilful in playing the lyre. David was the man chosen. 'And whenever the evil spirit from God was upon Saul, David took the lyre and played it with his hand; so Saul was refreshed, and was well, and the evil spirit departed from him' (v. 23). This is clearly a very different matter from the isolated incidents recounted up to now. A modern music therapist, Juliette Alvin, has analysed it with great insight in the context of the two men's relationship,[60] and concludes that in this instance the treatment failed. It appears from the biblical account to have become a daily occurrence until suddenly Saul threw a javelin at his therapist, fortunately missing him (I Samuel 18.10–11, repeated 19.9–10). From that time on their relations were severed, at least on Saul's part, and 'the Lord departed from Saul', leaving him at the mercy of his impulses. Everything that Alvin draws out of the story – the contrast between Saul's psychosis and David's gentleness and tolerance, Saul's possible homosexual attraction towards David and his dawning realization that David was in every way the better man – must have been plain long before the era of modern psychology to that most eloquent of biblical commentators, Rembrandt van Rijn.

As a contrast to the case of Saul and David, Alvin analyses a more recent and successful one: the treatment of King Philip V of Spain by Farinelli (1705–82). This singer, probably the most brilliant castrato of all time, was already rich and at the peak of an international operatic career when in 1737 he was invited to the comparative obscurity of the Spanish court. King Philip was in a state of nervous breakdown, unable to cope with the least responsibility, and the court was in despair. Every possible cure had been tried for the royal melancholy. At last it was arranged that Farinelli should come and sing, unseen, in an adjacent room. On hearing the voice, Philip began for the first time in months to take an interest in life. As the performance was repeated each day, the King allowed himself to be shaved and gradually returned to normal. When he was well enough to realize what had happened, he sent for Farinelli and invited him to name his own reward. His sole request was that the King resume his royal duties; and it was duly granted. But Philip's sanity remained dependent on his therapy, and every night until the King's death ten years later Farinelli would sing the same four arias that had first broken the spell. The singer never again sought a public life or returned to the operatic stage where he had made his name. As Alvin understands this strange relationship, Farinelli had already exhausted the creative possibilities of a virtuoso career and was looking for something less superficial: the expression of intimacy and pathos. At the same time, the two men came to enjoy a mutual confidence and real affection, which naturally put Farinelli in a position of considerable political influence. But Alvin cannot help wondering, as all do who know the story, what it meant to sing, and hear, those four arias about 3600 times. It reminds me of the Zen Buddhist saying related by John Cage: 'if something is boring after two minutes, try it for four. If still boring, try it for eight, sixteen, thirty-two, and so on. Eventually one discovers that it's not boring at all but very interesting.'[61] For boredom may eventually lead one to a state of meditation. Philip and Farinelli must both have come to a point at which the daily ritual was nothing less than a kind of yoga in sound.

The effects of music on Alexander, Eric, etc., seem to have been what medicine calls allopathic (curing by contraries). But Farinelli's cure of King Philip's melancholy by singing songs of the 'pathetic' type is closer to the more subtle homeopathic method, in which *similia similibus curantur* (like are cured by like). Sad music evidently does not make people unhappy, or else popular songs from the Troubadours to modern times would not dwell so insistently on melancholy themes. For an extreme example of musical melancholy I turn briefly to the music and words of John Dowland (1562–1625), whose song *Lachrymae* ('Flow my tears') was known, admired, and imitated throughout Europe. The words set, and possibly written, by Dowland in this and his other 'songs of darkness' present a dismal view of the world and, what is more, a complete rejection of hope, to a degree scarcely paralleled before the modern Existentialists. Here we meet such lines as 'Happy they who in Hell/Feel not the world's despite', 'Alas I am condemned ever,/No hope, no help, there doth remain', 'Mourn, mourn, look now for no more day nor night,/But that from hell,/Then all must as they may in darkness learn to dwell.'

Anthony Rooley, Director of the Consort of Musicke which has recorded Dowland's complete works, explains this[62] in the context of the religious stance known as 'Pessimist Gnosis', which works by 'spurning the world of sense as a most complex and horrid snare which traps and imprisons the soul, the only way back being through a total negation of the sensual world.' But as Rooley points out, 'a performance of this song ['Flow my tears'] is a most elevating experience. It is sad and lamenting, yes, but at the final close one feels uplifted, in a way cleansed.'

It is of course the beauty of Dowland's music which is responsible for this catharsis, just as it is the beauty of Shakespeare's language which makes us feel cleansed at the end of his tragedies. (We do not feel so after merely reading Dowland's poem or Shakespeare's plot.) This beauty does not belong to the sensual world, but bears witness to another order of things to which we ourselves have access. The metaphysician and art-historian Ananda K. Coomaraswamy calls Beauty simply 'a State', saying that 'there are no degrees in beauty; the most complex and the simplest expression remind us of one and the same state',[63] which is no less than that of the Supreme Spirit.

Melancholy words and beautiful music; the contrast of wretched earth-life with the Supreme Spirit. We are back again, at a deeper level, with music as an aid to meditation, whose ultimate purpose is the realization of that state.

Another famous homeopathic use of music is as the cure for tarantism.[64] A lot of colourful folklore has grown around this disease, which used to break out every summer in Apulia, the region of the 'heel' of Italy around Taranto. The cause was believed to be the bite of the tarantula, a large spider native to the region; but once bitten, one was liable to succumb again whenever the disease struck anyone else. It was a collective hysteria in which the victims, mainly women, would dance frantically for hours on end, sometimes singing, howling, laughing, weeping, and making obscene gestures. After collapsing exhausted, they would resume the next day. The only known cure was to play music, in the form of the Tarantella, repeating it without a break as long as the victim was possessed. This has now become a stock musical genre, a fast *moto perpetuo* in 6/8 metre. But originally there were many different kinds, sharing only the harmonic progression from major to relative minor, and the difficulty lay in finding exactly the right Tarantella for the occasion. Once this was found, the victim would dance in time with it, sweat out the poison, collapse and awaken cured – until next summer.

Tarantism is mentioned as early as the 1360s[65] and maintains all its classical features through the following centuries. It occurs in other regions than Apulia, and may not be dead even yet. In Aragon, Marius Schneider[66] interviewed two Spanish musicians who said that they had treated their last case in 1944, and Juliette Alvin writes[67] that it was still known in Apulia in 1968. That is no wonder if, as is generally believed today, the spider bite is not the actual cause but merely a time-honoured excuse for indulgence in hysterical behaviour that flouts all the rules of decorum. The maddening heat of summer and the restrictions of a very convention-ridden society are too much to bear, and tarantism becomes a safety valve that allows women, especially, to do things for which their husbands would normally beat them black and blue. The musical cure may in fact enhance the experience for them by bringing their frantic movements into a rhythm, while the constant repetition probably induces a kind of trance state, as in African tribal drumming or the rituals of the Whirling Dervishes. Henry Sigerist[68] points out that Apulia, once part of Magna Graecia, is a region where Dionysos and Cybele were worshipped in Classical times with rites that very much resemble the symptoms of tarantism. In such out-of-the-way places old traditions die hard, and the orgies of the Old Religion were very likely celebrated in secret long after Italy was nominally Christian. With the appearance of tarantism in the Middle Ages, the old rites were legitimized and their celebrants tolerated as victims of a disease, whose cure, ironically enough, actually aided the celebration.

Marius Schneider goes much further in regarding the Tarantella as the survival of a ritual dating from the Megalithic culture of the third millennium BC.[69] He says that the Tarantella is dedicated to the Old Spinner Woman, a goddess who symbolizes the negative polarities of Nature (winter, death, etc.). Its counterpart is the Sword Dance (still surviving in the Morris Dance tradition) which is dedicated to her polar opposite, the Young War God. Both dances are therapeutic, but within a world-view that regards disease and its cure as a meaningful, even an initiatory experience. (One finds the same in Shamanism, and in the function of Apollo's son, the physician-god Asclepius.) The Sword-Dance is performed vicariously: the sick person does not participate in it, but is represented by the Fool who, surrounded by eight other dancers, dies and descends like Eurydice to the Underworld. Accompanied by the music of wind instruments, he does battle with the demon of sickness, and as his head is struck off suffers the 'second death' which brings about recovery and return to the land of the living. The protagonist of the Tarantella, on the other hand, is accompanied by stringed instruments as she is led out of the state of possession by the Spider-Witch, enabled to resume her own identity and to perform a battle with the spider. The end of the attack is brought about by the intervention of 'St Paul': obviously a Christianized form of some ancient figure. In the Sword-Dance the Fool is likewise identified with St George, and the sickness-demon with the Dragon.[70]

Whereas musical melancholy leads to the formless contemplation of the Pessimist Gnosis, the cathartic orgy of the Tarantella belongs, in its highest interpretation, to the divine frenzy in which the world's norms are turned upside-down, so that the world itself may be forced to reveal its transcendent meaning. The spider hanging head downwards from its web; the Hanged Man of the Tarot; the word *tararot* in Catalan (*atarantado* in

Castilian) which means 'bitten by a tarantula', 'wild,' or 'foolish':[71] all these point to a symbolic complex of some magnitude, having to do with the reversal of all values in the interests of spiritual realization. The poor peasant women of Apulia who 'spent nearly all their money on music'[72] were partaking, after their own fashion, in this eternal quest.

The noble history of music therapy, with its heritage of heroes and kings, its marvels and miracles, tends to be more of a burden than an asset to the profession today. Modern music therapists have to work under people to whom the subject of this chapter would seem so much superstitious nonsense. Although doubly trained both in psychology and music performance, the therapists' status and salaries do not compare with those of clinical psychologists, psychoanalysts, or physicians. Their typical field of activity is the mental hospital, where they are usually restricted to giving weekly sessions to a room full of patients of every degree of need and responsiveness. Under such conditions it is impossible to demonstrate the full therapeutic potential of music: consequently it is not taken nearly as seriously as the more questionable therapies of drugs and electric shocks. Much of what is written on music therapy, especially in the USA, consists of statistical studies and reductions of it to some physiological basis, in a pathetic attempt to establish its credentials in a world of quantitative methods and behavioural psychology.

The climate is more receptive in Europe, where a whole range of music-therapeutical methods is emerging, each corresponding to a non–musical mode of therapy. They seem to fall into five distinct levels:

Musical Therapy	*Psychological Therapy*
1.	'Radio-One-Therapy'
2. Becoming conscious and consenting to participate in music	Basic care and amusement of the severely handicapped
3. Arousal of specific emotions (allopathic)	Behavioural modification; counselling
4. Individual exploration of emotion, leading to catharsis (homeopathic)	Psychoanalysis; encounter groups
5. Exploration of the self through music	Transpersonal psychologies (Jung, Assagioli, Maslow, etc.)

The first and lowest level, which is simultaneously a musical and a psychological therapy, is now being widely practised. It was first described in *The Lancet* of 16 October, 1971, in a letter from John D. Taylor, who reported an unusual experiment at the North Middlesex Hospital. Three patients with primary brain damage had been comatose for 63, 14, and 13 days before someone had the idea of putting earphones on them which played Radio One (the BBC's popular music channel) for ten hours a day. After two days of this, the patients were all speaking for the first time since their injuries, and after four or five days they were able to start walking and the treatment ceased. Taylor adds that the association may be fortuitous, but urges that the sense stimulation of comatose patients should not be abandoned just because they do not respond. He suggests that visitors should not sit in embarrassed silence, but should keep talking to them, and that 'Radio-One-therapy' be continued. As in some of the experiments with plants, it seems that sound alone is a potential agent of awakening: something whose deeper meaning will appear at the end of Chapter Two.

At the second level of therapy, the patients are conscious, but desperately handicapped by brain damage or congenital retardation. The therapist's goal is to involve them in music by singing, playing percussion, or simply listening with enjoyment; in short, fostering a positive response to life, no matter how disadvantaged they may be. Mary Priestley, an English music therapist and pupil of Juliette Alvin, describes such sessions with remarkable tolerance and humour, though sometimes her main concern has been to get out of the room with her violin still in one piece.[73] It is difficult to prove whether music achieves the goal of the second level any differently from craft work or physical games. Certainly it gives great pleasure to some severely retarded people, and it may be that it has an incalculable effect on their souls, which one assumes are not retarded *per se*.

The experience at the third level is definitely a musical one, and is designed to arouse specific emotions. It is more applicable to people who have once been 'normal', but who have developed mental afflictions as a response to traumatic experience. In cases of actual demoniacal possession, of which mental hospitals may be fuller than they realize, music is probably of little use: it did not work with Saul. But where the affliction has its seat in the person's emotions, there the allopathic method of Pythagoras will hold good. The therapist will seek to calm the manic and cheer the depressed – though this will be difficult if they are in the same room. Hence individual or select group therapy alone makes sense from this level upward, though unfortunately it is rarely made available.

Dowland's melancholy and the Tarantella, described above as specimens of homeopathic music therapy, belong to a fourth level where the purpose is not so much to change the patient's emotional state into its contrary as to work with that state and bring it to a climax. Obviously this method will not do for everyone: it would be foolish to apply the principle to a homicidal patient. But if madness can be made to yield its meaning, something has been gained from it. This kind of therapy, like its opposite number, psychoanalysis, is for the comparatively sane as well as for the sick: it is a way to self-knowledge, and presumes a mind of at least average capabilities. Even more than third-level therapy, it belongs in the private session, or at least in a thoroughly supportive group such as is used in encounter therapy. Mary Priestley describes many cases[74] in which typically the patient (untrained in music) improvises on percussion instruments while the therapist responds on other percussions or piano, sometimes in dialogue, sometimes in conflict. Often the catharsis is violent, as the patient suddenly breaks through his inhibitions and lets his negative emotions explode on gongs, cymbals, and drums. The transmutation of emotion into sheer sound avoids the labyrinth of words – for music cannot lie – and helps the patient to objectify his feelings. The success of this therapy depends very much on the capacity of the patient to respond to the emotional qualities of music. It works best with those of average musical intelligence, professionals being too aware and critical of what they are hearing or playing.

Transpersonal psychology, as the name indicates, is centered not on the personal Ego but on the higher Self which transcends the personal dimension and links the individual with the greater realities of Humanity, the Cosmos, and God. The transpersonal therapies begin with self-analysis but end with the dawning of Self-knowledge: beyond them there stretches the spiritual path. Music is rarely used in them at present, but they are after all a new departure in psychotherapy. It opens up many fruitful avenues to those who have made it a part of their practice, or at least as part of their repertory for use with selected patients or clients.

The Berlin psychologist and musicologist Hildemarie Streich has found in many years of analytic practice that music can be activated by the unconscious for its own purposes, while the patient is asleep.[75] Having collected hundreds of musical dreams from people of every kind, she concludes that the appearance of music in dream tends to mark important stages in the processes of healing and individuation – as if the unconscious of modern man is supplying the ancient function of musical therapy as it was practised in the healing centres of Antiquity.

From a more external point of view, Alexander Pontvik (sometime head of the Stockholm Institute for Music Therapy and Music Education) recommends the use of music in the conscious state, with concentration on 'the objective representation of the regular structure of the work in itself,'[75]

38

meaning that the client should contemplate the musical work apart from all personal and emotional associations. Pontvik regards J.S. Bach as the central source for such therapeutic music 'in the sense of a symbolic representation of archetypal contents or ordering principles', and attributes to music, thus used, a healing force quite independent of any associated knowledge. I suppose he envisions it as a kind of musical mandala, presenting a state of wholeness and perfection with which the psyche is to be identified.

Other possible uses of music at the transpersonal level actually exploit the aspects which Pontvik's Apollonian approach avoids. Music which has a strong personal meaning or is rich in associations from one's past can be used to recapture that part of one's life, to live it through again in the imagination, and to understand better how one has come to be what one is. Music which plays strongly on the emotions (such as Wagner's or Mahler's) can bring a glimpse of a 'cosmic joy' and 'cosmic sorrow' that have nothing personal about them but lead one beyond the ego's concerns. Likewise, one may use the extremes of musical emotion as a springboard to lift one onto a plane of serene detachment. Then there are the astonishing powers of music to evoke imagery from the unconscious which, like dreams, can be worked on subsequently by therapist and client. And if the client can perform music, not merely listen to it, there is a whole range of possibilities for developing self-awareness and exploring the body-mind relationship. In musical practice, this soon reveals itself as the eye-ear-hand-body-intellect-memory-emotion-criticism relationship, which is enough to keep anyone occupied. Books are beginning to appear on self-development of this kind,[77] and a few pioneering therapists are laying the groundwork for a future long-term therapy of the individual that will use music as its principal tool.

There is one place today where music therapy at every level is accorded its full value and flourishes in an atmosphere of complete acceptance. That is the Anthroposophic Movement, a worldwide enterprise based on the spiritual science of Rudolf Steiner (1861–1925).[78] Steiner himself wrote some of the clearest explanations ever made of the nature of music, which we will call on later in this book. His insights into music as a manifestation of realities of a higher order convinced him of its overriding importance to healing and education alike. Steiner's educational philosophy is based on respect for every child as a soul whose destiny is some day to enter the spiritual world in full consciousness. Music provides one of the closest images of that world; hence its value for reawakening the soul's prenatal knowledge of spiritual realities. Therefore one cannot begin too soon to make this art an accepted and loved part of a child's life, and this is done today in the many Waldorf Schools that follow Steiner's principles.

While Steiner's educational philosophy is itself revolutionary by comparison with the common view of the child as a *tabula rasa* to be scrawled on by parents and educators, his ideas on the mentally retarded or congenitally handicapped are doubly so. In his view these are otherwise normal souls who for some reason have taken a harsh burden on themselves. Steiner education is particularly effective in these difficult cases, and much of its success is attributed to the environment of live music which is created, and which the patients themselves create, around them. The therapists Paul Nordoff and Clive Robbins[79] record countless instances of music effecting a breakthrough with autistic, psychotic and subnormal children, including blind and supposedly deaf ones. At the other end of life, music can penetrate senility and give fresh meaning to the lives of the very old, preparing them for a harmonious transition to what Steiner called 'the world between death and rebirth'.

Music therapy as practised by Anthroposophists is, at its best, an element in an integral philosophy that covers every department of human existence, and tends to thrive in more or less self-contained communities. This is probably why, like other of Steiner's systems (education, agriculture, eurhythmy) it has made less headway in the non-Anthroposophic world than it deserves. But it is not necessary to assent to Steiner's revelations *in toto* in order to take advantage of some of them.

So far I have considered the effects of music from the point of view of the individual. Parallel to these in every respect are the effects that have been claimed for it at the collective level. In the *Li Chi*, the ancient Chinese Book of Rites whose compilation was begun by Confucius (551–478 BC), there is a long discourse on how music should be used in conjunction with ceremonies to bring civilization into a proper state of harmony and order. This is how the functions of the two are described:

Harmony is the thing principally sought in music: – it therein follows Heaven, and manifests the expansive spiritual influence characteristic of it. Normal distinction is the thing aimed at in ceremonies: – they therein follow Earth and exhibit the retractive spiritual influence characteristic of it. Hence the sages made music in response to Heaven, and framed ceremonies in correspondence with Earth.[80]

Music, which derives from inner experience, and ceremonies, which are derived from observing the situation in the outer world, are seen as complementary powers, as are their respective origins, Heaven and Earth. Music brings about in mankind the unity of purpose and of feeling, reflecting the perfect harmony of the heavens, without which civilization cannot stand; ceremonies assign to everyone his distinct place in the earthly hierarchy. Politically speaking, one might say that fascism is the attempt to rule with ceremony alone, while communism believes idealistically that one can rule with music alone. The disciples of Confucius who wrote the *Li Chi* knew that both harmony and hierarchy are indispensable, given the dual nature of Man as a being who belongs in one respect to Earth, in another to Heaven.

The book as we have it dates only from the Han Dynasty (202 BC–AD 220), a time of consolidation after many years of war and anarchy. Its compilers thought of the great age of music as being long past, and of themselves as reinstating, to the best of their ability, the ancient ceremonies and music with which the mythical philosopher-kings had once ruled so well: an early example of a conscious renaissance of past culture.

The *Li Chi* envisages music as being used publicly in conjunction with dance and pantomime, in shows which were staged for the benefit of everyone. 'High and low, old and young, listen together to it, and all is harmony' – because they all share the same emotions. And such harmonious effects were not limited to the human domain. As in many ancient nations, the ruler was deemed responsible for the behaviour of Nature as well as of his human subjects. The lower creatures, being servants of mankind, reflect unconsciously the current state of the human spirit, as the body may reflect by its sickness or health the state of the psyche. If all is well with Man, all will be well with Nature, too. In the following description of Nature flourishing under the rule of the 'Great Man', notice also an echo of Hans Jenny's idea of music as a formative force which embodies the laws of organic growth, the patterns of curling sprout and horn.

Therefore, when the Great Man uses and exhibits his ceremonies and music, Heaven and Earth will in response to him display their brilliant influences. They will act in happy union, and the energies of nature, now expanding, now contracting, will proceed harmoniously. The genial airs from above and the responsive action below will overspread and nourish all things. Then plants and trees will grow luxuriantly; curling sprouts and buds will expand; the feathered and winged tribes will be active; horns and antlers will grow; insects will come to the light and revive; birds will breed and brood; the hairy tribes will mate and bring forth; the mammals will have no abortions, and no eggs will be broken or addled, – and all will have to be ascribed to the power of music.[81]

Mao Tse-tung himself, like the Emperors of old, began his reign by decreeing the music and ceremonies of the new People's Republic. But he made a great mistake. In his 'Talk to Music Workers' of 1956 he said that the traditional Chinese folksongs needed to be 'elevated' and made more 'scientific' by adoption of Western traits.[82] Consequently his nation suffered the common cultural problem of the Third World: how to benefit by the Western experience without getting served up with the worst the

West has to offer. A Chinese Communist official recently had cause to complain about the infiltration of Westernized pop-music, or 'yellow music' as he calls it:[83]

Yellow music refers to decadent songs that nakedly express sex. The content of the lyrics advertises sex, the melody is languid and vulgar, and it gives to people a kind of disease-inducing stimulus to the sensory organs.

In one sense, this reaction is only to be expected in a country with a vast problem of overpopulation, whose official propaganda warns young married people that much lovemaking is bad for their health. But as we shall see in Chapter Four, it is with good reason that this Western export is mistrusted.

The idea of music as an actual instrument of well-being in the state is best known to the West through the political works of Plato. In *Republic*, IV, 424c, Socrates quotes an eminent musician, Damon of Athens,[84] to the effect that 'Musical styles are nowhere altered without changes in the most important laws of the state.' For Socrates, who has been elaborating an ideal republic, such change is to be avoided at all costs: he has already said that it is through music and the arts that lawlessness gains a hold over the entire community. But in order to make the republic ideal, it is necessary first to have purged its music. Hence Socrates allows into the city only two of the many current Greek Modes: the Dorian and Phrygian, 'the violent and the willing, which will best imitate the accents of brave and moderate men both in misfortune and prosperity' (III, 399c). The other modes are classed as the lamenting ones, dismissed as 'useless even for women who are to be good' (398e), and the relaxed ones which accompany drunkenness and idleness. A musical censorship is to be enforced, which only makes sense if it is believed that certain styles of music – for it is thus that we should understand the modes here – have power to make or mar the public character. If this is so, then music is far too serious a matter to be left in the hands of musicians, 'because poets are more depraved than the Muses' (*Laws*, II, 669c): it must be determined and limited by the Guardians of the city. In the *Laws*, from which the last quotation comes, Plato limits music still further, to use in religious ceremonies only. The Athenian Guest, who is the main speaker of that dialogue, places it in a context of Bacchic choirs, hymns and encomiums sung to the gods, daemons and heroes. In Book VII he describes dance-rituals which seem closely related to what the Confucians also understood to be the proper use of music in the service of the state. In the *Li Chi* public music was divided between the warlike kind, in which the performers brandished shields and axes, and the peaceful, in which they waved plumes and oxtails.[85] Similarly, in the *Laws*, Pyrrhic dancing imitates the dealing and dodging of blows; 'pacific' dancing (corresponding to Plato's personal view of the Phrygian mode) represents 'the prosperous condition of the temperate soul in moderate pleasures' (VII, 815).

Probably music has always had a part to play in ideal political states, wherever on the globe they may be. Just as the Confucians looked back nostalgically to the period of the great sage-kings, and Plato to the theocracy of ancient Egypt, so Richard Wagner also believed that there had been a time when music fulfilled its true civilizing function. The distant ideal for Wagner was the public theatre of classical Greece: he imagined music working there, in harmony with the arts of the other Muses, to create a ritual drama which served as the spiritual focus of all citizens. By assembling them in the theatres to witness their own mythology, it bound them socially and improved them individually. With his own music dramas and the building of the Festival Theatre in Bayreuth, Wagner was consciously working, as far as a single nineteenth-century man could, to give humanity a glimpse of this way of being which invested all the arts with a solemn and sacred purpose, and which he was sure would return at some future time.

The Russian composer Alexander Skryabin (1872–1915) was also convinced of the tremendous power which music might have for the spiritual well-being of mankind. He devoted the last years of his short life to planning a 'Mystery': a synthesis of all the arts with religious ritual that would combine poetry, drama, dance, music, coloured lights, and even fragrances. It was to be held in a hemispherical temple in India containing an artificial lake, so that the audience or congregation would seem to be enclosed in a perfect sphere. The effects of the Mystery were to exceed by far any Platonic or Wagnerian ambitions: beginning with the enlightenment of its beholders, it would spread worldwide to bring about the Apocalypse and usher in the New Age. But by the time he died he had only written some of the words and sketched part of the music. Skryabin's vision of a spherical auditorium as the perfect vessel for the music of the New Age was partially realized when the works of Karlheinz Stockhausen (b. 1928) were performed in the geodesic sphere of the West German Pavilion at the 1970 Osaka World Fair.[86]

Utopias apart, has music really affected the course of civilization, or are kings and battles the decisive factors, as our school histories taught us? One person thoroughly convinced of the importance of music was Antoine Fabre d'Olivet (1767–1825), one of the most extraordinary characters of the Romantic era and a key figure in the history of speculative music. In his *Histoire philosophique du genre humain* (1824) he tells a strange tale (since become a familiar one in the annals of Theosophy) of Atlantis and of the Universal Empire of Aryan India, giving actuality to figures such as Rama and Krishna and confidently describing events of the seventh millennium BC and earlier. Even Fabre apologizes for the strangeness of what he is going to say before he states that it was a revolution in speculative music that brought about the demise of this Universal Empire. The Empire apparently followed a religion of the Divine Unity until 'one of the sovereign pontiffs, examining the musical system of Bharata . . . perceived that it was not thus with it and that it was necessary to admit two Principles into the generation of sounds'.[87] As a result of this, the philosophers were also compelled to abandon their monism for a belief in an 'absolute Combined Duality' of two Principles: Ishwara (the God of created beings) and Prakriti (the universal feminine principle, or Matter). The people then attached themselves variously to the new male or female Principle, which led to schisms, wars, and eventually to the collapse of the Empire.

What did the Pontiff discover? We can piece it together from the surviving fragments of Fabre's book on music[88] and from his other writings; but the point here is that he accords this epoch-making influence to music not simply as sound, but in its philosophical or speculative dimension, which Pythagorean and medieval theorists have always regarded as the superior one. Fabre was an admirer of Plato and of the Chinese philosophers, and believed with them that as a nation's music, so will its morals be.

Music, envisaged in its speculative part, is, as the Ancients defined it, the knowledge of the order of all things and the science of the harmonic relationships of the Universe; it rests on immutable principles which nothing can impair.[89]

Therefore a nation which respects music and makes the laws of harmony the foundation of all its laws, measures and philosophy, will be in accord with things as they are in the cosmos. It was observance of these principles, says Fabre, that endowed the civilizations of Egypt and of China with their thousands of years of stability, with which he invites us to compare the fate of Europe since the death of Plato and of the Pythagorean ideal.

About a hundred years after Fabre d'Olivet, the English Theosophist and composer Cyril Scott (1879–1970) made the pioneering attempt to survey the whole of Man's history in the light of music. Scott was a composer of some renown, and less concerned with the speculative dimension than with actually sounding music. His book *Music: Its Secret Influence Throughout the Ages* (1958) was formerly entitled *The Influence of Music on History and Morals: A Vindication of Plato* (1933), since it revived the Platonic doctrine that music does act on the soul, for better or worse.

In Scott's view, the great collective movements of the human soul have always been anticipated by innovations in music. He suggests, for example, that the 'simple grandeur' of Handel's oratorios acted as a brake on the licentious tendencies of eighteenth-century England, ushering in a more sober age that would in turn stultify in Victorian prudery.[90] Then again, the refined music of Chopin awakened a new desire for culture, producing the Aesthetic Movement and the desire of women for emancipation from the bondage of the Victorian family structure,[91] while the sympathetic and compassionate music of Schumann and Mendelssohn awakened social concern and led to the abolition of child labour and slavery.

Scott made the link between musical and social phenomena too much of a causal one, but he had to counter the current dogma that the arts are merely the byproducts of social or personal circumstances. A more balanced approach might see the epochal changes to which humanity is destined as manifesting first in the more subtle and sensitive consciousness of composers and artists, only later permeating down to social institutions and physical life. But then the repeated performance and hearing of the music corresponding to a certain change will reinforce its qualities, whether they be bad or good, imprinting them as it were on the collective soul. This is the subject to which we will return in Chapter Four.

CHAPTER TWO

Hearing Secret Harmonies

In the last chapter we rose from the effects of music on the mineral, vegetable and animal kingdoms to its effects on Man, both as an individual and in society. Now we continue the ascent of the Chain of Being and listen to the reports of those who have heard music not of this world.

Before we even leave the Earth, we must remember that we share the planet with the race of elementals: beings made from the subtle essences of the elements, rather than from the physical matter that constitutes our own bodies. Nowadays they usually escape our perceptions, but to some individuals, and even to whole races like the Celts and Scandinavians, they are an accepted reality, being frequently felt and heard, and sometimes even seen. People see and hear them as fairies, leprechauns, elves, gnomes, trolls, and in many other picturesque forms. This little anecdote from the Isle of Man, taken from Evans-Wentz's *The Fairy Faith in Celtic Countries*, contains in a nutshell the favourite themes of musical fairy-lore:

William Cain, of Glen Helen, was going home in the evening across the mountains near Brook's Park, when he heard music down below in a glen, and saw there a great glass house like a palace, all lit up. He stopped to listen, and when he had the new tune he went home to practise it on his fiddle; and recently he played the same fairy tune at Miss Sophia Morrison's Manx entertainment in Peel.[1]

Here are the mysterious music heard at dusk, the crystalline palace of the Otherworld, and the fairies as sources of inspiration for mortal musicians. Later we will hear of people who have actually visited this Otherworld, and of higher sources of inspiration still. But to fairy music heard on our own soil, with waking earthly consciousness, the folklore of all races attests. As one might expect, it is especially likely to be heard at places of ancient lineage and high magic like the hill of Tara, spiritual centre of all Ireland, and near megalithic structures – stone circles, barrows, etc. At Tara an old man told Evans-Wentz:

As sure as you are sitting down I heard the pipes there in that wood . . . I often heard it in the wood of Tara. Whenever the 'good people' play, you hear their music all through the field as plain as can be; and it is the grandest kind of music. It may last half the night, but once day comes, it ends.[2]

Sometimes the fairies are seen as well as heard. They may appear as a busy troop of 'little folk', singing and dancing, whose effects on the human witness are not always of the best; for fairies, being soul-less and hence completely amoral, are as likely to steal away one's babies and replace them with their own ugly (but precociously musical) changelings[3] as they are to adopt rejected stepsons and teach them the piper's trade.[4] And the Celtic fairies are not always so little: they can even be mistaken for humans. Many are the tales of the slightly undersized character, always with red hair, who appears unexpectedly at taverns and parties, plays music of entrancing beauty and irresistible power, and leaves without a trace, only then to be recognized, as the spell wears off, as a fairy visitant. St Patrick himself relates a meeting with a 'wondrous elfin man' whose minstrelsy put him to sleep, saying of the music: 'Good indeed it were, but for a twang of the fairy spell that infests it; barring which nothing could more nearly resemble Heaven's harmony.'[5] Here the borderline between the true fairy and the fairy-inspired mortal becomes blurred: did Patrick meet a human minstrel and believe him to be a fairy? It is of the essence of fairytale that one cannot always be certain which is which: but the experience remains inviolate.

Picturesque tales are told in other folklores, too, of how one can learn music from the elementals. The Näkki, a Finnish water-sprite, will teach it to you if you take your fiddle to his waterfall on Midsummer's Eve, or on the Eve of Lent or Easter. After that you can make people dance, whether they will or no, and your fiddle may play by itself, even if it is broken.[6] Taking lessons from the Norse Fossegrim is a more painful affair. You must visit him on a Thursday evening with the offering of a white he-goat. If the goat is thin, you will get no further than tuning your fiddle. But if it is a good, fat beast, the Fossegrim will seize your hand in his, squeezing until blood flows from it. When your hand is recovered, you (like Orpheus) will be able to play so that trees dance and waterfalls stop flowing.[7]

Since the time of Paracelsus, the elementals have been the subject not only of folklore but also of serious research, and present-day occultists hold a sophisticated view of them. This does not diminish their poetic qualities, as one can see from the account given to Evans-Wentz by an Irish mystic and seer (probably the poet George Russell, known as 'A.E.'), to whom initiation into otherworldly vision came by way of the fairy music:

The first time I saw them with great vividness I was lying on a hillside alone in the west of Ireland, in County Sligo: I had been listening to music in the air, and to what seemed to be the sound of bells, and was trying to understand these aerial clashings in which wind seemed to break upon wind in an ever-changing musical silvery sound. Then the space before me grew luminous, and I began to see one beautiful being after another.[8]

He describes them as tall, self-luminous, opalescent beings whose sight brought joy and ecstasy, then goes on to explain their ontological status, different classes, and astral anatomy, in terms which only serve to illustrate the fundamental agreement between all accounts of this kind.

Belief in the elementals is a way of saying that everything is alive – that there is a spark of divine consciousness in every particle of matter. Anthroposophists and others, following Paracelsus, personify this universal life, regarding the origin of matter itself and all natural processes of growth as the action of elementals working on the subtle planes: not anthropomorphic little folk, of course, but beings of many different classes, powers, and degrees of consciousness intermediate between ourselves and the Angelic Hierarchy. Ernst Hagemann, the commentator on Rudolf Steiner's musical lectures, writes that they especially use the arts of speech and music to form a kind of magnetic channel through which the Angels can work upon the human race.[9]

According to the complex system developed by Steiner out of his own clairvoyance, some elementals are free, while others are in bondage to material objects and places. The forging of metal tools and machines, for instance, captures elementals, not altogether willingly, in the finished objects, and this accounts for the dangerous as well as the helpful qualities of such instruments. Elementals are continually being freed, as others are becoming bound – and this exchange, this perpetual sacrifice, is Life. In music, the composer's Ego summons certain elementals to a state of enchantment in tone, the quality of his own soul dictating whether these are of a good or evil nature. In performance, their influence is conveyed to the Sylphs and Undines (spirits of air and water) who are bound in the environing air and 'ether'. These carry the tone to the listener, and as soon as it is experienced in the inner ear, they are released from their enchantment. This psycho-acoustical theory is similar to that of the early days of modern science, mentioned in Chapter One, which posited the link of a subtle aether, except that here the intermediate substance is personified.

The inevitable question, which could not have arisen before Edison's phonograph (1877), is: What happens when the tones are reproduced mechanically via a record or tape? Rudolf Steiner, speaking in 1923 shortly before his death, had condemned the gramophone as a source of music. Of course the gramophone of that time could only produce a travesty of live music, but according to Hagemann the rejection was more than aesthetic. In an extraordinary passage which is not without its comic moments, Hagemann described his own research with various clairvoyantly gifted people in order to find out what happens to the elementals' function when music is mechanically reproduced. Not every detail was satisfactorily explained, but the consensus of several clairvoyants working independently was as follows.

On applying their second sight to the surfaces of gramophone records, they found them thronged with elemental forms – all dead. Looking through a magnifying glass, they could see even more of them! These, they said, are the lifeless replicas of the elementals who were constellated in the air, entered the microphone, and were 'shadowed' upon the record matrix during the original live performance. In order to carry over these dead copies into the physical world via the reproducing device, one needs the cooperation of other, living elementals – tiny Gnomes, to be precise – whom the clairvoyants were able to perceive in the diamond or sapphire stylus. (One recalls that gemstones are traditionally associated with these earthy spirits). Through the Gnomes' agency, the very same kinds of elementals – presumably Sylphs and Undines – could be seen emerging from the loudspeakers as had originally been captured in the recording process.

So far the inadequacy of recordings is not proven. But the clairvoyants had more to say.[10] At live concerts they did not just enjoy the visions of beauty which the music throws off into the air above the stage, visions which several artists have tried to capture.[11] They also saw the concert-hall beset by Spirits of Ugliness: vile, spider-like beings who swarm around whenever beauty is manifest, and crawl into our ears and noses while we are entranced by it. Everything must have its opposite; in order to create beauty, Man has to have the stimulus of the ugly. The greatest artistic natures, Hagemann says,[12] are those who have felt this conflict the most keenly – even to a physical degree. During recording, however, it is only the beautiful forms who enter the microphone and whose fair corpses litter the grooves of our records. The ugly spirits (who actually are no more evil than the manure with which we nourish our roses) are absent, and so the full artistic experience is lacking.

In this chapter, fact and fiction will mingle indistinguishably, for in matters such as these the distinction is not hard and fast. Someone may have had an authentic clairvoyant or mystical vision; once told or written down, it becomes part of the collective mythology. People have dreams which reflect it; authors and poets (dreamers all) draw on it for their own writing, which may in turn become a source of mythical, and an impulse towards mystical, experience.

Many people have heard music that seemed to speak to them of another world, another order of being than the one presented by the external senses. A fairly typical experience is that of synaesthesia, in which the music is instantaneously translated into other sense-impressions, usually visual ones. Some people, like the composer Olivier Messiaen (born 1908),[13] are naturally gifted with it, and cannot hear music without seeing colours with their inner eye. Others have had the experience as the result of psychedelic drugs. Here is a typical report from a lysergic acid (LSD) trip which shows the blurring of the visual and aural categories:

I was listening to a record of Mozart's Clarinet Quintet. I did not hear a note of music: the whole piece was translated into visual imagery of a highly coloured and emotionally delightful nature. Most of it is lost now, but I do remember the Minuet and Trios. They took me to a place of fantastic organic architecture – rather Max Ernst-ish – around which brightly-coloured dragons were playing some intricate team-game or ballet. One of them was the clarinet part (though nothing could have been more distant than any idea of instruments and players), and in the second Trio this solo dragonlet performed some daring and comical turns which, since they verged on the indecent, required some urging by the others: 'Go on, go on!' (These were the phrases on the strings preceding the clarinet's low triplet arpeggio.) Nothing, I thought afterwards, could have been more Mozartian in its combination of innocence and naughtiness.[14]

In a time when so few people acknowledge the world of the Imagination as a reality and a source of transcendent knowledge, psychotropic drugs have served to open a window on it for some. At the end of Aldous Huxley's last novel, *Island*, the hero Will Farnaby takes the extravagantly-named 'moksha-medicine' and, while listening to Bach's Fourth Brandenburg Concerto, has a vision that begins with joy and beauty but goes on to the terrible realization that sorrow and pain are inevitable elements of existence. Like the earlier hero of Huxley's *Point Counter Point*, who listens to Beethoven's *Heiliges Dankgesang* while awaiting his execution by the Fascists, Will finds his way through music to the acceptance of suffering and death.

But drugs can only give a temporary glimpse of such things. Unless one can earn the right to them by one's own efforts, the apparent revelations of psychedelic experience do not permanently elevate the soul, and may have to be paid for by a long period of purgation. Carlos Castaneda's story (whether fact or fiction) is a fable for our time in this regard: in his first book the Mexican shaman Don Juan uses drugs to shake him out of his rational social-scientific ignorance,[15] but later Carlos has to become a magician through will alone. And among musicians, Pete Townshend, the leader of The Who and a long-time symbol of Dionysiac behaviour, has gone on record as saying that, after years of habitually listening to music while 'high', he realized that he had to go back to the beginning and recapture his ecstasies without the aid of the drugs which were ruining his life.

Psychotropic drugs can force open the 'doors of perception' on to a sort of heaven, but, as Huxley well knew, they can also lead one into Hell; and it is thither that we must cast an apotropaic glance before continuing our ascent. For Hell is also a musical realm, in its own way. As everyone knows, the Devil himself is a fiddler, and a damned fine one at that. The violin virtuoso and composer Giuseppe Tartini (1692–1770) once dreamed that he had made a pact with him, and that the Devil played such music that it made Tartini want to give up the violin then and there. (Instead, he wrote his famous 'Devil's Trill' Sonata as a reminiscence.) But the Devil's musical skill serves one purpose only: the seduction of souls. He inverts the purpose of God-given harmony, using the power of music to drag the soul not up but down. It was from fear of this that the Fathers and Doctors of the Church mistrusted all music that was unsanctified by a sacred text – a fact which held up for centuries the development of instrumental music – and the exoterically-minded Mullahs of Islam invoked the Prophet Muhammad's authority for an absolute (and always unsuccessful) ban on all music whatever.

Once the Devil has souls in his grip, seduced maybe by songs of love and ease, they are condemned to a Hell where the perversion of harmony into horrendous cacophony[16] is relieved only by the hopeless and still more horrible silence of its frozen depths.[17] The excruciating discords of Hell inversely reflect the perfect concord that reigns in Heaven, whether as the song of angelic choirs or as Pythagorean number-principles (see Chapter Three). Hence the medieval term for the dissonant tritone (B-F), *Diabolus in Musica*, and its gingerly treatment in earlier music. Similarly, the silence of the lowest Hell is a reflection of the silence that fills the highest Heaven, as we will find it described by Synesius at the end of this book.

The Romantic novelist Heinrich von Kleist gives a vivid picture of the marriage of divine and demonic music in his short story, *St Cecilia, or The Power of Music*. Set in the epoch of religious wars, it tells of the miraculous intervention of Cecilia, patron saint of music, against four Calvinist brothers who had set out to desecrate a convent. While present at High Mass with the intention of disrupting it, they fell under the spell of the performance, under the Saint's own inspiration, of an ancient Italian mass setting. It left them the victims of a grotesque religious mania, and they spent the rest of their days in an asylum for the insane. This is how their first act after their conversion is described to their mother:

Suddenly the clock struck midnight, your four sons listened attentively for a moment to the dull sound of the bell and then all at once rising simultaneously from their seats . . . they started to intone the *Gloria in excelsis Deo* with a dreadful ghastly voice. The sounds they made were not unlike those of leopards and wolves howling to the sky during the icy wintertime. The pillars of the house, I assure you, shook, and the windows, hit by the visible breath of their lungs, threatened to shatter as if one had thrown handfuls of sand against their surfaces.[18]

For ever after they lived in the asylum, never speaking, eating and sleeping very little, just sitting around a table contemplating a crucifix and rising twice a day to repeat their hymns. In ripe old age they died a serene and cheerful death, after they had howled the *Gloria* for the last time.

Drugs and insanity are certainly not the only means of embarking on one's voyage to the Otherworld. The mystical alchemist Thomas Vaughan (1622–66) says that the soul 'has several ways to break up house, but her best is without a disease. This is her mystical walk, an exit only to return.'[19] Some of the ways thither are through fantasy or active imagination in the waking state; through dreams, trances, or visions; and after death, when we can all expect to enter it. In exceptional cases, among which Pythagoras is the most famous ancient example, a person may be so gifted as to enter the state at will, even without the extinction of normal consciousness.

In ancient times it seems that the door to these realms stood wider open. One reads of the many people in folklore who have strayed into the realm of Faërie through chinks in the rock or holes in the ground, or got lost in the woods like Dante himself at the beginning of the *Inferno*. Once inside, they may simply enjoy a kind of guided tour, but there is also the chance of a more serious involvement. Then all manner of difficulties and obstacles may appear to challenge the traveller: rivers and oceans to be crossed, wild animals and fierce men to be overcome; walls of fire and of ice, razor-edged bridges, steep mountains, and the very spheres themselves to be scaled. The medievalist Howard Patch, in his study of hundreds of legends concerning the Otherworld, found certain recurrent features both in the journey and in the realm itself. He notes that the latter usually contains

a garden with a fountain or several fountains, and one or more conspicuous trees laden with fruit. The perfume of the place is sometimes marked with peculiarity, and the birds are especially to be noticed for the quality of their song. Other familiar motifs include the pavilion or dwelling place, a castle or a palace, jewels in the garden or in the decoration of the palace, the music which is heard, the predominance of crystal in the building, the effect of eating the fruit there, and a mention of the abnormal passage of time – short or long – during the visit.[20]

Faced with the plethora of literature devoted to this visionary realm, one feels like a legendary voyager, adrift in a sea of wonders so vast that he does not know whither to steer. But there is one body of writing that is most consistently and delightfully musical: that of the Medieval Celtic period; and it is to this that we will restrict our view here.

The Celtic Otherworld has a constant quality peculiar to itself, which I believe to be the result of more than a purely literary tradition. Its landmarks are as unmistakable, its atmosphere as marked, as that of the Muslim Paradise with its greenery and houris, or of the Renaissance alchemical engravings with their formal gardens and fabulous beasts. As befits an island literature, that of old Ireland teems with visions and voyages to other lands and other worlds. Some of these are to isles beyond the sea, which less imaginative scholars have tried to identify with actual lands. Of course, Irish saints may have been blown off course and ended up in the Bahamas, but this in itself is not sufficient reason for the tales they told, any more than the natural sound of whistling wind can explain away the fairy music mentioned earlier in the chapter. Other journeys are to lands in the ocean-depths, no less musical than the others, as the hero Brian found when he plunged down with a crystal diving-helmet and saw the red-haired ocean-nymphs making music like the chiming of silver bells.[21] Perhaps it was the same sound as is heard from the submerged cathedral of Ys, the Breton town sunk beneath the waves. Then again, the Otherworld may appear on one's own familiar soil, produced like a mirage or suddenly revealed as the encircling mists clear away. It may be entered beneath the hollow hills or fairy mounds, and here it becomes inextricably confused with the Fairy Kingdom. Most typically, it is presented as a voyage to one or many islands, usually in the West, which from the point of view of Ireland represented the great unknown.

One explanation of the nature of these isles and their inhabitants is given in the Voyage of St Brendan (ninth century), when he and his companions visit an island called the Paradise of Birds. The birds here are white and so numerous that they entirely cover a giant tree. In response to Brendan's questioning, one flies down, 'making a noise with her wings like a hand-bell,' and explains that the birds are souls that were destroyed in Lucifer's rebellion, though not complicit in his sin: 'We wander through various regions of the air and the firmament and the earth, just like the other spirits that travel on their missions. But on holy days and Sundays we are given bodies such as you now see so that we may stay here and praise our creator.'[22]

And when the hour of Vespers comes, all the birds chant together the versicle *Te decet hymnus, Deus in Sion* for about an hour. Likewise, at each of the eight Canonical Hours (the services sung each day in monastic communities), they sing the appropriate psalms and other verses.

When one compares the account given to St Brendan with modern Celtic fairy beliefs, it is clear that the same beings are in question, and their musicality comes as no surprise. Of all the theories put forward by the old

53

people interviewed by Evans-Wentz in the early years of this century, the most widespread holds the fairies to be fallen angels who remained neutral in Lucifer's war.[23] As a Breton source puts it, 'after the angels revolted, those left in paradise were divided into two parts: those who fought on the side of God and those who remained neutral. These last, already half-fallen, were sent to earth for a time, and became the *fées*.'[24] Or, from a Welsh woman, 'I think there must be an intermediate state between life on earth and heavenly life, and it may be in this that spirits and fairies live.'[25]

From the human point of view, this intermediate state populated by fallen but not evil angels is none other than Purgatory. St Brendan continued to wander from island to island for seven years before his ship pierced a ring of dense fog and the voyagers suddenly found themselves at their goal, the 'Promised Land of the Saints', where there is no darkness, Christ being the only light. This is the transition from Purgatory to Paradise. Here the unfallen angels still take on the guise of bird-cantors, as several other related works of Celtic Christianity bear witness. The tenth-century *Adventures of St Columba's Clerics* takes us to the very throne of the King of Heaven, on which are perched three birds who chant the eight Canonical Hours.[26] So does the eleventh-century *Vision of St Adamian*, who did not go by boat but was taken up to Heaven by an angel.[27] The *Voyage of the Huí Corra* (also eleventh-century) is more specific: the traveller Lochan, before embarking on his voyage, has a dream in which he 'beheld the Lord Himself on His throne, and a birdflock of angels making music to Him. Then I saw a bright bird, and sweeter was his singing than every melody. Now this was Michael in the form of a bird in the presence of the Creator.'[28]

There is a characteristic passport to the Celtic Otherworld, reminiscent of the famous Golden Bough with which Aeneas descended to Hades in Book VI of Virgil's *Aeneid*. It is a silver branch with golden fruits, three or nine in number, which – and here is the typical Celtic touch – strike together to make an enchanting melody.[29] The branch itself doubtless comes from that same magical tree on which the eloquent birds were perched in Brendan's story. In *The Sickbed of Cuchulain* we meet the tree again in the island palace of Labra, actually giving off its music:

> From a tree in the forecourt
> Sweet harmony streams;
> It stands silver, yet sunlit
> With gold's glitter gleams.[30]

The hero Bran was lulled to sleep by sweet music, coming from he knew not where. When he awoke – or, perhaps more accurately, when he entered a lucid dream-state – he discovered a musical branch by his side. Going

home with it to his palace, he met there a strange woman who sang him a
long song of the wondrous isle whence the branch had come: an island of
perpetual youth, health, pleasure, laughter, feasting, and of course 'sweet
music striking on the ear'.[31] Another legendary king of Ireland, Cormac
MacAirt, came upon the selfsame branch in the hands of an unknown man:
its music seduced him so that he sold his own wife and children in exchange
for it.[32] It was his quest, Orpheus-like, to retrieve them that led him
through the mist to a Paradise teeming with white birds and watered by a
fountain with five streams 'more melodious than mortal music'.[33]

These and other musical themes recur in the Celtic stories like leitmotifs
in some great opera. There are musical stones, like the 'conspicuous stone' in
Bran's voyage, 'from which come a hundred strains',[34] and the 'three
precious stones with a soft melodious sound, with the sweetness of music at
every two choirs' (in *The Adventure of St Columba's Clerics*).[35] Sometimes
one cannot be sure exactly what the poet has in mind, though the last
quotation seems to resonate with another mysterious episode in St
Brendan's Voyage.[36] One of the islands visited by his party is extraordinarily flat, spacious, treeless, but covered with white and purple fruit. There
they see three choirs of boys, separated by a slingshot's distance from one
another but continuously moving. Singing both antiphonally and in
unison, they chant the eight Canonical Hours, just like the birds, but unlike
those fallen spirits they also celebrate the Mass. Lastly, there is the impressive
vision of the Crystal Pillar. In Brendan's Voyage[36] it rises out of the sea: a
vast column, each of its four sides seven hundred yards long, the whole
thing draped in a silvery net with meshes big enough for the boat to pass
through. In the *Voyage of Maelduin*[37] (early ninth century), the pillar and its
net are encountered again, and a voice speaks from the top of it. In the
Voyage of the Huí Corra[38] the net is a brazen one, spread on a brazen palisade
surrounding another island, and the wind makes music on it which puts the
voyagers to sleep for three days and three nights.

The Celtic legends leave an unforgettable impression of a dreamlike
existence suffused with music: an Elysium of musical trees, fruits, fountains,
stones, nets, choirs, and birds upon birds. Taken as discrete symbols, one
could analyze and explain them, but this would be to lose the environing
atmosphere of a world with its own nature and its own inner consistency.
To ask what the crystal pillar 'means' is as pointless as for a visitor in Paris to
ask the meaning of the Eiffel Tower: it is just what one finds there, and the
striking image is its own meaning.

But where exactly are all those worlds and planes situated? Certainly there
was a time when it made sense to place them somewhere on the Earth,

underground, or in the visible heavens: hence the legends of subterranean kingdoms (still in vogue among the 'hollow-earthers'), of Lost Eden, the Fortunate Isles, Shangri-La, Shambhala, and other places that the medieval cartographers confidently marked on their maps. Hence, too, the situation of Purgatory on a mountain, as by Dante, or in the spheres of the seven planets that circle the Earth in the Ptolemaic system. But these have become an anomaly since the voyages of exploration and the revolution in cosmology, and it is pointless to pretend any longer that the images presented to the Soul are anywhere in the physical universe.

An important distinction must now be drawn, as we scrutinize more carefully what has hitherto been called variously the Otherworld, the World of the Imagination or of the Soul, the fantastic world, the trance-, dream-, or ecstatic state. The distinction is between fantasy or reverie that one invents for oneself, and the objective but nonmaterial world that is presented as images to the inner organ of imaginative perception. These latter images have their own independent source, existence, and meaning. A Jungian would distinguish the two types as coming respectively from the personal and the collective unconscious, while occultists would tend to identify the latter as an Astral World of many planes. Since my concern here is ultimately with the hearing of music, I will follow the approach of the French savant (and passionate musical amateur) Henry Corbin and call it simply the Imaginal World.[39] Corbin's approach, while very far from being a sceptical one, was phenomenological and scholarly rather than vatic or theoretical. His personal experience apart, a vast knowledge of sources ranging over the whole Western and Near-Eastern tradition gave him abundant evidence for the existence of a world where 'autonomous archetypal Images are infinitely realized, forming a hierarchy of degrees varying according to their relative subtlety or density.'[40] Those are the words of Quṭbuddīn Shīrāzī, a commentator on the *Oriental Theosophy* of the twelfth-century Iranian sage Suhrawardī. Now let us hear that master himself, speaking from his own experience:

On each of these levels species exist analogous to those in our world, but they are infinite. Some are peopled by Angels and the human Elect. Other are people by Angels and genii, others by demons. God alone knows the number of these levels and what they contain. The pilgrim rising from one degree to another discovers on each higher level a subtler state, a more entrancing beauty, a more intense spirituality, a more overflowing delight. The highest of these degrees borders on that of the intelligible pure entities of light and very closely resembles it.[41]

The Imaginal World has its elements, its cities, and its heavenly spheres. Although they do not have a material substratum, they are objective and entirely real. Among the marvels there is the immense 'city' Hūrqalyā, which contains in exemplary form both Heavens and Earth: here are the archetypal Images of all individuals and corporeal things in the sensory world, as well as of the heavenly spheres. Shīrāzī says that it was in these celestial spheres of the Imaginal World that Pythagoras heard the Music of the Spheres. 'Afterwards he returned to his material body. As a result of what he had heard he determined the musical relationships and perfected the science of music.'[42]

Armed with the concept of the Imaginal World, we can make an intelligent approach to the age-old myth of the Ascent through the Spheres and the music that is heard there. While most of the Celtic adventures take place on the Imaginal Earth, the accounts of ascent must refer to what we may call the 'Imaginal Heavens.' In the classic version of the ascent, the soul rises above the Earth (which it may even look down upon from a distance, as did C.G. Jung in the visions of his old age[43]), and finds itself in the region of the planetary spheres. The Pamphylian soldier in Plato's 'Myth of Er'[44] saw the system of the seven planets and the fixed stars with a Siren standing on each sphere, 'uttering one tone varied by diverse modulations; and the whole eight of them together composed a single harmony.'[45] Following in Plato's footsteps, Cicero also ended his *Republic* with a cosmic vision, though this time presented as a dream. Scipio Africanus, the Roman hero, saw nine spheres (including the Earth), making a 'grand and pleasing sound.'[46] His deceased grandfather, who acted as his guide, explained that it came from the rapid motion of the spheres themselves, which although they are nine, produce only seven different tones, 'this number being, one might almost say, the key to the universe'.[47] Plutarch's Timarchus, who voluntarily entered the oracular Crypt of Trophonius in order to find out about the mysterious Sign of Socrates, lost consciousness of his body and, as he seemed to exit through the top of his skull, 'faintly caught the whirr of something revolving overhead with a pleasant sound'.[48] When he saw the glorious spectacle of the revolving spheres, he 'fancied that their circular movement made a musical whirring in the aether, for the gentleness of the sound resulting from the harmony of all the separate sounds corresponded to the evenness of their motion'.[49]

All these voyagers returned to Earth for the edification of their fellows: they did not pass through the spheres of the Imaginal World which resounded so marvellously in their ears. For an account of the journey's ultimate goal and meaning, we cannot do better than to read the Hermetic book *Poimandres, the Shepherd of Men*.[50] In this dialogue, Poimandres, the World-Mind, explains to Hermes that when a person dies, the physical body is first surrendered to its natural fate of decomposition. Next the 'ethos', the instinctive or habitual nature, is given back to the Daimon, and the senses, passions and desires return to their sources in irrational Nature. What is left of the person – the only immortal part – now enters what Poimandres calls the Harmony, a term that emphasizes the musical nature of the planetary spheres. At each one it is disburdened of the power which that planet rules. At the sphere of the Moon it leaves behind the power of growth and waning; at Mercury, the power of devising evils; at Venus, the illusion of desire; at the Sun, the arrogance of domination; at Mars, impious boldness and rashness; at Jupiter, striving for wealth by evil means; at Saturn, falsehood.

And then, with all the energies of the Harmony stripped from it, clothed only in its proper Power, it enters that Nature which belongs to the Eighth Sphere, and with the beings there it sings hymns to the Father, and all who are there rejoice at its coming.[51]

Perhaps St Brendan's seven-year voyage to the Promised Land of the Saints should be seen as analogous to this journey through the seven spheres. Certainly the Hermetic ascent corresponds to the purgatorial process in Christian pneumatology. But in its own context, the purification described in *Poimandres* is not from sins committed on Earth, so much as from the very fact of having been incarnated. The ascent through the spheres presumes a prior descent through them, in order for the soul to have acquired these contaminating planetary powers. As in every gnostic doctrine, it is assumed that the soul once enjoyed a pristine state in Heaven from which, for one reason or another, it descended to take up its abode in an earthly body. The actual manner of realization of each planetary power is shown forth in the natal horoscope cast for the moment of incarnation: here each planet occupies a definite zodiacal degree and is in certain relationships with the others. In C.G. Jung's words, 'The ascent through the planetary spheres therefore meant something like a shedding of the characterological qualities indicated by the horoscope, a retrogressive liberation from the character imprinted by the archons [planetary rulers].'[52] And again, in more psychological terms; 'The journey through the planetary houses, like the crossing of the great halls in the Egyptian underworld, therefore signifies the overcoming of a psychic obstacle, or of an autonomous complex, suitably represented by a planetary god or demon. Anyone who has passed through all the spheres is free from compulsion: he has won the crown of victory and become like a god.'[53]

In other words, the journey is an initiation, or a series of initiations, taking place in the Imaginal World, either while still associated with one's earthly body or after one has discarded it. The music that is heard there and whose supernatural beauty is always remarked upon is none other than the knowledge gained in these initiations by those who have attained the requisite stage of psychic growth, being exempt from desires and vices to which nearly everyone on earth is subject. As the late Neoplatonist Simplicius puts it:

If anyone, like Pythagoras, who is reported to have heard this harmony, should have had his terrestrial body exempt from him, and his luminous and celestial vehicle, and the senses which it contains, purified, either through a good allotment, or through purity of life, or through a perfection arising from sacred operations, such a one will perceive things invisible to others, and will hear things inaudible to others.[54]

In this dense passage, Simplicius sets out the three conditions under which the secret harmonies may be heard. The 'good allotment' is the grace or genius with which exceptional people are born, apparently free from the vices that beset others and already endowed with superhuman powers. 'Purity of life' is gained by asceticism and persistent self-denial: the vices are conquered in this life. 'Sacred operations' are theurgic or magical practices that aid the soul's ascent through sacramental means. The reward of all of these is knowledge or Gnosis, of a sort inaccessible to the uninitiated.

The Ptolemaic cosmos with its concentric spheres is an adequate and symbolically accurate projection of the Imaginal Heavens on to physical space, the seven planets being the visible manifestations of the seven ruling powers of the soul, and the journey through them being the necessary prelude to eternal life beyond the Eighth Sphere. But the heliocentric cosmos, physically correct though it be, can no longer accommodate this symbolism. If the soul were to rise from the earth and head for the stars through the Copernican–Newtonian cosmos, not only might it miss several spheres altogether, but far from breaking out of the limits of material existence to emerge in Heaven, it would continue endlessly through star-scattered space. Certainly the physical universe is indefinite in extent, but it is not infinite,[55] that is to say it does not exclude the existence of other worlds and other modes of being, for which the Ptolemaic cosmos wisely left room outside the Starry Sphere.

Geocentricity is wise in another sense, too, because to put Earth at rest at the centre of all things agrees with the evidence of the unaided eye, thereby enabling simple people to live in a cosmos that makes sense to them. Heliocentricity requires one to disbelieve the still earth under one's feet and the moving Sun in the sky. One makes such leaps of faith only on the basis of overwhelming conviction. But what peasant could understand the proofs, say, in Galileo's *Dialogue on the Two Principal World Systems*? The heliocentric dogma requires him to believe it solely on the authority of his betters, the scientists, just as the Church required belief in the invisible and the improbable solely on the witness of its Scriptures and Saints. But to what end? There the parallel breaks down. In true religion one believes in order some day to 'see face to face', but science craves, even compels, our assent lest its single vision fail and its topless tower fall. For the human microcosm, the geocentric system remains the most accurate map: the four sluggish elements of body are surrounded by the volatile and musical spheres of the Soul, and all a mere bubble in the infinite space of the Spirit.

The heliocentric cosmos, however, contains its own truth: one which, going as it does against the evidence of the senses, is esoteric in nature. In turning the focus of our system inwards, from the invisible Primum Mobile to the visible Sun, it reflects the doctrine that the Divine is not to be found in external forms, nor is it vastly remote from us, but on the contrary shines in the centre of our own being as the Kingdom of Heaven within. The structure of the physical universe corresponds to this teaching, as the Pythagoreans and Kepler knew, but in its intellectual and esoteric aspect, not its sensual and public one. When in the seventeenth century this structure was revealed and generally accepted, it was misunderstood, its literal sense supplanting its symbolic meaning, and, like all initiatic secrets when disclosed to the profane, it worked negatively: in this case toward the devaluation of Spirit and Soul and the destruction of Man as microcosm. That is why the music of the spheres fell almost silent for two hundred years.

Although hearing the planetary music is usually reserved for those in supernatural states, there is a widespread and recurrent tradition that the Sun, at least, makes sounds which are audible on Earth. The Indians of the Peruvian Andes, who have a cosmological system as rich and complex as any in the Old World, say that the Sun makes a sound on rising.[56] The Greek historian Strabo[57] writes of the sound which it makes on setting in the sea between Spain and Africa, beyond the Pillars of Hercules. A curious Jewish tradition, reported by the Italian Rabbi Moscato (sixteenth century) is that Joshua heard the pleasant melody of the Sun in the middle of battle with the Amorites and was seriously distracted, which is why he said 'Sun stand thou still upon Gibeon' (Joshua 10.12), meaning 'Stop singing!'[58] (If such an interpretation had been acceptable among Moscato's Christian neighbours, Galileo and his doctrine would have had an easier time.) A passage in the Talmud regards the Sun's noise as something to be taken for granted, unnoticed by its very familiarity like the din of the Nile cataracts, the Catadupa, to which classical writers often compared the music of the spheres. 'Why is the voice of a man not heard by day as it is heard by night?

Because of the wheel of the Sun which saws in the sky like a carpenter sawing cedars.'[59] The medieval Grail poem *Titurel* gives a more flattering description of its sound, saying that 'the sounds of the rising Sun surpassed the sound of strings and the song of birds, as gold surpasses copper in value.'[60] And Goethe, in the Prologue to *Faust*, has Raphael say at dawn: 'The Sun sounds forth, in age-old fashion.'

If we do not hear it ourselves, perhaps we should listen to the Dawn Prelude of Ravel's *Daphnis and Chloë*. Or, if that is too elaborate, imagine the Sun's sound as a single, piercing note. 'A distant sound that seems to come from the sky, the sound of a twanged string mournfully dying away': that is the mysterious offstage sound that comes twice in Chekhov's *The Cherry Orchard*, itself suggestive of the 'Cry of Memnon' – the sound like a snapped string which the rising Sun used to evoke from the Colossus of Memnon in Egyptian Thebes.[61] Perhaps it is the sound of the Archer God Apollo twanging his bow, as he sends out his arrows of light.

'Look at the Sun! It is the triad from which the chords of the stars shower down at our feet to wrap us in their threads of crystallized fire! A chrysalis in flames, we await Psyche to carry us on high to the Sun!'[62] Thus the German Romantic fantasy writer E.T.A. Hoffmann puts in a couple of lines the whole doctrine of musical ascent, invoking the antique image of the Soul as butterfly. Here on Earth we are like mere caterpillars until we let ourselves be entranced and enwrapped by the music which has its origin in the starry spheres – the silken harp-strings of the stars. Then we await the moment, whether in trance or at death, when our cocoons will fall away and we will awaken as winged soul-beings who can fly back to our true home of light.

There is plenty of evidence that it is music itself that can set us on this journey. That is how the Irish hero Bran began his quest. Athanasius Kircher relates how one evening, after listening to a particularly beautiful concert by three lute players, he fell into a deep trance in which he ascended through the seven planetary spheres and even glimpsed the Divine Light beyond.[63] Blessed Angela of Foligno (thirteenth century) rose to the Uncreated Light as the organ played the *Sanctus* in the Church of St Francis.[64] And in our own day, Warner Allen[65] writes of the Timeless Moment which he experienced during a concert in the Queen's Hall, between two consecutive notes of Beethoven's Seventh Symphony. Or again, the music may be heard internally. Hildemarie Streich, the therapist mentioned in Chapter One, writes that:

There are dreams in which music acts as a kind of leader of the soul into the life after death. The music to be heard in such cases is mostly of indescribable beauty and leaves behind a feeling of consolation and of a certainty of the existence of timeless forces which exist beyond death and transcend human experience.[66]

Here is an account of one such dream:

Sick with a fever, I fell asleep brooding over the meaning of harmony. . . . Some hours later I awoke, but not into the earthly environment: it was an awakening to a state that was at once a Pleroma of perfect fullness and a Void of perfect emptiness, through which – though far less real than the state itself – the heavenly choir and orchestra played tremendously the theme E E E C. (The theme came from Charles Ives' 'Concord' Sonata, where it occurs as a reminiscence of Beethoven's Fifth Symphony.) After a while I came gradually back to my ego, trailing like a melody a sublime feeling of peace. That theme had also answered my question about harmony.[67]

Both inner and outer music can serve as *psychopompos* – as leader of the Soul – to realms more real than Earth. In some of the examples already given in this chapter it would even be difficult to say whether the music heard was objective or subjective. Music can start one off on the journey, it can accompany one on the way, and it may even be there at the journey's end. All the religious traditions have known this, and put this knowledge to use in their different ways. In the remainder of this chapter we will see some of these applications.

The Christian tradition, while recognizing the great psychological value of music, has seldom used it for esoteric or initiatic purposes. The reason lies in the situation under which early Christianity, both esoteric and exoteric, developed. Under the Roman Empire music was associated with all the things the Christians shunned: the ecstatic worship of pagan divinities, frivolous entertainments by virtuosi, sexual licence and the horrors of the circuses. The Church Fathers allowed the singing of hymns, but could not conceive of anyone actually listening to music except for mere sensual enjoyment. Not for many centuries did the organ, the instrument of the circus, become a fixture in Christian churches, and other instruments were never completely at home there. The fears of the Fathers were justified in post-Reformation times, when the High Mass and major Offices tended to degenerate into concerts, the congregation into an audience – a degeneration in the liturgical sense, even if the music was a cantata by Bach or a Mass by Haydn. The reader may judge whether the situation has improved since the Second Vatican Council (1962), with the modernist trend in both Catholic and Protestant churches being to use music, and language, to which no one could possibly respond aesthetically, thus forcing a retreat into religious or at least communal aspiration.

A miracle occurred, however, during the Dark Ages, when the simple hymns of the Church Fathers blossomed into plainchant. What we know as Gregorian Chant is only one branch – the best organized and the best preserved one – from the fertile stem of Christian monophony. The others are suppressed, lost, or largely forgotten. But at a time when even Gregorian Chant has virtually disappeared from use, there is no need for quibbles. Two French composers have said, once and for all, what needs to be said about plainchant:

It is the prayer and the music of the Church, it is impersonal, it is above the weakness of a composer, it is sheltered from attack or criticism, it is as solid as Earth and as tranquil as Hope. It is the only worthy musical office. Plainchant itself is above all composers, past, present and future.

Charles Gounod, 1873[68]

[On liturgical music] There is only one: *plainchant*. Plainchant alone possesses all at once the purity, the joy and the lightness necessary for the soul's flight towards Truth.

Olivier Messiaen, 1977[69]

A plainchant liturgy certainly does not exclude the use of other religious music, as Messiaen is quick to add, but it should form the daily bread to which other musics are as garnishes.

For monastic orders, the daily singing of plainchant has been a way of life for a millennium. If the liturgy is performed in its entirety, as in the contemplative orders, the Mass with its dozen sung items, and the eight daily Canonical Hours or Offices with their numerous psalms, hymns and antiphons, provide several hours' singing each day. In a monastery this is the work not of a professional choir but of every monk irrespective of musical talent. Like many good things, its value was only recognized in its absence, as witness the following true story.[70] When after Vatican II the Trappist monks of an American abbey obediently discontinued the singing of their daily Offices in Latin, all manner of things began to go wrong. Most noticeably, they found that they could no longer survive with only four or five hours' sleep a night, as some of them had done for years. Other troubles followed: sickness and psychological disturbances that threatened to upset the even tenor of their contemplative lives. After trying various conventional remedies, all unsuccessfully, they began to wonder whether the cause of their ills might have been the loss of the hours they used to devote to singing the liturgy in Gregorian Chant. So with special dispensation they went back to their old routine, and their troubles gradually disappeared.

The lesson of this anecdote is that singing was instituted in the contemplative orders not only for the glory of God but also as a practical means of harmonizing the personality, and the community, in a situation of great psychological stress – for in no other way can one describe a life devoid of normal human intercourse. The use of the voice is a human need no less compelling than sexual desire. The Trappists, forswearing conversation, nevertheless exercised their voices in song, and it was the removal of this sublimation that brought disharmony to their lives.

Plainchant is the perfect devotional music for singer and listener alike. It does not demand the complications of professionalism; as Gounod points out, it bears the stamp of no personality; it avoids emotionalism. At the simplest level, as demonstrated above, it is therapeutic. Its resonances, especially when enhanced by the Romanesque and Gothic buildings in which it is at home, have a beneficent effect on the body and psyche. It calms, it awes, it uplifts. But there is more. It is a vehicle which can take one as high as one is capable of going, whether on the path of identification with the inner tone, as for the singer, or, for the listener, on that of entry into 'those temples in the high spheres that can be opened through song only'.[71] For the seven notes of the modes can be heard as the notes of the planets, the wandering of the melody through them felt as a journey around the spheres. Or even their differences can be transcended, and the whole entered as a pleroma, like the Hermetic soul breaking through to the Eighth Sphere. Plainchant, like the mystery of the Mass, offers to each what he or she is able to receive.

Not so the music of Protestant sects, which has always been more self-conscious and specifically emotional. Protestantism has periodically given a home to the more Dionysian impulses, and to a cruder type of congregational participation in the service, like that of the eighteenth-century Methodist sect called the 'Jumpers' from their dancing and leaping during services, or the present-day Pentecostal and Revivalist sects, especially in the American South, which combine repetitive music with rhythmical movement to induce a sort of ecstatic trance in which visions, glossolalia (speaking with tongues) and healing may occur. However, this is quite a different matter from the use of music as an initiatic means, for the practices are open to all, not controlled by a Master, and the ecstatic states are not accompanied by any metaphysical understanding. It is intoxication without knowledge.

Apart from the experiences of individual mystics, music is missing from Christian esotericism except in the speculative form favoured by the Platonists as an intelligible image of cosmic and metaphysical realities. For a deliberate application of *musica instrumentalis* for higher ends we must look to the mystical schools of the other branches of Abrahamic monotheism, first Judaism, then Islam.

The writings of the Jewish Kabbalah contain a vision of a harmonious universe in which 'not only the angels sing: the stars, the spheres, the

64

merkavah [Chariot-Throne] and the beasts, the trees in the Garden of Eden and their perfumes, indeed the whole universe sings before God.'[72] Although this source says that only Moses and Joshua could hear such music, in later Kabbalistic schools, and especially in Hasidism, the privilege is extended to the zaddiks or living spiritual masters. It is their part then to pass on its benefits to their disciples for their healing and purification, either directly by singing to them some semblance of it, or indirectly through the wisdom with which it has imbued them: for we must not forget that music, on that level, is synonymous with Gnosis.

The human voice is better for this purpose than any instrument, being as it is said 'of a noble corporeality',[73] on the confines between spirit and body (compare our earlier association of music with *spiritus* and the quintessential aether). When the zaddik is truly possessed by the experiences of his soul, his singing may go beyond anything of which his voice is normally capable: 'Thus one zaddik stood in prayer . . . and sang new melodies, wonder of wonder, that he has never heard and that no human ear had ever heard, and he did not know at all what he sang and in what way he sang, for he was bound to the upper world.'[74]

Such melodies are generally wordless: 'For the songs of the souls – at the time they are swaying in the high regions to drink from the well of the Almighty King – consist of tones only, dismantled of burdensome words.'[75] As early as the fourteenth century, Rabbi Solomon ben Adret issued a formal decree against the use of wordless chant as practised in Kabbalistic circles,[76] but such chant, though only admitted to the public Jewish liturgy (as to the Christian) under the guise of extended melismata on words such as 'Hallelujah', re-emerged as a favourite devotional means of Hasidism. In the Hasidic communities of Eastern Europe, which by the end of the eighteenth century contained as many as a million Jews, singing and dancing were cultivated as the perfect expression of God's people on earth. When practised communally they tend to adopt the features of folk-song and dance, both local and Near-Eastern. When given forth by one inspired person the Hasidic song is an emotional outpouring, joyful or sad as it may be, of the soul to God, 'capable of transforming the soul of the singing worshipper to such an extent that definite stages of a mystic approach to God could be reached, stages which otherwise were most difficult to attain'.[77] We must mention one further variety of song, typical of the Hasidic blend of mysticism with humour: the type with a 'doodling' refrain. *Dudeln* in Yiddish means to play on the bagpipe (*Dudelsack*) or just to 'tootle'. But *du* is also the familiar 'thou', and the sense of the song is an address to a God who is found everywhere: wherever the singer looks, it is *du-du-du*, 'Thou, Thou, Thou'.[78]

A song without words is perhaps the best image of the secret harmonies: yet in a religion whose esoteric schools have always had such an interest in words and language – believing Hebrew, in fact, to be God's own tongue – it would be surprising if one did not find a corresponding elevation of the word. Here we should distinguish between individual mysticism and the work of collective redemption. To the mystic belong the wordless, timeless, wandering melodies whose wings carry his soul to higher realms, even to temporary union with the eternal *Du*. But to every Hasidic Jew, as to the Boddhisattva of Buddhism, belongs in addition the task of redeeming the Universe: aiding the return not only of his own inner spark to its Origin but of all the other myriad sparks imprisoned in the manifested world. In Hasidic life this is done, constantly, by the intentional performance of every thought, word, and act. In a profound passage, written as early as 1908, Martin Buber explains something of this miraculous process.

From time immemorial speech was for the Jewish mystic a rare and awe-inspiring thing. A characteristic theory of letters existed which dealt with them as with the elements of the world and with their intermixture as with the inwardness of reality. The word is an abyss through which the speaker strides. 'One should speak words as if the heavens were opened in them. And as if it were not so that you take the word in your mouth, but rather as if you entered into the word.' He who knows the secret melody that bears the inner into the outer, who knows the holy song that merges the lonely, shy letters into the singing of the spheres, he is full of the power of God 'and it is as if he created heaven and earth and all worlds anew'. He does not find his sphere before him as does the freer of souls, he extends it from the firmament to the silent depths. But he also works towards redemption. 'For in each letter there are the three: world, soul, and divinity. They rise and join and unite themselves, and they become the word, and the words unite themselves in God in genuine unity, since a man has set his soul in them, and worlds unite themselves and ascend, and the great rapture is born.' Thus the acting person prepares the final oneness of all things.[79]

But perhaps there is no real divide between God's music and his words. Abraham Abulafia (thirteenth century) compares the intellectual exercise of the Kabbalist, working on his letter-combinations, to that of musical composition, as exerting a similar influence on the soul. As explained by Amnon Shiloah, 'the combination of letters creates enjoyment in the soul just as musical harmony does, because of the unveiling of secrets confined in such combinations'.[80]

In the public worship of Islam, music has no place beyond the simple chanting of the Quran. As if in compensation, the Muslim esoteric orders – the Sufis – have made music one of the strongest features of their own religious practices. The general term for it, *samāᶜ* 'audition', stresses the passive nature of this musical way: whereas the Hasidim are transported by their own song, the Sufis' is the more inward path of the concentrated listener. Perhaps in this one can see a reflection of the earth-embracing mysticism of the Jew *vis-à-vis* the earth-forsaking flight of the Oriental mystic. At first the *samāᶜ* referred simply to the hearing of the Quran being recited or sung. Devout listeners would be transported into ecstasy by certain passages: some would pass into unconsciousness, or even, if we credit the many reports, die. Others would moan, move about, wave their arms, arise and begin dancing. From these spontaneous beginnings grew an institutionalized *samāᶜ* with strict rules of conduct and decorum, allowing as the impetus to these ecstasies not only the canonical text but also devotional songs and instrumental pieces.

Everyone knows of one such development: the 'Whirling Dervishes' of the Near East. Properly called the Mevlevī Order, and founded in Konya, Turkey, by the Persian poet Rūmī (1207–73), these still practise a *samāᶜ* of whirling dance accompanied by the music of the *nay* or reed flute. They dress in tall felt hats like truncated cones, and white gowns with broad skirts that stand out as they whirl. Their hats are said to be tilted at the same angle as the Earth's axis, and their dance to symbolize the movements of the planctary spheres as they circle in perfect order and love for their Lord. Rūmī, in one of his poems, explains the purpose of this devotion:

> We all have been parts of Adam, we have
>   heard those melodies in Paradise.
> Although the water and earth of our bodies
>   have caused a doubt to fall upon us,
>   something of those melodies comes back
>   to our memory.

(*Mathnawī*, IV, 736–7)

Not all Sufis were as disciplined and elegant in their *samāᶜ* as the Mevlevī. In books of instruction dating from the eleventh century there are sections on what is to be done when an auditor or dancer begins to tear off his clothes, what someone should do who catches a torn garment, etc. If deriving from someone in a high spiritual state, such rags could become relics. But apparently there were abuses, especially with regard to attractive women looking on (they never seem to have participated) and to attractive boys gradually divesting themselves of their clothing. So one finds, just as in Christian and Jewish medieval writings, long and dreary polemics both for and against the admissibility of music in religious devotions. Both sides tirelessly quote the few applicable passages in the Quran, and the numerous Hadith or stories of the Prophet's life, in which his every yawn or smile is interpreted as an absolute principle. From the Sufis' point of view, they were fighting for their lives against a centralized, legalistic, exoteric Islam such as again threatens today. Taking up a previous theme of whether words or music are closer to God, one can at least say in favour of music that tones can never be twisted and interpreted, as words can, to condemn one's fellow man out of God's mouth.

What happens to the Sufi during the *samāᶜ*? I will summarize the accounts of the philosopher brothers Al-Ghazālī: Abū Ḥāmid (1058-1111) and Majd al-Dīn (d. 1126), who both wrote treatises on Sufi music and dance. Both agree that *samāᶜ* can bring one to states that are otherwise very difficult to attain. Above all, it arouses one's love and longing for God – just as for the ordinary fellow, love songs arouse his sexual longing – and from this single-minded devotion comes a purification of the heart. Following purification come visions and revelations that surpass all other ambitions:[81] a hundred thousand states in a world of lights and spirits otherwise undiscoverable even through the most perfect religious observances.[82] In truth, these states are incapable of expression through words, or of imagination by those who have not experienced them. But a parallel is given us by the two types of music, vocal and instrumental. In the first, the poetry tells us what we are to feel – fear, grief, joy, etc. – and we can put our feelings into words. But instrumental music gives us feelings, no less intense, which we cannot describe, and longings which are felt most powerfully, even by common people, without knowing what it is that they long for.[83]

Suhrawardī, who has already explained to us the ontology of the spheres, is more able to find words for the inexpressible.

The suprasensory realities encountered by the prophets, the Initiates, and others appear to them sometimes in the form of lines of writing, sometimes in the hearing of a voice which may be gentle and sweet and which can also be terrifying. Sometimes they see human forms of extreme beauty who speak to them in most beautiful words and converse with them intimately about the invisible world; at other times these forms appear to them like those delicate figures proceeding from the most refined art of the painters. On occasion they are shown as if in an enclosure; at other times the forms and figures appear suspended.[84]

Suhrawardī's own other-worldly experiences, as one can tell from his writings in general, were mainly visual, that is to say perceived with the inner eye. Nevertheless, he does not discount the music that is heard with the inner ear, for he says: 'Thus it is conceivable that there are sounds and melodies in the celestial spheres which are not conditioned by the air nor by a vibratory disturbance. And one cannot imagine that there could be melodies more delightful than theirs . . . '.[85]

During *samāᶜ*, he says elsewhere, 'the soul deprives the ear of its auditory function and listens directly herself',[86] meaning that what is heard in the state no longer bears the slightest resemblance to the music that is going on.

Olivier Messiaen, in the speech already cited, says that religious music in its widest sense stands above liturgical plainchant, but even above that he places a third kind of music which he calls 'coloured'. Evidently more a gift of the listener than of the composer, coloured music means synaesthesia, the perceiving of sounds as colours and of colours as sounds – or perhaps of both as something not definable through either sense. He describes the effect of this as an *éblouissement*, a 'dazzling' or 'dizzying': when we stare at a stained-glass window 'we do not understand, we are *éblouis*'. This experience, he says, puts us in touch with another reality. It shows us that God is beyond words, thoughts and concepts. Most of all, it prepares us for the life to come in the Resurrection Body, when we will know God. In Messiaen's closing words,

This knowledge will be a perpetual *éblouissement*, an eternal music of colours, an eternal colour of musics.
'In Thy Music, we will SEE Music'.
'In Thy Light, we will HEAR Light'.[87]

Rūmī projects the experience into Paradise past, Messiaen into the Celestial City to come, and Suhrawardī knows in the present. But since it is beyond determination of time, it is plain that all three know of the same thing, though perhaps to differing degrees of intensity.

As one looks further East, to the Hindu world, the use of music for the attainment of higher states merges into a whole science of sound and its practical application in Yoga. The important distinction to be made here is between Mantra-yoga and Shabda-yoga.

Mantra-yoga uses as a focus of concentration a mantram: syllables, words or sentences which may be spoken or intoned out loud or may be pronounced with one's inner voice. The sounds used (e.g. OM MANI PADME HUM) always have a symbolic meaning, but whether one's practice involves knowledge or consideration of that, or combines the mantram with visualization, or concentrates exclusively on the sound, is a matter for schools and individuals to decide. So is the degree of repetition, and so is the extent to which mantra in general are invested with cosmic or magical significance. The underlying principle is as follows. When one tries to control the mind in meditation, one discovers two major adversaries: the inner ear and the inner eye. The one hears a perpetual running commentary, the other watches an endless filmstrip. To overcome them is not, for most aspirants, as easy as switching off a television. So one tries to replace them, the chatter by a mantram, the flicker of images by a deliberate visualization. One way is to try to hold steady the picture of a written mantram while simultaneously hearing it, as for instance a vividly coloured Sanskrit or English OM-syllable.

Eventually a state of inner quietude may be reached by this means, in which the proper work of meditation can begin. I say this advisedly, because the public image of meditation as the simple repetition of a mantram in order to induce a relaxed state, although therapeutic, has little to do with Yoga properly so-called. The mantram is only an aid on the path: a stick to support one and to beat off the assailing thoughts, which one eventually discards. For the same reason some Sufis urge one to dispense as soon as one can with the outward music and ritual of the samā^c, the goal being the capacity to enter the states at will and eventually to sustain them unbroken so that one 'hears from every object in the Universe'.[88]

In Shabda-yoga, one does not begin with a tool ready to hand: one sets out to discover the Inner Sound and to identify oneself thereby with the universal Sound Current. The inner ear may perceive it at first in multifarious forms: noises as of bells and other instruments, of animal and human voices, of waters and thunders are mentioned, sometimes in systematic sequence and with reference to various energy-centres in the body in which they seem to occur as one's practice progresses. Some sounds are not of this world, and bring ineffable states with them. Others represent the action of vast cosmic forces into which one's little self is absorbed. Clearly the Shabda-yogin is exploring the same worlds, or states, as the Jewish and Muslim mystics, only more particularly in aural mode.

Terrestrial music lets us hear a feeble echo of those sweet modulations which the ear of common mortals cannot grasp, and awakens in them the uplifting memory of what they heard in a previous life. Purifying their souls, it inspires in them a passionate love of divine things; it seizes them from the earth, to the point of making them forget to eat or drink, and lifts their desires towards the starry heavens, which they will attain when they are free of their envelope of clay. Of all instruments, the seven-stringed lyre is the most apt for recalling to men the eternal concert of the grand cosmic symphony. Those who cultivate the art of music are preparing themselves a path through the heavens to the place of the Blessed, just as surely as the most powerful geniuses. And the choir of divine singers exhorts the soul which rises to accomplish this ascent, or rather each one salutes it on its way as it mounts from one heaven to another . . . . Macrobius says that 'The laws of many people and lands set down that one should accompany the dead to their burial with song: this usage is founded upon the belief that souls, on quitting the body, return to the origin of music's magic, that is, to heaven.'[89]

Thus Franz Cumont (1868–1947), interpreter of the spiritual world of Late Antiquity, puts in his own words the doctrines that form the basis of this chapter, and leads us upward to the angelic realms. As late as 1747 Johann Mattheson was taking pains to prove that there must be music in Heaven, and that such music existed before the creation of Man, just as it will last for all eternity. Mattheson was famous throughout Europe for his musical writings; having become deaf, he turned as others have done from audible to intelligible music. Railing against the accepted philosophies of his time, he complains of how positivism (*Demonstrier-Sucht*) and mathematics have become too bold, venturing into the supramundane where they do not belong. How, he says, can one subject the Holy Spirit to syllogisms?[90] In such a climate angelic music is dismissed as a mere allegory, its critics naïvely believing that they have closed the matter by proving that music such as our own cannot exist in Heaven. Of course it does not, says Mattheson: heavenly music can and must be far superior to anything we can imagine.[91] Christians seem to be capable, after all, of believing much more improbable things![92] Why should there not be air in Heaven, or ears, or dancing, or trumpets and trombones? God says in Revelation 21.5: 'I make ALL things new.'[93] In such words Mattheson is defending the existence of the Imaginal World, 'peopled by Angels and the human Elect',[94] containing the Archetypal Images of all things in the sensory world – including music. Such a defence is even more necessary in our time than in his.

Visions of this world which included heavenly music became especially common in the Middle Ages when the liturgy began to reach out to the common people, encouraging them not merely to be present at services but to understand and experience them subjectively.[95] Consequently their mystical visions often take on a liturgical character, the inhabitants of Heaven being perceived by the inner eye and ear as celebrating what we might call the Archetypal Images of ecclesiastical services. We have met this already in the musical birds of Celtic mythology, singing the Canonical Hours. St Hildegard of Bingen's visions (*c.* 1143–50), as described and illustrated in her *Scivias*, conclude with the following:

Next I saw the most lucid air, in which I heard . . . in a marvellous way many kinds of musicians praising the joys of the heavenly citizens . . . And their sound was like the voice of a multitude, making music in harmony . . .[96]

Hildegard's is the apocalyptic vision, first recorded by St John the Divine (Revelation 19.6), of the 'multitude which no man can number' praising God. But others have had more homely visions, such as that of Christ and Mary leading the procession to a church, in which Christ then celebrated the Mass, himself singing the Preface and bidding the congregation at the appropriate place to sing the *Sanctus*.[97] Much earlier, in the mid-ninth century, Aurelian of Réôme tells of how a report of heavenly music actually enabled the earthly liturgy to be amended.

There was a certain monk of the monastery of St Victor, near the city of the Cinnamanni, who by the grace of prayer arrived at the basilica of the Archangel Michael on Mount Gargano. Holding vigil by night before the porch of the church, he heard a choir of angels singing the responsory which is sung at the Nativity of Apostles . . .. When he came to Rome he repeated it to the clerics of the Roman Church and left a record of it as he had heard it. They changed one verse, and thus it is now sung not only by them but by the whole church.[98]

Even more significant than these eyewitness (or earwitness) accounts are the experiences of mystics who have actually taken part in a higher kind of music. Foremost among them is the remarkable testimony of the Yorkshire mystic Richard Rolle of Hampole (d. 1349). He describes his states as progressing from one of inner heat (*calor*) to one in which his whole being was as though suffused with an inward song (*canor*). Far from finding earthly music useful as a stimulus to mystical experience, after the fashion of the Jewish and Muslim groups mentioned earlier in this chapter, Rolle found it unbearable. His 'sweet ghostly song' may be discordant, he says, when heard with bodily ears, and fits ill with the songs and organ music used in church. 'But among angels' tones it has an acceptable melody and with marvels it is commended of them that have known it.'[99]

A German contemporary of Rolle's, Blessed Henry Suso (*c.* 1295–1366), not only heard and saw angels playing rebecs, fiddles and harps, just as they are shown in fourteenth-century paintings:[100] he joined with them in round-dances, such as Dante had recently described in his *Paradiso*.[101] Suso, a follower of Meister Eckhart, lived as a monk and wandering preacher. He appears in his autobiography as a deeply romantic soul, visited by glorious visions and witness to strange phenomena, but also addicted to gruesome ascetic practices. One stage of his mystical progress is interesting enough to quote at length:

Now, on the night before the feast of All Angels, it seemed to him in a vision that he heard angelic strains and sweet heavenly melody; and this filled him with such gladness that he forgot all his sufferings. Then one of the angels said to him: – Behold, with what joy thou dost hear us sing the song of eternity; even so, with like joy do we hear thee sing the song of the venerable Eternal Wisdom. He added further: – This is a portion of the song which the dear elect saints will sing joyously at the last day, when they shall see themselves confirmed in the everlasting bliss of eternity. At another time, on the same festival, after he had spent many hours in contemplating the joys of the angels, and daybreak was at hand, there came to him a youth who bore himself as though he were a heavenly musician sent to him by God;

and with the youth there came many other noble youths, in manner and bearing like the first, save only that he seemed to have some pre-eminence above the rest, as if he were a prince angel. Now this same angel came up to the Servitor [Suso] right blithely, and said that God had sent him down to him, to bring him heavenly joys amid his sufferings; adding that he must cast off all his sorrows from his mind and bear them company, and that he must also dance with them in heavenly fashion. Then they drew the Servitor by the hand into the dance, and the youth began a joyous ditty about the infant Jesus, which runs thus: *In dulci jubilo*, etc. When the Servitor heard the dear Name of Jesus sounding thus sweetly, he became so blithesome in heart and feeling, that the very memory of his sufferings vanished. It was a joy to him to see how exceedingly loftily and freely they bounded in the dance. The leader of the song knew right well how to guide them, and he sang first, and they sang after him in the jubilee of their hearts. Thrice the leader repeated the burden of the song, *Ergo merito*, etc. This dance was not of a kind like those which are danced in this world; but it was a heavenly movement, swelling up and falling back again into the wild abyss of God's hiddenness.[102]

All religious traditions that acknowledge the existence of angels concur in giving them musical attributes. Since it is not clear in visual representations when someone is singing, they are usually given musical instruments to make their function plain. One can see such angels in the Courts of Heaven as pictured in Iranian manuscripts. They appear in Hindu temple sculptures as the seductive Gandharvas, of whom the *Mahabharata* has much to tell. In some *tankas* of Mahayana Buddhism they surround the central figure, and in certain meditations of Tantra one is instructed to imagine one's guru attended by beautiful *dakinis* singing, dancing and playing. One need scarcely mention the musician-angels to be found in the sculpture, wood-carving and stained glass of innumerable European churches, or in the paintings of manuscripts and altarpieces. Finally, the Kabbalistic tradition of Judaism tells of a song which the angels sing whenever Israel sings her song of human praise, the two resounding together.[103]

In Kabbalism there is an interesting development of an idea we have already met with in Rolle and Suso: that of the angelic reaction to human song. Apparently the angels draw as much profit from hearing us as we do if we are fortunate enough to hear them. In a passage from the *Zohar* (compiled in the thirteenth century), Rabbi Eleazar is thus quoted:

It is also known and believed that those angels who sing by night are the leaders of all other singers; and when on earth we living terrestrial creatures raise up our hearts in song, then those supernal beings gain an accession of knowledge, wisdom and understanding, so that they are able to perceive matters which even they had never before comprehended.[104]

In another place, 'the Holy One and all the righteous in the garden' listen to the voice of the pious man.[105]

The reason for this is the centrality of the human state (which of course is not restricted to humans living on this planet) *vis-à-vis* all other beings. Kabbalism expresses this by the task of universal redemption laid to Israel's charge. Buddhism puts the insight in another way, regarding the human state as the only one from which a being can achieve Liberation from the Wheel of Death and Rebirth, and perforce take up the redemptive work of a Boddhisattva. Christianity gives its assent by having the Logos incarnate not as angel but as man, and by the Good Friday Mystery whereby, in the esoteric teaching of the Grail, all Nature is redeemed. In Islam, Allah has the angels pay homage to the newly created Adam; and Muhammad says: 'I have a time with Allah in which no angel who is brought near Allah's presence or prophet who is sent on a mission is enough for me.'[106]

Man is a symbol of Universal Existence: a microcosm that potentially spans all the states of being, and even those states 'above' or 'prior to' being as well.[107] The human being is the potential place of a knowledge of Allah unmediated even by the loftiest Archangel. As the metaphysician René Guénon (1886–1951) says,[108] the celestial hierarchies certainly exist as states of being, populated by entities of the appropriate order, but there is no reason to be particularly concerned with them, any more than with the states of sub-human being that we see all around us. None of these states is in any way absolute or ultimate; all must be transcended by us in order to achieve Liberation.

In the world-view of the Middle Ages and Renaissance, these states were pictured as an orderly hierarchy, a 'Great Chain of Being' stretching from Earth to Heaven. At the bottom of the chain are the minerals and rocks, the vegetable and animal kingdoms; then come the elementals, whose highest members merge with the spirits of the planetary spheres. Above them are the spirits of the fixed stars, and then the angels in their ninefold hierarchy. At the lower end of this angelic hierarchy are the beings concerned with the nature and government of the material world. Plato shows them to us in the Myth of Er as Necessity, holding the spindle of the cosmos on her knees, and her three daughters, the Fates who turn the whorls of the universe and sing of past, present and future.[109] By holding the World-Axis, Necessity creates Space, for the Axis is a line and hence the first development of the primal, dimensionless point into a geometric figure with two ends. This is the birth of opposites to which our world is 'of necessity' subject. Her daughters Lachesis, Clotho, and Atropos create Time in its triple aspect, and with it spin and cut the thread of each mortal life. The French Romantic writer François René de Chateaubriand (1768–1848) described this scene in an early novel, *Les Natchez*, freely adapting it to his theme of the ascent of two saints to present a petition to the Blessed Virgin:

This golden axis, living and immortal, beholds all the worlds turning around it in rhythmical rotations. At equal intervals along this axis are seated three grave Spirits: the first is the angel of the past, the second the angel of the present, the third the angel of the future. They are the three powers who let time fall upon the earth, for time does not enter into heaven nor descend from thence. Three lower angels, similar to the fabulous Sirens in the beauty of their voices, sit at the feet of these first three angels, and sing with all their strength, while the sound which the golden axis of the world makes by turning about itself accompanies their hymns. This concert forms that triple voice of time which tells of past, present and future, which the wise have sometimes heard on earth by pressing their ear to a tomb in the silence of night.[110]

Chateaubriand has separated the twin functions of Plato's cosmocrators, the creation and singing of Time, perhaps feeling that song or music can only exist where there is already temporal succession. Other writers in this chapter will prove him mistaken, for there is an intellectual music that is not subject to the laws of time. However, we will continue with him and hear his description of what the two saints find when, far beyond these Fates, they come to the fields of Heaven itself, described in the pure spirit of early Romanticism:

The waters, trees, and flowers of these unknown fields have nothing resembling our own but their names; it is the charm of verdure, of solitude, of the freshness of our woods, and yet it is not that; it is something whose existence cannot be grasped.

Music never ceases in these places: music which one hears everywhere but which is nowhere; sometimes it is a murmuring like that of an Aeolian harp which the soft breath of Zephyr strokes on a night in springtime; sometimes the ear of a mortal believes it hears the plaint of a divine [glass-]harmonica, those vibrations which have nothing terrestrial about them and which swim in the middle region of the air. Voices, brilliant modulations, suddenly break from the depths of the celestial forests, then dispersed by the breath of the Spirits these strains seem to have expired. But soon a confused melody revives afar off, and one distinguishes perhaps the velvet sounds of a horn wound by an angel, or the hymn of a seraph who sings the splendours of God on the banks of the River of Life.

A gross daylight like our own never lights these regions, but a soft brightness falls noiselessly on the mystic lands, almost as it were snow; it enters into everything and makes it lambent with the loveliest light, giving it a perfect beauty to the eye. The ether, so subtle, would still be too material for this place; the air one breathes is divine love itself: air which is like a sort of visible melody which fills all the white plains of souls with splendour and harmony alike.[111]

In his efforts to convey the flavour of Heaven through images of sight and sound, Chateaubriand makes a point vital to grasp at this stage. He talks, as we do, of 'ascent' to the heavens, picturing them as inconceivably further off than the most inconceivably distant galaxy (which, in his words, would take a musket-ball a million years to reach!). But of course they are also present here, in this room, and, to use a Muslim expression, 'closer than your own jugular vein'.

What Chateaubriand is describing, as best one can and with all the ardour of youth (he was in his twenties and just back from exploring America), is an earthly landscape perceived in a 'heavenly' or mystical state. At about the same time, William Blake was writing and speaking such descriptions without any pretence of fiction, for to him the very streets of London were transparent to the visitations of angels.

There are plenty of other witnesses to the possibility of living earthly life in such a state of angelic consciousness. Theosophers of every persuasion confirm this. Some explain that, just as every person contains in potentiality the qualities of Universal Man, so the three states of consciousness with which we are daily familiar – waking, dreaming, dreamless sleep – embody experiences in the three worlds: elemental, planetary or astral, and angelic. In a lecture on music Rudolf Steiner succinctly describes the transformation of these states when a sufficient degree of spiritual consciousness or initiation has been attained.[112] The Astral world, he says, is experienced as a glorious play of light and colours, indeed as being oneself light and colour. After a transition of deep peace and silence comes the entry into the angelic world or Devachan (*deva* = angel or lesser god in Sanskrit). This announces itself by the sounding of a tone, and Devachan is essentially perceived by the initiate as a world of tones, though still co-present and illuminated by the Astral. Chateaubriand seems to have had a similar intuition in describing the unearthly colours and visible forms of his heavenly fields as shot through with angelic tones.

Pierre Teilhard de Chardin must have been alluding to an experience of this kind – rising through the Astral to Devachan, though perhaps he would not have favoured these terms – in his *Hymn of the Universe*. Here he speaks of the 'intense yet tranquil rapture of a vision whose coherence and harmonies I can never exhaust,' and goes on to say that 'the powers of my inner being begin spontaneously to vibrate in accord with a single note of incredible richness wherein I can distinguish the most discordant tendencies effortlessly resolved'.[113]

While theorists of the planetary spheres, ancient and modern, have been at pains to demonstrate that the cosmos is musically or harmonically organized, those who describe the highest world do so with a confidence in its harmony that needs no proof. The sixth-century mystic who first wrote on the Angelic Hierarchies, Dionysius the Areopagite, assumes harmony to be the universal condition of all God's creation, from the Seraphim down to our own intelligence.

For that superessential harmony of all things has provided most completely for the holy regulation and the sure guidance of rational and intellectual beings by the establishment of the beautiful choirs of each Hierarchy; and we see that every Hierarchy possesses first, middle and last powers . . . . He also divided each rank in the same divine harmonies, and on this account the Scriptures say that the most divine Seraphim cry one to another, by which, as I think, it is clear that the first impart to the second their knowledge of divine things.[114]

The Song of the Angels is their Gnosis; or, to put it another way, what they know cannot be spoken, only sung.

This tradition has been continued by two myth-makers of our own time. In J.R.R. Tolkien's *The Silmarillion*, the first chapter is entitled 'The Music of the Ainur', and it describes how 'Eru, the One, who is called Ilúvatar' declared a mighty theme to the Ainur ('the Holy Ones, that were the offspring of his thought'). Ilúvatar said:

'Of the theme that I have declared to you, I will now that ye make in harmony together a Great Music. And since I have kindled you with the Flame Imperishable, ye shall show forth your powers in adorning this theme, each with his own thoughts and devices, if he will. But I will sit and hearken, and be glad that through you great beauty has been awakened into song.'

Then the voices of the Ainur, like unto harps and lutes, and pipes and trumpets, and viols and organs, and like unto countless choirs singing with words, began to fashion the theme of Ilúvatar to a great music; and a sound arose of endless interchanging melodies woven in harmony that passed beyond hearing into the depths and into the heights, and the places of the dwelling of Ilúvatar were filled to overflowing, and the music and the echo of the music went out into the Void, and it was not void.[115]

Tolkien's epic account of Creation and Fall – truly a *Paradise Lost* for our century – continues by describing the discords introduced into this harmony by the Evil one, Melkor, and its consequences. His cosmogony holds out the promise that a greater music still 'shall be made before Ilúvatar by the choirs of the Ainur and the Children of Ilúvatar [mankind] after the end of days. Then the themes of Ilúvatar shall be played aright . . .'.[116]

It is this re-creation that C.S. Lewis depicts in his novel *The Magician's Nephew*, which tells of the founding of the fairytale land, Narnia (evidently the realm of Hūrqalyā under yet another name). Narnia is sung into existence by the lion Aslan, who in the first published volume of the 'Chronicles of Narnia', *The Lion, the Witch and the Wardrobe*, suffers death at the hands of the Witch. Now, true to Johannine theology, this redemptive Christ-figure is identified with the Creative Logos or Word of God by whom all things were made. Thus Lewis describes his song:

77

In the darkness something was happening at last. A voice had begun to sing. It was very far away and Digory found it hard to decide from what direction it was coming. Sometimes it seemed to come from all directions at once. Sometimes he almost thought it was coming out of the earth beneath them. Its lower notes were deep enough to be the voice of the earth herself. There were no words. There was hardly even a tune. But it was, beyond comparison, the most beautiful noise he had ever heard. It was so beautiful he could hardly bear it. . . ..

Then two wonders happened at the same moment. One was that the voice was suddenly joined by other voices; more voices than you could possibly count. They were in harmony with it, but far higher up the scale: cold, tingling, silvery voices. The second wonder was that the blackness overhead, all at once, was blazing with stars. . . .. You would have felt quite certain that it was the stars themselves who were singing, and that it was the First Voice, the deep one, which had made them appear and made them sing.[117]

After the 'morning stars have sung together', Aslan's song forms the hills and valleys, then brings into being the vegetable, animal and elemental kingdoms in turn. Finally his song turns to speech as he makes certain of his creatures 'talking beasts', endowing them with reason and the freedom to sin.

In an age which believes neither in the creative power of sound nor in a musical cosmos, such ideas must enter the collective mind through the back door of fantasy. Written ostensibly for children but, as reviewers like to say, 'for children of all ages', this is eminently a genre for a civilization and a period which, more than any other, needs to rediscover the childlike state that can receive these perennial truths.

PART II

THE GREAT WORK

CHAPTER THREE

Musical Alchemy

It is no doubt a wonderful thing to have heard the Secret Harmonies, the Music of the Spheres, or the Song of the Angels, but what we want, those of us who are still chained by the ears to earth, is to hear those musics ourselves, as best we can, and for this purpose we need not mystics or theorists but composers and performers.

The role of the composer and performer is obvious after what has been said in the preceding chapters: they are the alchemists who help to transmute the Earth by making its substance and souls resonate with echoes of the heavenly music. In so doing, these earthly echoes also became audible in Heaven, and the gulf between the two thereby closes by another hairsbreadth. This is the accomplishment of the Great Work of musical alchemy which, like alchemy proper, aims towards the redemption of all Nature as well as to the reunion of Man with his Overself.

In order to undertake this work, the true composer, like the alchemist, does not choose his profession: he is summoned to it by a call that cannot be ignored. One of the signs of such a call is that he will possess the double endowment of skill and memory. Not without reason was Mnemosyne, Goddess of Memory, called the mother of the Nine Muses. What this memory is of, has been well explained by Rudolf Steiner. I mentioned in the previous chapter his words on deep sleep and the experience therein of the Astral and Devachanic worlds that everyone visits each night; also the fact that the initiate does so consciously, whereas the vast majority remain unaware of where they have been. There is another stage, intermediate between these, which is the experience of the inspired creative artist: he may not remember consciously where he has been, but still he is able to reproduce something of what he saw or heard there. In the same lecture of 1906, Steiner speaks of the capacity of certain painters to create colour tones and harmonies that go beyond those of the physical world (he mentions Leonardo da Vinci in particular) and asks: ' . . . where could he have experienced them? They are the after-effects of night-time experience in the Astral world. Only this flowing ocean of light and colours, of beauty, of radiant, glimmering depths, where he has lived in his sleep, enables him to use those colours among which he dwelt'.[1] Then Steiner turns to music:

The musician, on the other hand, conjures up a still higher world. In the physical world he conjures up the Devachanic world. Indeed, *the melodies and harmonies that speak to us from the works of our great masters are faithful copies of the Devachanic world*. If we can obtain a shadow, a foretaste of the Devachanic world in anything, it is in the effects of the melodies and harmonies of music, in their effects on the human soul. . .[2]

Man's original home is in Devachan, and the echoes from this homeland, this spiritual world, resound in him in the harmonies and melodies of the physical world. These echoes pervade our world with the presentiments of a glorious and wonderful existence; they throng through his innermost being and thrill it with vibrations of purest joy, of sublimest spirituality, which this lower world cannot provide.[3] [My italics.]

The Memory of which Mnemosyne is patroness is not the everyday memory that recalls things from the past, but the power of recapturing our other modes of being: of remembering whence we came, who we really are, and where we are going. But memory alone is not sufficient to make an artist. Mnemosyne is the Muses' mother, but their leader is Apollo, god of order and beauty, supreme wielder of the bow and lyre. It is sad to think of the well-meaning artists in every genre who have tried to reproduce their memories without his blessing. Their experience may have been intense, even genuinely mystical, but how tedious is their ecstatic verse, their cosmic art, their musical improvisation. For them it is the very embodiment of unforgettable raptures, yet to others it seems inflated, pretentious or inept. Such people can never understand why the world will not listen to them.

On the other hand, there are those endowed by Apollo but wanting in Memory. Everything comes easily to them: they can paint anything, make words or notes do their will. But their deep sleep is spent in vain: they return from it with their vision still bounded by Earth's horizons. They can enchant the mind, captivate the feelings, and arouse the chthonic daemons, but never stir the immortal Spirit. Fame comes readily to such artists; unlike the cosmic amateurs they enjoy a harmony of ends and means, and within their chosen limits achieve a kind of perfection akin to that of the master-craftsman who works with earthly substances.

At the same time as Rudolf Steiner was lecturing on music, Marcel Proust was also considering these matters in his magnum opus, *A la recherche du temps perdu*. This book is about Time and Memory, but also about the relation of the most outwardly profane occupations – sex and social climbing in *fin-de-siècle* Paris – to the deep currents of human destiny and existence. Proust shows his philosophical intention frequently in the first volume, *Swann's Way*, alerting one to read subsequent volumes in the same spirit, and never more explicitly than in the passages concerning music. I would juxtapose to Steiner's words on the treasures to be found in deep sleep these thoughts of Swann:

He knew that his memory of the piano falsified still further the perspective in which he saw the music, that the field open to the musician is not a miserable stave of seven notes, but an immeasurable keyboard (still, almost all of it, unknown), on which, here and there only, separated by the gross darkness of its unexplored tracts, some few among the millions of keys, keys of tenderness, of passion, of courage, of serenity, which compose it, each one differing from all the rest as one universe differs from another, have been discovered by certain great artists who do us the service, when they awaken in us the emotion corresponding to the theme which they have found, of shewing us what richness, what variety lies hidden, unknown to us, *in that great black impenetrable night, discouraging exploration, of our soul*, which we have been content to regard as valueless and waste and void.[4] [My italics.]

Swann's reflections are aroused by his intense response to a little phrase in a sonata for violin and piano by the fictitious composer Vinteuil. He feels as if he has known the phrase, as one knows a friend, all his life: but that

it belonged, none the less, to an order of supernatural creatures whom we have never seen, but whom, in spite of that, we recognize and acclaim with rapture when some explorer of the unseen contrives to coax it forth, *to bring it down from the divine world to which he has access* to shine for a brief moment in the firmament of ours.[5] [My italics.]

This secret function of musical creation and performance 'made of that stage on which a soul was thus called into being one of the noblest altars on which a supernatural ceremony could be performed'.[6]

There are only a few real artists, composers, or poets, meaning those abundantly endowed with both the memory of the realm of Ideas and the skill to embody that memory. Theirs is the privilege to conceive the progeny of the Gods, called by the alchemists the Philosophic Egg. At the appointed time these divine children are brought forth for all to behold, incarnated in bodies of paint, of marble, of vibrating air. For a time these substances undergo a veritable transmutation, becoming transparent to realities of a higher order. Paint may last a few centuries, marble and words a few millennia. But musical entities are more reluctant: no sooner are they born, with the indispensable help of the performer as midwife (or, to continue the alchemical analogy, as *soror mystica*), than they vanish. Again and again they have to be conjured back to earth on the altar of stage, studio, or living-room. No art so closely parallels those religious rites, such as the Mass, which demand constant re-enactment.

But although to the outward eye the music seems to be over as soon as the last chord has sounded and the celebrants have dispersed, this is not the case. Something has also been created on a subtle plane, and remains like an exquisite flower hovering over the sanctuary. One can sense it in the stillness that ought to follow a musical performance. Clairvoyants assure us that they see it, but that it can be shattered by the sound of applause. Alas, one seldom has the pleasure of inhaling its full fragrance in silence, unless it be at home – where, in turn, one seldom enjoys live performances by the greatest interpreters. The French writer Camille Mauclair, who was most sensitive to these things, describes the howls, stampings, and cheers of an intoxicated audience as the growling of savage beasts before Orpheus.[7] Yet he recognizes it as the sad but necessary means by which they re-enter ordinary life after musical ecstasy, and also as their way of compelling the performers to acknowledge *their* 'music' and to become merely human again. In any case, no musical vibrations are ever entirely lost: even though they are dispersed, they will go on vibrating through the cosmos for eternity. Mauclair also writes of this, in an essay on 'Occultisme musical', saying that 'All our symphonies are recomposed in unknown worlds, as if on prodigious phonographs, and if, as I like to believe, they make music on other planets, it is quite possible that they will send us its echoes one day.'[8] This is a modern recasting of the ancient idea of human music being heard by the angels (see previous chapter), according to the conventional equation of the planetary spheres with celestial states of being.

There would be material for another book if one were to examine all the statements of composers for evidence that they, too, understand their inspiration as having its source on another plane. One would find ample corroboration from the composers of the Romantic era, especially:

When I compose, I feel that I am appropriating that same spirit to which Jesus so often referred.[9] (Brahms.)

When in my most inspired moods, I have definite compelling visions, involving a higher selfhood. I feel at such moments that I am tapping the source of Infinite and Eternal energy from which you and I and all things proceed. Religion calls it God.[10] (Richard Strauss.)

I have very definite impressions while in that trance-like condition, which is the prerequisite of all true creative effort. I feel that I am one with this vibrating Force, that it is omniscient, and that I can draw upon it to an extent that is limited only by my own capacity to do so.[11] (Wagner, reported by Humperdinck.)

There are other ways of communing with God besides attending Mass and confession. When I am composing I feel that He is close to me and approves of what I am doing.[12] (Puccini.)

My most beautiful melodies have come to me in dreams.[13] (Max Bruch.)

We composers are projectors of the infinite into the finite.[14] (Grieg.)

These quotations are from the interviews of Arthur Abell (1868–after 1955), an American music critic who during his twenty-eight years' residence in Europe set out to collect composers' own accounts of their inspiration. Brahms, whom he interviewed in 1896 in the presence of Joseph Joachim, was so explicit about his religious convictions that he forbade Abell to publish their conversation (recorded by a bilingual stenographer) until 50 years after his death, which occurred the following year. Grieg and Strauss made similar restrictions. When eventually Abell published the interviews in 1955, their style and subject were too 'earnest' and old-fashioned to attract serious attention. Inspiration was no longer *à la mode* in an age of disillusion and objectivity.

Perhaps in the present reaction of neo-romanticism and 'postmodernism' it is coming back. When Karlheinz Stockhausen (born 1928) speaks of his own origins on the star Sirius, which he says is the source of all great composers, he is after all fully in accord with the Hermetic tradition. It is as if to say that the greatest music does not simply derive from the music of the planets (which is reflected in us at the psychic or astral level) but from the Eighth Sphere and beyond: the realms of pure Intelligence. Who is to say that certain composers are not creatures of some higher type who have voluntarily taken on human incarnation in order to bring gifts to Mankind? No matter that their personal life may not always measure up to the highest moral standards: being moral exemplars is not their task. There are other souls who may have incarnated for that purpose: we call them Saints, and we do not expect them to be great artists! The arts have all had their avatars, especially in periods of rapid change such as the past thousand years. No merely earthly chain of development can account for such sudden apparitions as the Gothic Cathedrals, the four-part polyphony of Perotin, the works of Shakespeare and J.S. Bach, try as people will to interpret these as effects of some known cause. It takes a 'pure fool' to penetrate the fogs of reductionist scholarship and perceive the miracle which is there for all to see. But whether such miracles can only be brought about by superhuman beings descending to Earth, or whether they can also be the work of men who in the course of long striving have managed to enter the portals of Heaven, I would not like to say. The answer lies hidden in the mysteries of each person's pre-existence.

There are three main levels of musical and artistic inspiration. The highest is the 'avataric' level that has a historical function in addition to, or even surpassing, its intrinsic value. The works of such composers serve, in their own domain, like the visions of meditating saints which become the icons of religion. They become objects of contemplation for every subsequent

85

composer, being constantly re-interpreted and imitated, just as, for instance, the painting of Jesus and his mother originally attributed to St Luke became the model for every subsequent 'Virgin and Child'.

In slowly changing civilizations such as those of Antiquity or the East, a single revelation is sufficient to sustain and nourish a whole epoch of creativity. Such avatars are thenceforth celebrated as divine or semi-divine revealers of wisdom: Hermes, inventor of the lyre; Jubal, 'father of all such as handle the harp and organ' (Genesis 4.21); Sarasvati, Hindu goddess of learning and player of the vina; the Chinese Emperor Fo-Hi, 'discoverer of music' and inventor of the lute. Next to these may be placed the human but still almost mythical founders of historic musical eras, such as the Greek innovator Timotheus, contemporary of Plato; St Gregory the Great, to whom all of Gregorian chant was at one time attributed; Ziryab (eighth-ninth centuries), court lutenist in Baghdad and Córdoba, who 'received his best melodies from spirits';[15] Magister Perotinus of Notre-Dame (c. 1200), creator of the first polyphony in four parts. Each left his stamp permanently on the music of his civilization.

In every culture except the post-medieval West, the task of the creative artist has been to work within the traditional forms bequeathed by such masters, filling them more or less adequately as his own capacities permit. An icon painter, for example, repeatedly copies the best image he can find of the Virgin and Child, either having it before him or else holding it in his imagination. The monks who composed the 'Gregorian' chants listened inwardly to a source of music in their souls: a kind of mental improvisation which anyone can practise who has sung enough chant. At its best, this is inspiration of the second degree. The *spiritus* that is *in*haled is the breath of the archetype: that is the element of Memory. Such an artist refreshes his memory every night in deep sleep – so Rudolf Steiner has told us – but to jar it into action each morning he needs the exemplars of those with still clearer vision who have preceded him and created the style or models within which he works. At this second level – and it is no denigration to say so – the maker of songs is in no wise different from the maker of lutes: each is a re-creator after a revealed pattern. The arts and the crafts, in short, are synonymous. Even nowadays, do we not revere the violins of the craftsman Stradivarius after our own fashion (by putting a price on them) as much as we do the works of his artist contemporaries Corelli or Vivaldi? Stradivarius did not invent the violin (we do not know who did: it was surely one of the avataric revelations), but was able to hold fast to its archetypal form and, with a skill that verges on the alchemical, to infuse that form into matter. While Stradivarius was a young man, Jan Vermeer of Delft was performing a similar work. His *prima materia* was not wood but paint, his memory not that of a shape and a sound but of a certain quality of light. Yet he, too, was a craftsman working in an old and accepted tradition which he was able to raise to a transcendent level.

The third degree of inspiration is not strictly speaking inspiration at all, because it no longer has a connection with Memory. I have already mentioned it as the creativity that proceeds only from the creator's own ego, from the models he sees around him in the world, and from his subconscious (not his superconscious) mind. Having used the example of Vermeer, one could now cite that of his contemporary Jan Steen, the painter of amusing tavern-scenes and pictures of domestic disaster. The history of the arts in the West is largely the history of this type of inspiration – that is why it is so enthralling. But in a traditional culture there is no call for 'self-expression': artistic gifts are put to use by simply copying the canonical works of art or craft, models which supply the necessary Memory. Talented but uninspired artists may achieve unusual feats of virtuosity within their medium. But more than that, they will very likely graduate one day to the second degree of true inspiration, the constant contemplation of the models having awakened in them their own souls' Memory.

This leads us in our descent through the creative hierarchy without a break to the position of the artist's audience. For the beholder or receiver of the work of art, contemplation of beautiful objects should awaken (to paraphrase Plato[16]) the memory and finally the awareness of that Intelligible Beauty that is their source. This is the ulterior purpose of art and craft alike. In the traditional crafts it is reached by means of symbols, like the geometrical patterns or animal emblems on textiles or pottery, or the elements of masonry, whose meaning is revealed in craft initiations. In traditional 'arts' – which means in effect those crafts employed in the service of religion – the symbols are overt, though their range of meaning will not be appreciated by all alike. It is up to the beholder to follow the symbol as far as his capacity allows, but his effort is sanctified by the fact that the object is true to its source. The only such musical art in the West is plainchant.

I have been considering the arts and their inspiration as found in traditional societies, leaving to the next chapter the special case of their development in the modern West. But now that we come to analyse the experience of the listener, less distinction is necessary. People, after all, are not very different in their needs and desires, wherever and whenever we look at them. There are certain needs which music best fulfils, but it may be music of many types. I make the first division according to the three regions of the human being: belly, chest, and head. Every developed culture has music aimed at each level. There is visceral music, usually marked by strong rhythm, which makes one feel physically powerful (the battle march) or sexually aroused (the harem dance). Next there is the music of the heart and its emotions, with lovesickness always in pride of place since this is the strongest emotion one can feel, with the exception of bereavement. Thirdly there is music which sets thought in motion: the thought of the connoisseur who understands what is going on in the composer's mind or in the performer's actions and follows it with dispassionate interest. Just as in Robert Fludd's diagram (see p. 174) these three bodily regions correspond to the three macrocosmic realms of the elements, the planets, and the angels, so in a humble way these ordinary musical experiences exercise body, soul, and intellect.

This is true, at least to a degree, whether or not one is consciously involved in the music. Much of the time the listener is absent, either by accident as when one's mind wanders in a concert, or by design, as when one hears music as background to some foreground activity such as reading, watching a film, dining, working, etc. The choice of background music, as the specialists in Muzak and film scores know, is a delicate matter even if people never notice it. For a film it must intensify the prevailing mood, hence be aimed at the visceral or emotional level. For the other purposes it must be unobtrusive, familiar in style, constant in mood. It works through the unconscious mind to harmonize the being – and this is meant literally, for the sounding of consonant harmonies and regular rhythm does have a harmonious and regularizing effect on the body and psyche. When used as a background to reading or other work of the mind, it serves to give the emotional and physical bodies something to attune themselves to, so that they do not obtrude on the desired field of consciousness. Where mealtime music is concerned, it contributes to psychic harmony by covering awkward gaps in the conversation, while its rhythms aid the body's digestion.

It has also been known for centuries that music helps people work, and the more boring or disagreeable the work, the more it is welcome. Classical writers mention the songs of galley-slaves; nowadays it is the drudgery of factory work that is relieved by specially designed Muzak. If factory-workers are left to do their job in silence, they all too readily begin to dislike and resent it, envy those whose fortunes they are helping to make, and take frequent breaks for gossip. Muzak provides a clever solution to this problem by attacking on two levels simultaneously. Subconsciously, it again presents an example of regularity and harmony to which the worker's body and psyche naturally attune themselves. Consciously, it provides pictures, usually of a pleasantly romantic nature, to keep the imagination or fantasy occupied. Watered-down versions of popular love-songs therefore make the best factory music, just as the romances of film-stars and other princesses make the most popular reading-matter. They create a mild erotic haze in which the work-day passes quickly and easily.

Even in more elevating surroundings than factories, the commonest use of music is to feed the fantasy. Most concert-goers, though they may not realize it, are 'lookers' to a far greater extent than they are listeners. The music creates scenes, events, journeys, pictures in their imagination, working like a kind of low-grade synaesthesia (the function mentioned in Chapter Two in which tones are transmuted directly into visions). Some kinds of music explicitly invite this level of listening by means of an extramusical programme or title. The Romantic era from Berlioz (*Symphonie fantastique*) to Debussy (*La Mer*, etc.) was the heyday of such programme-music: before then, it was a curiosity (Renaissance battle-pieces; Kuhnau's *Biblical Sonatas*, etc.); afterwards, rather an embarrassment. But outside Europe it is still the norm. In the traditional music of the Far East, most compositions are avowedly descriptive or evocative, usually of a natural scene: *Ducks Flying over a Moonlit Lake, The First Chrysanthemum, November Steps*, etc. The same may be said of Chinese and Japanese poetry and painting, for that matter, in which, similarly, scenes of natural beauty serve both to calm and refresh the soul and to carry a philosophical message to the intellect.

But there does not have to be a title for the listener to interpret the music programmatically. Westerners prefer, on the whole, to choose their tone-pictures for themselves. Besides, there are many other contributing factors, apart from the music. One's inner imagery may be blended with thoughts of current concerns at home or work: the concert may be spent in deciding how to redecorate the kitchen, or in imaginary conversations with colleagues, and yet afterwards one may say that yes, it was a lovely evening and the music was beautiful. Alternatively – or additionally, for all these modes of 'listening' may be exercised at one and the same event – the focus of attention and fantasy may be on the atmosphere of the setting, especially when this is something other than an ordinary concert hall: the splendour of a Rococo church or palace; the sanctity and resonance of a Gothic cathedral; the presence of Nature at outdoor events. It may be the other people there: the person one loves, the group of friends, the celebrity in the next row or in the Royal Box.

Coming closer now to the musical event in itself, the listener's primary attention may be on the performer(s). Certain individuals and even groups carry with them an aura so compelling that their own presence is the most felt reality, quite apart from the music. People will go to hear (or actually to see and feel) them no matter what they are playing or singing, knowing that the experience will be an intense one. At a slightly higher level, perhaps, it may be the composer's personality which one encounters. Several of the great composers have become heroic figures and exemplars for our culture, at the same time being individuals for whom one may have a deep love and respect. People identify especially with those who have suffered in their lives and transcended in their music. One need not look far to find examples of debilitating illness, deafness, blindness, poverty, loneliness, rejection, insanity, or sexual preferences outlawed by society. But in every case their music emerges supreme as the healing Elixir extracted from the soul's dark night. Another group, not necessarily separate but smaller, is constituted of those whose creative achievements exceed merely human limits, and it is these who have been mentioned before as the 'avatars' among composers.

Only when one's listening is concentrated unbrokenly on the music – no matter whether imagery, good or bad, is present – does one enter a phase comparable and complementary to the third degree of creativity mentioned above. This is the kind of creativity that comes from the composer's ego and skill alone, hence subject to his own psychological makeup. The listener then shares in his personality, for better or worse, by means of responses that again fall into the three main divisions of visceral, emotional, and mental, or those of body-music, heart-music, and head-music.

Body-music is strongly rhythmic and regular, thus resembling the physical constitution itself. It is best felt by actual participation in the movement and gesture, whether in the perfect discipline of classical ballet, the weightless swirl of the waltz, or the orgiastic contortions of popular and savage dancing. Even without this there will be some felt response on the part of the passive listener. For instance, the loud obstinate beat of rock 'n' roll raises the pulse and breathing rate, and the listener responds by foot- or hand-tapping. Some people, in fact, react to all music in this way or not at all. But in the more refined forms of body-music, the response takes place not in the physical but in the subtle body; to be precise, in the *linga sharira* or etheric body through which the movements of the will are transferred to the physical vehicle. This is the locus of those empathetic feelings of lightness and grace which one experiences at the ballet. As a subtle vehicle, it is capable of movements and impulses which, in the untrained person, cannot possibly be realized on the physical level. It dances with the dancer, who differs from ordinary people in having brought the two vehicles into unanimity.

Heart-music grips one by the emotions, which have their seat not in the physical or etheric vehicles (though they may affect these) but in the *kama rupa* or vehicle of passions and desires. For one's everyday emotions it substitutes the vicarious longings, the artificial sorrows and joys, for which art has always been cultivated. Since this is the centre of most systems of musical aesthetics, and of most people's experience, little need be said about it here. But again it is an important consideration whether the emotions generated are ennobling or debasing. Whether they are happy or sad is an incidental matter. Is the sorrow that of the hurt ego (the maudlin self-pity of the Blues) or of the higher Self entombed therein (the *St Matthew Passion*)? Is the joy that of sexual conquest or that of the praise-song that fertile Nature sings to her Creator? When it acts positively, heart-music aids in the refinement of our own emotions by displaying those of people better than ourselves. If it displays those of people who are worse, then persistent exposure will cause us to resemble them instead.

Head-music is perceived in the *kama manas*, the 'lower mind'. Here the music is transmuted into thoughts, usually visual in nature but far removed from the idle fantasies described earlier. This is the preserve of the trained musician, the *connoisseur* in the sense of being cognizant of what is going on. The music may be experienced as spread out over inner space, its different pitches and textures separated as in a score. Often the image of a keyboard, or the feel of one's hands on an instrument, appears as an aid to understanding. Words, too, explain the harmonies and forms in the language of musical analysis. Empathetic emotion is supplanted by the critical intellect (now using the term in its lower, more usual sense): the faculty that watches, weighs, and judges the work or the performer. Here, too, the connective thoughts have their place that comprehend the music in its historical context or in relation to the composer's other works. Musicologists commonly become addicted to this level of listening, and for some types of music it is the only proper response.

Composers have periodically delighted in their technical capacity to set and solve musical puzzles. Of course a composer is doing this all the time, to a certain degree, but I refer to virtuoso efforts, such as Guillaume de Machaut's rondeau *Ma fin est mon commencement*, in which the second part of the music is the first part played backwards, or the canonic tradition that runs from the late fifteenth-century Netherlands composers to J.S. Bach's *Goldberg Variations*, *Art of Fugue*, and *Musical Offering*. When the composer presents us overtly with a work of great ingenuity, the right response is to appreciate it as such, which means to think it through as he has done. The same applies to compositions by modern serial composers which are evidently first and foremost the work of cerebration. In the 1950s and 1960s it was quite common for such composers to explain how their compositions were constructed, using charts, diagrams, and tables, so that those few with the patience to follow them (usually other composers with similar intentions) could cerebrate in turn. This attitude was born from the discovery of the intricate structures that govern the works of the Second Viennese School (Schoenberg, Berg, Webern): a discovery that still continues as a veritable analytic industry.

This desire to uncover secret structures goes back at least to Albert Schweitzer's recognition, early in the century, of the symbolic meanings incorporated in J.S. Bach's music. Schumann's music, according to Eric Sams,[17] contains ciphered messages. Bartók and Debussy apparently made conscious use of the Golden Section or 'Divine Proportion' (the mathematical ratio ϕ or 1:1.618+), doubtless for philosophical as well as psychological reasons.[18] In other disciplines there are parallel searches for numerological schemes in poetry (Dante, Spenser, etc.) and geometrical ones in painting and architecture. The discovery by John Michell[19] and others of an ancient and universal Canon of measurement, cosmologically based and applicable to every creative activity, makes manifest the original and exemplary form of such 'Lawfulness'. But there is no suggestion that the proper use of a Gothic cathedral or of a Debussy prelude is to be measured. As Debussy himself said, once the work is complete, the scaffolding can be thrown away.

Listening with a combination of bodily, emotional and thinking responses can be an extremely rich and rewarding experience. It is the summit of 'third-degree' listening, in which the composer is paid the compliment of full attention, yet in which the higher faculties of the listener are still not involved. Another model is necessary as we proceed to the types of listening that compare to the second degree of inspiration, as defined above. Just as most composers never know this degree of inspiration, so most listeners never suspect its existence. Before entering on the difficult task of trying to explain it, I will anticipate the reader's question and say that I do not believe there is any form of listening that corresponds to the first degree of creative inspiration, the rare degree I have called 'avataric', for the simple reason that above the second level 'listening' as such ceases, and the activity that supersedes it is of the nature of mystical or philosophic meditation. This no longer requires any musical support, though as we have seen in Chapter Two music may be a helpful prelude to it.

The new model is a refinement of the body-emotion-intellect (or visceral-heart-head) scheme. It is based on three of the subtle centres of the individual, known to all esoteric traditions but most commonly referred to via the Hindu system of seven *chakras*. Those involved here are, in ascending order: (1) the *anahata chakra*, linked to the heart in the physical body and often called the Heart Centre; (2) the *vishudda chakra*, also known as the Throat Centre; (3) the *ajna chakra*, situated between the eyebrows and called the Third Eye.

When one listens to music – and it must be music of a suitable degree of inspiration – with one's consciousness deliberately focused in the Heart Centre, one may be able to enter a higher octave of emotion than that of ordinary heart-music. What is now felt is no longer the human emotions that heart-music represents, but the feeling-qualities that underlie that representation: the face behind the mask. These are cosmic feeling-qualities beyond joy and sorrow: they are experienced as an ever-changing dilation and contraction, tension and release, to which none of the five external senses offers any parallel but which find an echo in the astrological signs of the Zodiac. In Western music they are carried primarily by the harmony, but naturally this dimension of experience is not absent from unharmonized forms such as plainchant or Oriental music; it is present there as the tonal centre of gravity, to which all the other tones are related as specific feelings. Here as always, the convention of a language must be assumed, and as verbal languages differ, so one cannot normally expect to feel perfect empathy with musical styles which one has never learnt. Therefore the Westerner should attend to the harmony. Although all great composers have been masters of this dimension, some have had a particular genius for revealing it. They are the composers such as Chopin and Wagner, who, while commanding the widest harmonic palette, can still give to the simplest progressions an aspect of profound meaning. One could take as an example the chords with which Wagner awakens Brünnhilde in *Siegfried*, Act III, scene 3: E minor, C major, E minor, D minor. What do these simple chords mean? As soon as they are analysed or verbalized, the magic is lost. They do not even mean that Brünnhilde is awakening: that is a translation of music into the inferior language of drama. Like the Crystal Pillar of Celtic legend, mentioned in Chapter Two, they embody their own meaning, and the listener to the Heart has no need for explanation.

The Throat Centre (*vishudda chakra*) is traditionally connected with artistic creation and with the use of the voice, the primordial creative organ of both divine and human beings. So it is not surprising to find the key to it in melody. If one listens while one's consciousness is placed at the throat, the larynx may actually respond soundlessly as if one is singing the melody, just as the dilations of the *anahata chakra* may be felt physically around the heart. One should try to stop this natural reaction, because it tends to exteriorize the melody in an imaginary space of high and low notes, besides the possibility of one's response deteriorating into merely 'singing along'. Spatializing the melody leads readily into the observation of it characteristic of head-music. To avoid this, the listener should not observe the melody, but rather become identified with it as a golden thread that winds throughout the piece and provides a vehicle for its journey through time. Again, the melody should not be represented in any form other than itself. By listening in this way one comes very close to the limpid spring of melodic inspiration to which the composer has listened and from which he has been able to draw. It is an experience of the nature of Time.

Finally, one may place the attention between the eyebrows, closing one's eyes as one must, unless adept at meditation, for all these exercises. Now one is again 'looking at' the music, but at this higher level it has nothing of the visual about it. The vision of the Third Eye (*ajna chakra*) is more akin to insight. It is a concentrated attention without selectivity, from which one may merge and become identified with the music itself. Then the normal state, that of ego-bound consciousness, is supplanted by the state of music.

This total self-absorption in sound brings to being in us the primordial condition of the Universe, which, as Marius Schneider has eloquently described it, is musical and temporal in nature, not visual nor spatial. Schneider writes in many places[20] of the flowing primordial Waters whose rustling or roaring sound is the first created thing. Only later does a light shine in the subaqueous darkness (the Rheingold!), bringing with it the first duality: the distinction of light from darkness, hence by analogy of apparent good from apparent evil; and the first creation in space, the dimension of meetings, separations, and inevitable conflicts. The state of music is at least potentially beyond these, as is the condition of the person who has become assimilated to it. In the words of the ancient Chinese *Book of Rites*:

When one has mastered music completely, and regulates the heart and mind accordingly, the natural, correct, gentle, and honest heart is easily developed, and with this development of the heart comes joy. This joy goes on to a feeling of repose. This repose is long-continued. Persons in this constant repose become a sort of Heaven. Heaven-like, their action is spirit-like. Heaven-like, they are believed without the use of words. Spirit-like, they are regarded with awe, without any display of rage. So it is, when one by mastering of music regulates the mind and heart.[21]

Mystics, poets, and even ordinary people speak of those rare moments of self-forgetfulness when one becomes indistinguishable from one's object of perception. It is the moment sought by lovers of nature and of art alike. In the second act of *Tristan und Isolde*, Wagner shows it occurring between human lovers. Since freedom from the ego — and not necessarily from the body or its perceptions — is our higher Self's dearest wish, such moments of ego-extinction are remembered as supreme experiences, pledges of Heaven's joy. But it is foolish, if blessed with such moments, to let them become memories only: they should be repeatedly sought and seized, keeping in mind as a goal the condition of the liberated Sage, the *jivan-mukti*, who has extinguished the ego not for a moment but forever. To pursue this path of musical alchemy, repeatedly giving oneself up to conscious assumption of the condition of music, is a step toward the perfect harmony of the person whose leaden ego has been transmuted into the pure gold of the Self.

CHAPTER FOUR

Music and the Currents of Time

We turn now from our scrutiny of the transforming work of music within the individual to consider how it has worked, and is working, on the whole human race. And since this study has, for the most part, concentrated on Western civilization, it is particularly the development of music in Europe over the past nine hundred years that concerns us now.

Every historical account necessarily unfurls against the background of the historian's own assumptions concerning universal history. Usually these are unspoken, if not actually repressed, but even those historians who consider themselves agnostic already hold an assumption, namely that we do not and cannot know the wider context and above all the meaning of events. Esotericists do not hesitate to supply what the professionals disdain to consider, for they feel obliged to situate Man within his whole hierarchical and temporal being. So, because esoteric psychology (or, for that matter, esoteric musicology) explores dimensions that do not exist for the common variety, there are currents of history that we must take into account before we try to understand our present strange predicament and the musics that accompany it.

The Hermetic teaching is that if one can understand Man, then one can understand everything: and that means, in the first instance, 'knowing oneself'. For where else is one to start? Hermeticism also holds that 'what is above is like that which is below', and vice versa, 'for the perfection of the One Thing'. It is therefore through introspection that one comes to a vision of the universal, using the known to explain the unknown.

Let us now expand the alchemical analogy used in the last chapter to a macrocosmic scale, and cast God – that is, God the Creator and Demiurge, not God the Absolute, which has no hand in history – in the role of the Alchemist. The entire human race, body and soul, is then his *Prima Materia*. In this raw first matter lies hidden the seed or spark of divine light that, if properly cultivated, can come into manifestation as the Philosopher's Stone or the Tincture, able to transmute every metal into gold. Thus the human race might, if the experiment succeeds, become the agent for the transmutation of the whole Earth, and even more.

The alchemist is the most patient of men. Day in, day out, he works on the substance which he has gathered with such care: feeding it, cooking it, reducing it to a dry powder and revivifying it with dew and the extracts of green plants. He is always attentive to the configurations of the stars and planets; always he is praying. Sometimes he has to wait a whole year for the right season to arrive for a certain procedure; at other times he must seize the hour and minute, or all will be lost.

These 'years' and 'days', when we transpose them to the larger stage, are quite well known to that part of esoteric science that studies cosmic cycles. The Greeks and Romans knew of a Great Year (*magnus annus*), their longest measure of time, which approximates to the precessional period of 25,920 solar years. The twelve 'months' of this year are each about 2,160 solar years long, and they in turn are familiar as the astrological Ages, each named after the constellation of the Zodiac in which the sun rises at the Spring Equinox. The most recent ages are the Taurean (roughly speaking, the 4th and 3rd millennia BC), the Arian (2nd and 1st millennia BC), and the Piscean (first two millennia AD), which is now ending as the Aquarian Age begins.

Each of the civilizations and cultural periods that flourish on the surface of the globe lasts for a certain time, then declines and disappears. In his great *Study of History*, which among exoteric works of universal history comes closest to esoteric models, Arnold Toynbee recognized this as the predominant rhythm of the past. But what are these civilizations to Him in whose sight 'a thousand ages' are 'like an evening gone'? They are his day's work. Every morning there is something for the Alchemist to do in his laboratory. Every night, when the day's work is over, oblivion descends. Some days are simple repetitions of what was done the day before, and this may persist for months on end. (One thinks of the all but static civilizations of ancient Egypt or China.) On other days things move faster: the contents of the alembic may be suddenly transformed before his very eyes.

The work done on such a day will leave the material forever changed. These are the red-letter days, marking the stepwise progress of the Great Work. One day, when putrefaction occurs, as it must, the whole thing becomes a fetid, stinking mess. Yet by diligent washing and gentle cooking, this horrid and depressing sight will change into something glitteringly white, over which the 'Peacock's Tail' may flash with its unearthly play of colours, and from which a sweet perfume may arise. Can one not conceive of civilizations and cultural periods – days in the life of mankind – which correspond to all of these stages?

It must be obvious that our current civilization marks one of those crucial days, on which either the Work will move forward into a new phase, or else – to put it bluntly – the vessel, heated beyond endurance, will blow up in the

Alchemist's face. Then he will have to begin all over again, which doubtless he is quite prepared to do, having inexhaustible patience; and in any case, if what Plato tells of Atlantis is true, he has seen this happen before.

However, in this 'year' there is a difference. Whereas we may suppose that during the previous age of the world that esotericists call Atlantis, the Alchemist was working by the more usual method, known as the 'Humid Way', now he is following the 'Dry Way'. The latter is a much more rapid process that will yield tremendous results if it succeeds, but which is extremely hazardous because of the greater temperatures to which it subjects the matter in the sealed vessel. For that reason it is not the waters that inundated Atlantis that threaten now, but the uncontrollable transmutation of elements in a nuclear fireball.

The choice of the Dry Way is responsible for the unprecedented acceleration of historical events over the past five hundred solar years (about a week of cosmic time). It is also doubtless the reason that the Alchemist himself has been, to all appearances, absent so long that many people suppose him dead or never to have existed. For the Dry Way requires the crucible to be heated mercilessly, and no more dew, no green plants, can be fed to the matter within. The Alchemist, it seems, made his last direct intervention in the seventh century AD, with the revelation of the Islamic religion which considers itself, with reason, the last of the cycle. Now he awaits events within the flask that will either allow him to open it again in triumph, or will spell the ruin of all his work so far. Much of this will depend on the behaviour of the matter itself, over which he has little control, but which is ruled by the stars and by the degree to which it has been previously been prepared. No wonder that the period after AD 2000 is scarcely imaginable.

Western civilization has certainly been different from all other known civilizations, and esotericists tend to react to this difference in one of two ways. Either they are 'traditionalists', and regard it as an anomaly, not to say a monstrosity (René Guénon's words) which could only have come about at the end of a dark cycle (the Kali Yuga of Hinduism, the Iron Age of the Greeks). Or else they are 'evolutionists', for whom the Western experience, for all its aberrations, is a necessary step in the development of mankind as a whole. The first group bewails Western materialism, secularism, the decline of its traditional religions, its loss of philosophical certitude. The second extols the emergence of individual consciousness, freedom from dogma, global awareness. My alchemical analogy tries to hold these opposites in tension without deciding for either, because I find such a state more productive of insight than the dualistic taking of sides. The stage of the Great Work at which we find ourselves is, collectively speaking, full of obscurity − modern Man's ignorance of his own true nature − and putrefaction, his consequent suffering and that of the Earth under him. But he is being put through this stage deliberately (for is not even the Kali Yuga ruled by a Goddess?) so that a new Golden Age may one day emerge − and one that will be different from the last Golden Age.

As we come at last to review the history of Western music, we will find support for both the traditionalist and the evolutionary view. For while the former points out that music's development in the West has been altogether abnormal in the context of the world's music as a whole, does one not welcome an 'abnormality' that has produced J.S. Bach, Mozart, Beethoven? Yet how many people actually welcome the course that music has taken in the twentieth century? To judge by attendance at concerts of classical music (popular music is another matter), very few: most music lovers inhabit a musical museum which stopped acquiring in about 1910. Perhaps something has gone seriously wrong; or is it that people as a whole simply do not understand an art that has become so abstruse?

We must begin by looking back to the early Middle Ages, before the process of cultural acceleration got under way. At that period the styles and uses of music were fixed, forming a framework for musical craftsmen to work in without inviting individuals to make any fundamental changes to the art. Music was a handmaid to the traditional functions of worship, song and dance; it did not yet exist for its own sake. Some composers and singers, certainly, were acknowledged as better than others, just as some potters made better and more beautiful pots; but the music, exactly like the pots, was made to be used, not yet to be put on a mantelpiece or in a museum. If there was a kind of counterpoint or polyphony, as there seems to have been in every culture,[1] it was more a matter for the performer than for the composer. A piece of plainchant or a dance tune, once remembered, could be adorned by adding other melodies without the necessity for writing them down. Music resided not on parchment but in the memory: the capacious memory of oral tradition. Hence most of it is lost today.

There are many advantages in such a situation. Perhaps the greatest is that composer, poet and singer are often one and the same person, enabling inspiration to descend at any stage of the work, even spontaneously in performance. Relics of this unity would long persist: one thinks of the great composers of the Northern Renaissance − Dufay, Obrecht, Ockeghem, Josquin Desprez − all of whom were professional singers; of Caccini and Dowland around 1600, writing their own poetry and singing to their own lute accompaniments. But from the later seventeenth century onwards, when the composer becomes typically a keyboard virtuoso, this 'Orphic' heritage is lost, and the composers themselves re-enact the withdrawal of the divine Alchemist from active participation in his work. From the composer as image of the Deity, creating through the sound of his own voice, one moves to the eighteenth-century image of God as the supervisor of a clockwork universe, like the intricate but impersonal mechanism of organ, harpsichord, or piano. Later still, the composer is more often a conductor (the Creator as dictator), or else he just issues his scores and other people act on his directives, like servants of some distant bureaucrat. Perhaps this puts in a fresh perspective those composer–poets of Folk and Rock who are still unashamed to sing, and who are responsible for the only universal classics of our time.

In the latter part of the twelfth century, a new kind of architecture and a new kind of music were invented in and around Paris. While Abbot Suger was putting his ideas into action in the Abbey church of Saint-Denis, the first Gothic building, at Notre-Dame de Paris a master we know as Leonin was assembling a *Magnus liber organi*, the 'Great Book of Organum' consisting of settings of plainsong in two-part polyphony for services throughout the liturgical year. Vestiges of each new style had appeared earlier, but no precedent can be found for the magnitude of these projects and the assurance with which they were carried out. And, by the end of the century, each had found a successor to cast these new beginnings in a form one may well call classic: Suger's Saint-Denis in the new cathedral at Chartres (rebuilt after 1194), and Leonin in Perotin, the reviser and enlarger of the *Magnus liber organi*. The new cathedral succeeded in raising a vault of a width and height never before attempted, and in piercing the stone walls with a half-acre of stained glass. Perotin surpassed the work of Leonin by writing Organum in three and four parts, using a time-scale never equalled before (and seldom since) in his prolongation of the plainchant melodies he took as his basis, opening them up, as it were, to the luminosity of his counterpoint.

If Europe had been India, or ancient Egypt, music and architecture would have stopped developing then and there for at least 500 years in order to digest the implications of these new styles. Of course they did not. Now, in the thirteenth and early fourteenth centuries, it was the motet that became the laboratory for experiments of every kind in rhythm, harmony, and word-setting. Perhaps the most artificial of all musical forms, and the hardest to appreciate nowadays, the motet typically sets a phrase of plainchant, without its words, in a regularly repeating rhythm, and adds to it two higher parts, moving somewhat faster, each of which has its own text (the *mots* that give the motet its name). The texts may be Latin and religious, or French and amorous. Often one is of each kind, sung simultaneously. Sometimes there is a connection with the words that were originally set in the borrowed plainchant, but more often not.

No one listening to a motet for the first time can disentangle the two simultaneous poems, or perceive the underlying rhythmic structure. Were these pieces composed for connoisseurs who were willing to make the effort of understanding how they were put together, while other high-born music-lovers were content to listen to the monophonic songs of the Troubadours and Trouvères? One does not know: all we have are the manuscripts, preserved in mint condition with the mistakes uncorrected, as if they were treated as 'coffee-table books' and never sung from. It may be that, like the avant-garde compositions of the twentieth century, these works were intensely interesting to other composers, having great historical importance but barely touching the mass of music-lovers.

One of these motet composers, Philippe de Vitry, was well aware of the historical significance of his work. In his treatise *Ars nova* (*c.* 1325), he initiated the series of manifestos announcing the creation of a 'new music' that continues to this day. But every new music calls forth defenders of the old, and in the present case the traditionalist was Jacques de Liège, author of the longest of all medieval music treatises, *Speculum musicae* (between 1325 and 1350). Jacques deplored the neglect of the old Notre-Dame music (Organum and Conductus) in the current enthusiasm for secular songs:

Do not the moderns use motets and chansons almost exclusively, except for introducing hockets in their motets? They have abandoned many other sorts of music, which they do not use in their proper form as the ancients did; for example, measured organa, organa not measured throughout, and the organum purum and duplum, of which few of the moderns know; likewise conductus, which are so beautiful and full of delight, and which are so artful and delightful when in two, three, or four parts; likewise two, three, and four-part hockets. Among these sorts of music the old singers divided their time in rotation; these they made their foundation; in these they exercised themselves; in these they delighted, not in motets and chansons alone.[2]

Jacques was making a plea for sacred polyphony in an age whose composers were occupied almost exclusively with secular forms. There is certainly something incongruous in the fact that Francesco Landini, the greatest Italian composer of the Trecento and organist of the Duomo in Florence, should have left nothing but secular love-songs; and that Guillaume de Machaut, an ordained priest and canon of Reims, should have spent his creative life as epic poet and composer of courtly love-lyrics to various kings and noblemen, contributing to the liturgy only his single *Messe de Nostre-Dame*. But perhaps the Church had to reject a musical style

101

so obedient to secular impulses: to the composers' delight in their own ingenuity (the motets), and to the expression of the transient world of human emotion (the *chansons* and *canzone*).

This exploration continued at the end of the fourteenth century with the Mannerist schools of France and Italy. Fascinated by the confluence of their two national styles, composers made every song an exaggerated study in a single direction: in chromaticism; in notes of extreme speed or slowness; in exploring unusual voice-registers; in writing canons; in complex rhythms; in using circular or heart-shaped staves. Mannerism, or its close relative, Decadence, is a valid mode of artistic expression, allied to certain forms of eroticism that concentrate passionately on normally incidental things. It always comes at the end of an artistic cycle, after the possibilities of classicism and emotionalism are exhausted. In the present case it reflects the spiritual state of Europe at the end of the Middle Ages, for which the turning-point would come with the Renaissance and its public rediscovery of the Antique.

But was there a Renaissance in music? Certainly not in the early fifteenth century, when the remedy for Franco-Italian exhaustion came in the form of a new musical style from England, known as the *contenance angloise*. English polyphony had developed somewhat in isolation from the Continent in the thirteenth and fourteenth centuries, sharing a common root in the Notre-Dame style but going on to explore the possibilities of harmony for its own sake, rather than as the secondary result of combined melodies. Captivated by the English sound, the fifteenth century revelled in the sheer beauty of major and minor triads. The more contrapuntal parts were added (sometimes as many as 40), the more the music became a glorification of these chords. This tendency reached its height in English music of the fifty years around 1500 (the time of the *Eton Choirbook*, of John Taverner, etc.), in many-voiced Masses and antiphons in honour of the Virgin. If any music is an image of the Hosts of Heaven in their perpetual song, it is this, in which each voice blends perfectly with each but remains distinct, while the underlying substance is those primordial triads of which not just music but all harmony is made.

The Continental composers, in the meantime, were perfecting the art of imitative counterpoint, whose function is to unify the voices not just harmonically but thematically. In an imitative piece, all the voices sing similar melodies and take on equal importance: a situation unknown since the Conductus style of three centuries before. The Buddhist writer Marco Pallis (born 1896), co-founder of the English Consort of Viols, thus describes its symbolic nature:

102

This universe is characterized by the triple fatality of change, competition and impermanence; to speak of a world (any kind of world) is to speak of contrast or opposition, for distinction of one being from another inevitably imposes this condition; 'a world' is always a play of black and white, with all the intermediate shades of grey or, shall we say, all the changeful play of the spectrum: what then exactly happens when two or more beings are developing in the same world? These beings may either converge or diverge or, for a brief space, move parallel with one another (or almost so, since an absolutely parallel course is not a possibility) and this will from time to time bring the beings in question into contact or even collision: what happens then? In proportion as one being is carried along with greater force as compared with another, the latter will get pushed and deflected from its course until it is free to move again in its own direction; this fresh direction it will pursue until it again runs into opposition of some kind – perhaps this time its own impetus will prove the stronger and it will be the *other* being which will be deflected in its turn and so on indefinitely.

What does this picture suggest but a *counterpoint* which, by its continual interplay of tensions and releases, expresses that unity out of which all its constituent elements have arisen and which they are all for ever seeking to regain consciously or unconsciously? The musical parallel is self-evident and it is this, in fact, which confers on contrapuntal music its strange power to move the soul.[3]

One finds this symbolism at its purest in the vocal music of the later fifteenth and sixteenth centuries; in some instrumental music of the seventeenth century, notably the English fantasies for viols; and of course in the fugues of J.S. Bach. In the pure imitative style, the idea of polyphony reaches its classic expression, and its invention deserves to be placed among the very greatest achievements of European civilization.

However one defines the Renaissance – whether as the Revival of Learning or of Antiquity, as Humanism and the discovery of the individual, or as a movement of secularization – it is scarcely evident in the surviving music of the fifteenth and sixteenth centuries. In the period of the High Renaissance associated with the names of Leonardo da Vinci, Raphael, Michelangelo, Giorgione, Bramante, etc., two intentions were uppermost.[4] First, that the art of painting (up to then regarded more as a craft than as a creative art) should rival and even surpass the more honoured art of poetry in its capability to delineate character, tell stories, and depict the whole range of human emotion. Second, that the arts of the moderns should rival and even surpass those of Antiquity in beauty and in their power to move the soul. The visual arts, favoured by a combination of genius, patronage, and technical advances, were so placed around 1500 as to succeed in these ambitions, to judge by the consensus that has ever after regarded the High Renaissance as the zenith of Western art. Music was not so placed: not that it lacked genius and patronage, but because its current style did not suit the first intention, while current knowledge of Antiquity did not allow it to attempt the second. The great musical figure of the High Renaissance was Josquin Desprez, whom Leonardo must have known at the Sforza court in Milan: Josquin, regarded as without peer in musical expression as well as in contrapuntal skill. Yet how slight is his expressivity in comparison with the twisted faces of Leonardo's *Battle of Anghiari*, or the encyclopedia of gesture in Michelangelo's Sistine Chapel paintings! This is no disparagement, merely an indication that music had not yet followed the visual arts into an infatuation with representing the feelings. The style of imitative polyphony of which Josquin was supreme master is expressive, certainly – but it expresses the Intelligence that is above emotion and deeper than the outward personality. Moreover, it owes nothing whatever to Antiquity.

Polyphonic music is essentially a Gothic art, for it grew up at the same time as the Gothic cathedrals and replicates in its own way the same spiritual experience that was behind those. The nineteenth century, which accompanied its Gothic Revival in architecture with a rediscovery of the church music of Palestrina and Bach, may have been historically naïve in comparing architecture of 1200 with music of 1560 or 1720, but there was a correct intuition behind its enthusiasms. Just as in England, for instance, the Renaissance in architecture was delayed a hundred years or more, so it was in the art of music.

As long as music was conceived as the polyphonic interweaving of voices, there was only limited scope for the expression of individuality. If the singer is to come forward as a person and express what is peculiar to the individual, he or she must be free and alone, just as an actor is free to declaim the lines of a play without consideration for ensemble. Such music was already being cultivated in humanist circles of the later fifteenth century, but it is all lost. Marsilio Ficino, Leonardo da Vinci, and Castiglione's ideal Courtier, are all represented as having practised this art of singing to their own accompaniment. The instrument favoured was the *lira da braccio*, a bowed, chord-playing instrument, parent of the violin family. Pictures of the classical patrons of music, Orpheus and Apollo, often show them as just such solo singers. But this was first and foremost improvisatory music: a spontaneous rendition of one's state of soul, whereby others might be moved to feel the same state. Therefore it was never written down, to the historian's great loss. Moreover, the primary object presented to the listener was emotion cast in poetry. The music was secondary, supporting and intensifying the effect of the poem certainly, but by no means indispensable. In polyphonic music, on the other hand, what is offered as the primary object of contemplation is the music itself, doing precisely what words cannot do.

104

Towards 1600, the humanist singing his verses to a simple chordal accompaniment on *lira* or lute underwent a metamorphosis that may fairly be called epoch-making. A Florentine club of gentlemen-scholars called the Camerata, occupied with discussions about Greek music and drama, put its theories into practice in the production of the first dramas set to music in what they considered the best approximation to Antique style. But since there was no Leonardo da Vinci or Richard Wagner to take on the whole responsibility for theory, poetry, music, performance and stage production, the operas of the Camerata were collaborations. The role of improvisation was reduced and the music was written down. So it is from this time that we must date the first *surviving* evidence for a Renaissance in music, definable as the appearance of a style based on ancient Greek models which aims at conveying individual emotions. The humanist had become the operatic soloist.

In the brief springtime of opera, the time of Peri, Caccini, Cavalieri and the young Monteverdi (*Orfeo*, 1607; *Arianna*, 1608), the three elements of poetry, music and singing were held in balance by the higher intention of recapturing the marvellous effects of ancient Greek music. As Robert Donington has shown,[5] the first operas were no less than the sacred dramas of a revived Neoplatonism. These developments in Italy were exactly contemporary with those in France, England and Germany which Frances Yates has traced with such mastery: academies of poetry and music, Neoplatonic court drama, Rosicrucian philosophy, Hermeticism and alchemy, working together towards a hoped-for renovation of the whole world. But perhaps it was too soon. In any case, by mid-century most of these hopes had been dashed, while opera was no esoteric drama, but had become the most popular public show in every major city in Europe. In the process it had had to change its emphasis from philosophy to spectacle and from expressive recitative to melodious aria. So opera, as it was enjoyed throughout Europe by 1700, depended mainly on its stage-effects and the voices and fame of its singers.

Italian opera between Monteverdi and Mozart is seldom heard today, but one cannot understand the period in which it was the dominant musical form without having at least an imaginary conception of what it was about. First, it was about the heroic virtues. Its stories were usually taken from the Roman historians or from later epics such as Tasso's *Jerusalem Delivered*, and worked over by the librettists in such a way as to display superhuman beings undergoing the extremes of emotion. The libretti were set again and again by composers: no one minded hearing last season's story, so long as it was set to new music. The characters of heroic opera are taken through the most complicated adventures involving mistaken identity, transvestism, betrayal, self-sacrifice, unjust imprisonment, seduction, rescue, and the miraculous conversion necessary for a happy ending. The villains, until the last moment, are black as black can be; the heroes and heroines whiter than white. What is touching about these operas, when viewed from our own uneasy age, is their total absence of self-doubt, cynicism, even irony. They are as pure and idealistic as the Hollywood movies and Broadway musicals of the between-wars period, and the comparison is informative, for these art-forms, so different in time and style, served very similar social and commercial purposes. They display people larger than life, who exemplify the archetypal virtues and vices in plots which, against all probability, bring events to a happy ending.

It was during the same period that instrumental music first gained complete independence from vocal models, dance and background usage. Although nowadays one thinks above all of J.S. Bach in this context, at the time he was a peripheral figure. The composer who is central to this event is Arcangelo Corelli (1653–1713), who initiated the stream of musical classicism that runs uninterruptedly through the pure instrumental music of Handel and the Bachs to Haydn, Mozart, Beethoven, Schubert, Schumann, Mendelssohn, Chopin, Brahms, and even beyond. In this body of work both composer and listener give their assent to certain inner laws of form and tonality, requiring nothing beyond or outside themselves. It is the discourse of pure Intelligence.

Corelli showed his allegiance to these ideals as no other composer before or since. He wrote only instrumental music, while all around him were writing operas. He used only stringed instruments and continuo (i.e. harpsichord, lute or organ, according to circumstance). His oeuvre is the tidiest thing imaginable: Opus 1, 2, 3, and 4 each comprise twelve trio-sonatas; Opus 5, twelve violin sonatas; Opus 6, twelve concerti grossi. That is all. But Corelli was also the first international success in instrumental music, and the first to awaken the possibilities of commercial music publishing. His sonatas and concertos appeared in hundreds of different editions and arrangements: every fiddler in Europe knew them. Lesser composers imitated his style as best they could, while those such as Vivaldi, Handel and J.S. Bach learnt its lessons then deliberately went beyond its bounds.

Siegmund Levarie and Ernst Levy, in their remarkable *Musical Morphology; a Discourse and a Dictionary*, call such pure instrumental music *musica musicans*, defining it as 'music determined by immanent laws of musical structure and by the grammar of musical language' (as opposed to *musica musicata*, which serves 'the unfolding of the passions').[6] These 'laws' are the natural laws of harmony in its wider sense; the 'grammar' is a consensus, as any language is, as to how the elements of melody, rhythm and harmony should be used to fill up a determinate tonal and formal framework. Its dialects vary only slightly as the period progresses (how often before Schubert did the first modulation in a major key go anywhere but the dominant?) As far as tonality is concerned, all classic movements tell the same story of leaving the home key, exploring other key areas, and returning. It is an archetypal tale one never tires of hearing, whether in its simplest form as the binary dance (minuet, waltz, etc.) or in the epic complexity of a symphonic movement by Beethoven or Brahms.

All the musical categories reviewed so far are rich in symbolic and allegorical meanings. The earlier polyphony reflects the ideal hierarchical world of the Middle Ages in which each being knows its place, whether on earth or beyond. Imitative polyphony allows for more flexibility, more communication between levels; the hierarchy begins to dissolve and reform (though it did not find as happy a resolution in sixteenth-century society as it did in music). With the invention of opera, the individual steps forward and plays out a drama of passions on the stage, just as the exploration of the emotions and the exercise of heroic virtues were replacing other-worldly salvation as the perceived purpose of life. In a more subtle way, the tonal journeys of the pure instrumental style are allegories of each one's potential for making a unique and individual exploration of a given world. The tonal form is like an alembic for self-transformation, rather rigid and conventional in Corelli's day but becoming, by the time of the Revolutions of 1776 and 1789, ever more adventurous, conflicting, and individualistic. Finally, in the late works of Beethoven, the vessel no longer serves the experiment and is consequently broken, though others will continue to find it useful.

This new vision of the individual as an explorer of new worlds and a barometer of the passions found its foremost spokesman in Jean-Jacques Rousseau (1712–78). The conflict of ideas between Rousseau and the composer Jean-Philippe Rameau (1683–1764) gives us a remarkable insight into currents which flow far beyond their own time.[7] Their difference, in brief, hinged on the question: Is the essence of music harmony, or melody? Rameau, the professional theorist and founder of the modern understanding of harmony, writes of it in 1742:

What fecundity there is in this phenomenon! So many consequences follow from it of themselves. Can one refuse to consider a phenomenon which is so unique, so abundant, so rational, if I may use this term, as a common principle of all the arts in general, or at least of all the fine arts?

107

Is it not reasonable, in fact, to believe that *Nature, simple as she is in her general laws, might have only a single principle for all things* which seem to be related to one another in that they excite the same sensations in us, such as the arts destined to give us the feeling of beauty?[8] [My italics.]

For Rousseau, the gifted amateur and enthusiast for the melodious Italian opera, harmony deserves no such primacy in music. Writing in 1755 to answer Rameau's criticisms of his *Encyclopédie* article, Rousseau points out that harmony as distinct from melody was unknown in Ancient Greece, and that folk singers today have no natural feeling for it.[9] 'By what right does harmony, which cannot give itself a natural foundation, pretend to be that of melody, which was working miracles two thousand years before there was any question of harmony or of chords?'[10] These 'general laws' asserted by Rameau seem to Rousseau an unwarranted extraction from the multiplicity of partials, mostly dissonant, that surround every note.[11] Therefore, he concludes, 'Harmony consists not in the relationships between vibrations, but in the concourse of sounds which result therefrom; and if these are null, how will all the proportions in the world give them an existence which they do not have?'[12]

As Lionel Gossman comments, 'Rousseau's rejection of the primacy of harmony involves a rejection of the entire world-view that the primacy of harmony supposed. And indeed Rousseau does separate man from the cosmos and gives him his own history and his own laws.'[13] But the matter cannot rest there. From another point of view, and one which is nothing if not aware of man's place in a harmonious cosmos, comes the contrary opinion. Albert Steffen, one of Rudolf Steiner's most eminent pupils, writes that as soon as melody is conceived of (as it was by Rameau) as inevitably carrying with it a 'fundamental bass' that may or may not be realized on an instrument, it is dragged down to earth. Until then, tone – which for Steffen is inseparable from melody – is a creature of the cosmos, the superphysical realm where the human being is truly at home. These are Steffen's words:

Rameau's discovery of the fundamental bass distances music from the human. The chordal theory that rests on it consequently emancipates itself from the living voice and allows the melody to perish. Tone thereby loses its 'atmosphere' ['*Stimmung*']. Its origin in the spiritual-soul realm, which is bound by Nature to man (but not necessarily to the instrument), disappears.

It is grasped more abstractly. That which precedes it, its inaudible life which is there before it is physically sounded, is scarcely experienced any more. It has no longer any genesis, any connection with the cosmos, any divinity. The melody of the spheres has become a phrase.[14]

Yet Steffen acknowledges this development – and for him it is Rameau who is more 'progressive' than Rousseau – as an inevitable part of the process by which man's senses must be emancipated from their archaic spiritual, clairvoyant state. 'That awakening of the Consciousness Soul in the fifteenth century, grasped musically, is heard as an earthquake of the Soul, and the fundamental bass is an echo of it.'[15] And he quotes Rudolf Steiner's dictum: 'The chord is the corpse of the melody.'[16]

If we reconsider this controversy in the light of that great period of pure instrumental music, and ask what one is invited to listen to in a Bach concerto or a Schubert sonata, the answer is surely not the harmonic and tonal structure – that is taken for granted – so much as an endless melody. The whole work is a melody in which the succession of phrases and themes is as perfect, on a larger scale, as the fitting-together of single notes to make each melodic phrase. Anyone can construct harmonic progressions or tonal schemes in classical style, but without the gift of melody they will be lifeless images. That is why we teach students to write harmony and counterpoint, which are no harder to learn than mathematics, but never attempt to teach them melody, which is a gift from the Gods. The analytical system of Heinrich Schenker (1868–1935) obeys a correct intuition in looking for quasi-melodic outlines behind classical pieces, although it can never explain why a certain second subject of Mozart is such a perfect companion to its first subject. Neither can any intellectual analysis, for the relationship is not an intellectual one. Harmonists such as Rameau are certainly right in recognizing the conventions of Western tonality as a manifestation of the natural laws of musical number; but Rousseau was right, too, in defending the ancient fount of melody which music can never dispense with, and remain music. All the arts, as Rameau points out, must have proportion and harmony (taken in its broader sense); but we must reply that only music has the capacity, through melody (also taken in its broader sense), to form and transform the substance of time.

In these classical works the transformation of time takes place, as we have said, within a vessel of form that has predictable proportions and sequences of events. The surprises are such as one would expect to find on taking a guided tour to a known destination. But what if we were to go blindfolded, and not know where we were going? That is the situation with the unique and unpredictable forms that begin to appear as the nineteenth century proceeds.

Beethoven, in his late works, is like a guide who takes us into virgin territory. Each of the last piano sonatas and quartets is a journey to a realm hitherto unknown in music. By now these places have become familiar, just as sites like Petra or Niagara, formerly accessible only to intrepid explorers, are now full of tourists. They have expanded the limits of our world. But now comes the crucial question to be posed to anyone who presumes to compose in this manner, that is to say, who tries to create a work unlike any before it: 'Have you really been there, or are you making it up?'

Many modern scores seem not to have arisen from a revelation to the inner ear, but to have been made by the clever constructive powers of the ego. They are inventions, not discoveries, belonging to the third degree of musical inspiration, as described in the last chapter (p. 87). Their composers, had they lived a few hundred years ago, working within a traditional style and not trying to astonish at every turn, might have turned out works as delightful as those of the many *Kleinmeister* of the past. But they were not content to do this, and neither would their time consent to it. The clock of history does not run backwards, and the world of musical classicism in whose nurturing embrace Beethoven wrote his early works no longer exists. Figures such as Rousseau, Goethe, and Beethoven himself stand as symbols of a new emancipation of the individual, heralds of the coming initiation of Mankind after which the power of the collectivity to nurture and control can only wane. The attempts of avant-garde artists to be innovative and original at all costs are gropings in this direction: they are pioneers who often pay for their self-separation from the masses by neurosis, but who nevertheless have set their feet on the path of individuation.

One of the hopes of the modern age, which was first enunciated publicly at the French Revolution, is that the social hierarchy will be broken down and that the opportunities it gives for the oppression of man by man (and of woman by man) will vanish. This is evidently part of the Great Alchemist's programme, too, since it can be detected as early as the Middle Ages. One might say that in previous stages of his work, he kept the four elements in separate development, in the form of the four castes decreed by the earliest lawmakers of India and followed there ever since, whereas in recent history they have all been permitted to contest for first place, as the elements are said to battle in the alchemical flask.

Western civilization started out with a caste arrangement exactly analogous to the Hindu one. First there were the clergy and monastic orders, comparable to the Brahmins (though not hereditary) and charged with the performance of religious duties, with learning, and with education. Second were the nobility, comparable to the Kshatriyas and comprising the entire secular hierarchy from the King down to the Lords of Manors; men united in their freedom from commercial and manual labour, in their right to bear the sword, and their duty to protect their country. Third came the merchants and free guildsmen – Vaishyas, in the Hindu system – who lived by trade or skill. Lastly, the class of peasants or serfs, like the Hindu Shudras, lived by their own physical labour.

Since the Middle Ages, each caste in turn has come to power in Europe, fulfilling the Hindu predictions that in this age the social order would collapse and all distinctions be broken down; but also giving hope to those religions – Buddhism, Christianity and Islam – which are explicitly opposed to caste distinctions. In theory, at least, the three later religions look forward to an age, or a state, in which each person will stand in independent and direct relationship with God, and in universal brotherhood with the whole human race.

Let us apply this historical pattern to Western music. Obviously polyphony, born and bred in the service of the Church, reflects the values of the first caste. The polyphonic era, from the ninth to the sixteenth century, is the era of music's domination by the Church, even if domination sometimes took the form of prohibition. When the power of the Church, already weakened by schism, took second place to that of secular rulers after the Reformation, the pictorial arts turned to the subjects of portraiture, classical themes, and beautiful bodies. Music, lagging behind somewhat, achieved its 'noble' form with the invention of opera, in which the same three subjects manifest as the expression of individual emotion, classical plots, and sexual intrigue. Opera was not only for the nobility, any more than the Church exists only for the clergy, but still it was the royal and titled patrons who first owned the theatres, provided the money, and dictated the style. This art of the second caste reached its apogee in the France of Louis XIV.

Whereas before the French Revolution a successful merchant had only to carry a sword to look every inch a knight, afterwards even princes wore the workaday black of the tradesman, and the only Kshatriyas who still looked the part were army officers. Opera survived, as church music did, but neither could serve the more intimate purposes of the newly propserous burgher who had the money to buy a piano, and a wife with the leisure to learn to play it. Abstract thought does not come easily to the man of the third caste, whose duty in life is to keep the material world running. He likes his paintings to 'look like something', hence his penchant for genre scenes (first cultivated in socially progressive Holland). He also likes his music to be anchored in what he knows as reality. What serves him best in this regard are songs and small-scale instrumental pieces that tell a story. On a grander scale he likes tone-poems, and will make up stories even to pure symphonic works. (Berlioz and Wagner obliged with hideous literary versions of Beethoven's symphonies.) But one should not disdain this world of bourgeois music lovers, which one sees at its best in Moritz von Schwind's

111

pictures of Schubert and his friends. 'Biedermeier' they may have been, but what serenity and charm there is in the Biedermeier of *Die schöne Müllerin*, or of Schumann's *Kinderszenen*!

Each caste has its characteristic virtues, and these, as well as its more obvious faults, also manifest as it ascends to the possibility of independence and self-consciousness. For the priest, the ideal is holiness; for the warrior, bravery and mercy; for the merchant, honesty and generosity; for the peasant, diligence. Anyone who aspires to self-realization must cultivate all four in himself; hence, in the larger world of collective evolution, our civilization has had the opportunity to govern its affairs according to each in turn. A primary function of the arts – one might say their main purpose – is to teach by displaying these virtues in idealized form. Of sanctity and nobility we have said enough. Bourgeois virtues are best seen in the unpretentiousness and directness of the character-piece, and in the cheerful plots of comic opera. In the best of these, as in the best genre scenes from Vermeer to Van Gogh, something sublime shines through and everyday life becomes transparent to the ever-present heart of things: there is no need to build cathedrals or go on Crusades, for perfection is here and now.

But pure instrumental music of the 'classical' kind belongs to no caste, even though virtually all its composers were born into the bourgeoisie. Too secular for the narrowly ecclesiastical mind, too intellectual for the extraverted warrior, too abstract for the tradesman, it is music that truly rises above caste. Its devotees may include Abbés and Archdukes, bankers and barbers, but they meet as equals in this freemasonry of all those who have won a deeper understanding of what music can be. This category reflects the best aspirations of an era in which Liberty, Equality and Fraternity were first proposed as ideals, however far they fell short of realization.

By the time of the revolutions of 1848, the fourth caste was beginning its ascent to power, though this would be through a destiny as pitiful as anything in history. For in the meantime the Industrial Revolution had called into being an entirely new way of working, cut off from the soil and from the age-old traditions of the peasantry. Peasant life, unless oppressed by the other castes, has a beauty and an integrity of its own, enhanced by an awareness of Nature and the cosmic rhythms, by traditional festivals, crafts and customs. But the industrial worker is deprived of these. As Karl Marx rightly perceived, the proletarian's labour is void of any meaning beyond keeping him alive to enrich his employer. Even if the means of production is made his own, the very nature of his work – unaesthetic, repetitive, and without cosmological foundation – alienates him from human as well as from spiritual reality. And proletarian music, which anyone can hear by switching on the nearest radio, mirrors this condition. It is as different as can be from the rich and beautiful folk music of Europe that inspired the Nationalist composers such as Liszt, Bartók and Kodály in Hungary; Smetana, Dvořák and Janáček in Czechoslovakia; Grieg in Norway; Sibelius in Finland; De Falla in Spain; Holst and Vaughan Williams in Britain; and almost every Russian composer from Glinka to the present. This is what might have been the popular music of our time; but the new proletariat does not listen to it. Having no indigenous artistic or caste-traditions of its own, it has fallen victim, since its birth, to the cynical purveyors of mindless and soulless trivia, from the banality of the music-hall to that of Radio One.

Plato had strong words for the effect of bad art on the masses: 'Bred among images of evil as in an evil meadow, culling and grazing much every day from many sources, little by little [they] collect all unawares a great evil in their own soul.'[17] But if one is to condemn any sort of art as actually evil, one must be precise about its nature, particularly since any evocation of Platonic censorship tends to court the disapproval of modern 'intellectuals'. Part of this evil, in the present case, lies in the shallow and false world-view that is presented in the lyrics of many popular songs, as by the mass media in general. Another part is actually inherent in the music, though this is harder for most people to believe – for what, they may ask, can make pure music harmful?

Setting aside what we have already said in Chapter One on the extraordinary powers of music and sound, there is the question of how 'pure' this music is. Most popular music is backed by a regular percussive beat that is strictly speaking not music or tone, but noise. Now percussion has its place in Western classical music, albeit a small one, while in non-Western traditions it often has a much more important role. But in these traditions it always approaches tone, through the use of tuned drums, etc., and is used as a vehicle for rhythmic subtlety, as in the astonishing patterns produced by African and Indian drummers. It is never a mindless repetition of the beat, that unhappy legacy of an American jazz that had wandered too far from its African roots. The thumping beat of Rock, the no less regular ticking behind most 'easy listening' music, serve to anchor the music in the physical body, which responds with minute internal twitches if not with overt movements. Factory workers have to learn to shut out the regular noises of their machinery, but this ubiquitous beat enters subliminally into minds that do not just accept noise but apparently cannot take in musical tone without its accompaniment. Like the excessive sweetening or salting of commercial foods, it dulls the perceptions of the finer tastes that should be, but often are not, present – in music, the finer points of melody and harmony. And nothing could be more contrary to the cultivation of inner stillness that is the most desirable background to all activity, and to which the silence points that broods over all true music. At rock concerts, the beat reaches its apotheosis with a noise level so high that it has caused permanent hearing impairment to a whole generation. It propels its feelers – one cannot say its listeners – into a trance-like participation which is a perverted image of the higher modes of listening described in the last chapter.

The evil in popular music, and in mass culture in general, lies also in its addictive nature, which robs the individual, often during childhood, of the capability for choice and rejection. One has only to think of the television addiction of children and adults, and of the use of pop music as an omnipresent background in the home and at work. Constant exposure to banality, triviality and phony sentiments, whether expressed in words or in music, breeds anaesthesia, suitable enough for the dentist's surgery but more fit for the cattle suggested by Plato's words than for human beings.

Finally, there is the question of the images on which popular songs and their singers build, which are held up – again, above all, to the young – for admiration, and to which their musical style is directed. The melodies of plainsong and polyphonic music made the human voice sound like the voice of an angel. Those of opera make it sound like a superman. The Lieder-singer sounds like a lyric poet. And the melodies of popular music? I search the dial of my radio for a random sampling of current predilections and hear several whores, two hermaphrodites in distress, a street-fighter, and a few lachrymose labourers. I would not let them into my house: who could possibly want to let such voices, sinister carriers of psychic influences, into their minds?

There is a positive side even to this. This concentration on the outcast, the misfit and pervert, the harshness and violence of life, is exactly what we find in the 'highbrow' art of about a hundred years ago. These characters could have stepped out of the pages of Baudelaire, or Beardsley. What we have here is the very stuff of the alchemical *Nigredo*: the Putrefaction, the journey through the Inferno where one must behold Man's every sin, without which the Work cannot proceed with its purgative process and its paradisal conclusion. Popular culture, in so far as it presents these negatives for contemplation, even for admiration, is a proletarian version of what Mario Praz called the 'Romantic Agony'. It enables the masses, for better or worse, to pass vicariously through regions that were minutely explored by certain artists and writers from de Sade to the Surrealists.

To accept Putrefaction is necessary, but there is always the danger that this exploration of the Underworld will lead to the loss of the soul, as

Orpheus was unable to retrieve Eurydice from Hades. The rock musicians who have fallen victim to drugs, drink, or suicide are like that legendary singer, torn to pieces by the Maenads – or like all those poets and artists, albeit in more elevated style, who have cracked under the tensions between the demands of art and those of normal life. The sadism, masochism and homosexuality, the drugs and alcohol, the fascination with low life, even the Satanism, are nothing new. And everyone who enters on the quest for spiritual regeneration is going to encounter them at some stage.

There is another side to popular music, too, which is more positively a reflection of the quest that is now being offered not only to initiates but to Everyman. This is its truly Aquarian aspect, if the Age of Aquarius is to be one in which hidden knowledge is poured out for all of mankind. The Rock music of the 1960s and early 1970s was full of idealism, and a powerful support for the many 'New Age' impulses that had their rise then: the Peace Movement, ecology, the awakening to the Orient, consciousness expansion, the desire for freedom from pigheaded authority. Meditation was never a respectable practice in Western society until the Beatles lent their name and fame for a while to Maharishi Mahesh Yogi's 'TM' movement. And although in the past every war has had its songs, the Vietnamese one gave birth for the first time not to songs of jingoism but of virulent opposition to the whole machinery that thrives on war. This is to say nothing of the music and lyrics in that period that actually showed an awareness of the spiritual quest, on which I have written elsewhere.[18]

As I write, there are new stirrings in the air: *We are the World* tops the charts in the USA, while *Pie Jesu* has reached them in Britain. Perhaps as the Demiurge subjects the world to a further turn of the screw, popular culture can find a better response than the nihilism of Punk Rock or the anodynes of the 'Me Generation'.

In the world of modern 'classical' music there is even more evidence of the forced and accelerated growth to which Western culture has been treated, having to do with the realization of musical potentials hitherto unknown. Since the beginning of the twentieth century, every possible scale has been explored, including those that require a revision of the entire tuning system (e.g. – and these lists are by no means exhaustive, merely suggestive – by Debussy, Hába, Bartók, Partch, Messiaen); every rhythmic device exploited (Strawinsky, Bartók again, Carter, Nancarrow, Lutosławski). Every kind of structure and performance situation, and the absence of any of these, has been tried out (Satie, Cage, Stockhausen, Cardew, Xenakis). The gradual acceptance through history of smaller and smaller intervals (and their inversions) as consonances, i.e. as not requiring resolution to a purer consonance, has now embraced the whole range of harmonic possibilities within the tempered chromatic scale, culminating in atonality with or without serial organization (Schoenberg, Webern, Babbitt). The acceptance of every possibility of tone as musically viable leads logically to the inclusion of noise within the musical domain (Antheil, Varèse, Pierre Henry), and finally of silence, too (Cage, Feldman). And one need not be 'absolutely modern' either: in the spirit of the Renaissance, one can return to a past epoch for inspiration (Strawinsky, Hindemith, Rochberg, Del Tredici). Or one can build bridges to other musics, especially the popular and Oriental ones (Cowell, Hovhaness, Bedford, Reich, Glass).

Even by the end of the 1950s, most of these things had already been tried and taken to their logical conclusions, and there was little left to be done in the way of innovation. But now a vast mass of musical possibility – a veritable new *Prima Materia* – lay ready to hand, with none of the restrictions that had limited composers in the past. This is the raw musical matter of the new age that has been laboriously gathered and poured out, to be used by each composer according to his own lights. It is like the spiritual heritage of the whole world that is now offered, for the first time, to anyone who can read.

Whereas in the past the stylistic boundaries were defined both for composers and for those following a religious impulse – e.g. the symphony orchestra and sonata form for the one, Roman Catholicism for the other – now the first thing a person has to do is to choose his or her own style or path from the many available options (the musical or spiritual supermarket, as it has been called). In the case of the composer, he or she has to decide whether or not to use electronics, serialism, chance, historical references, and a dozen other fundamental things. Once these choices are made, the question remains as to whether the material will be used well or poorly.

If the composer is one of the very few who are really summoned to be composers and endowed with commensurate inspiration, these choices will be made by inner necessity. Thus Strawinsky said of *The Rite of Spring*: 'I heard and wrote what I heard. I am the vessel through which *The Rite* passed.'[19] In such a case, the new style is not an invention of the ego but the revelation of an archetype from the collective unconscious: and one can tell such a work by its fruits. The power of *The Rite of Spring*, like that of Wagner's operas or Beethoven's symphonies, has not waned with time, but radiates outward to touch more and more people. One cannot say the same of many of Strawinsky's other compositions (and he made no such claims for them), in which the power at work is rather his personal unconscious or merely his gifted ego. But this is no censure: only a handful of works are needed as vessels for the initiatory rites of their age.

Whatever may be thought of their music and its effects, the major composers of the twentieth century seem to have been without exception paragons of sincerity and humane concern. Many of them are also religious, even mystical (Webern, Messiaen, Stockhausen, Maxwell Davies), while some have actually been involved in esotericism (Debussy, Satie, Skryabin, Schoenberg). Among the many other composers, living or recently dead, whose historical stature has yet to be determined, allusions to mysticism or esotericism are positively in vogue. Although such allusions are no guarantee of profundity or musical worth, they show, like parallel phenomena among popular musicians, a sensitivity to the currents of the time.

One of the most respected of living composers, Elliott Carter (born 1908), said on accepting the 1983 Edward MacDowell medal:

I have a feeling that somehow there are these shadowy things behind me, these compositions, which are in a way not me, myself; really, they deserve the medal and not me. They have this strange life; I'm not sure that I invented them. These strange beings began to come to my mind and gradually somehow insisted on being written in their strange and unusual way, difficult to some people, and profoundly exciting to others. I was just sort of something that wrote them down, because they were telling me they had to be done this way and they were rather trying and sometimes difficult and demanding. And sometimes they did things I have never done before and made me do things that bothered me and upset me and sometimes excited me – and puzzled me, too, sometimes.[20]

Carter's words bear an intriguing resemblance to the accounts of people in Jungian and other forms of analysis who have encountered the energies of the unconscious in personified form. Perhaps a lot of modern music has come into being as part of an individual process of therapy: as an exploration and casting-off of psychological complexes in the form of sound. This would certainly assimilate it to the more patently confessional and cathartic role of much modern literature and painting. It would also explain the compulsion toward the ugly and the discordant (judged against the laws of harmony that are intrinsic to the human ear[21]) that is one of the most striking, and to many people upsetting, features of modern music. These are the musical images of the demons within that have to be raised and faced in any analysis. And to the degree that the contents presented by the music derive from the personal rather than the collective unconscious, it would account for the general absence among modern composers of the Pentecostal gift – speaking to each one in his own tongue – that was possessed by the great voices of the past.

The composers, poets and artists of today are the nervous system of a civilization in transition. They suffer its tensions and display them for the education of the world. One finds expressed in modern art the most contrary impulses, from utter degradation to pure spirituality – and often both by the same person. Here again, Baudelaire is the prototype of the modern artist, crucified between these extremes, who in turn is the prototype of modern Man. In music, the closest correspondence would be Arnold Schoenberg, already as a Viennese Jew born to experience in the highest degree both the intellectual ferment and the political evil of our time. One the one hand he aspired to the heights of a Swedenborgian heaven (*Séraphîta*[22]) in which one can move freely in every dimension – such being one of the symbolic meanings of atonal music, liberated from the gravitational pull of tonality. On the other hand, he was attracted to the gruesome decadence of the *Pierrot Lunaire* poems, vacillating between nihilism and nostalgia. In his religious life, too, he felt the conflicting currents of Judaism, Christianity and modern agnosticism. As a composer, the anchor to which he eventually held firm was the twelve-tone system, which served him perhaps much as the sexual theory of psychology served Sigmund Freud, as a bastion against the forces of musical or psychic dissolution. It enabled him to exercise complete theoretical control over the musical chaos that threatened to overwhelm him. So he could set, for example, the horrors of *A Survivor from Warsaw* within a structure of the utmost law and clarity, thus purging himself of emotions almost too strong to be sustained in sanity. Nevertheless, in contrast to the great music of the past, there remains a large gulf between means and ends in Schoenberg's music, namely between the hyperorganization that continues to supply doctoral students with analytical dissertation topics, and the emotional contents which can actually cause nausea in sensitive listeners.

For Schoenberg's pupil and friend Anton Webern, the twelve tones and the serial system derived from them became something quite different, which Schoenberg himself might have realized had not his historical position and emotional nature been what they were. The serial world, in Webern's pieces, is a musical image of the Pleroma, the divine fullness in which every possibility exists in perfect orderliness. Ever since ancient China, the twelve chromatic notes have symbolized musical fullness, from which selection is then made according to the demands of mode or key. But in Webern's twelve-tone music the notes are still in their primal state, prior to the selection of five- or seven-note scales. Symbolically speaking, this is the music of the Eighth Sphere, the realm of the twelvefold Zodiac, prior to descent along the scales of the planets. It is also prior to the domain of physical manifestation, in which the notes inevitably form a hierarchy in the order of the harmonic series. This is why the idea of Webern's twelve-tone music is, on the whole, more satisfying than the music itself. When materialized in performance it suffers from a brevity that makes it incongruous in any normal concert setting: how can one play a five-minute string quartet of Webern's beside a thirty-minute one of Beethoven's and expect the audience to treat them as the equals which they may be in the Realm of Ideas?

In the 1950s, with the rediscovery of Webern's music, several composers developed the serial principle further, applying it also to durations, registers, dynamics, timbres, etc. Milton Babbitt (born 1916), who has remained the most faithful as he was the earliest exponent of this idea, admits that totally serial music is and will always be a concern for the very few. 'Who cares if you listen?' is the title of one of his articles. Yet for those who have penetrated his music, there is a satisfaction akin to that of higher mathematics, in which a perception of order upon order, of realms of totally logical organization, reunites the cerebral intellect with the sense of wonder and the charm of scintillating tone. In Babbitt's compositions the goal is reached of a musical microcosm, complete, balanced and account-able in its every detail, obeying laws sufficient to itself. And although from his articles he might seem the least mystical of composers, he has chosen to set texts such as Gerard Manley Hopkins' 'That Nature is a Heraclitean Fire', with its concluding lines:

> I am all at once what Christ is, since he was what I am, and
> This Jack, joke, poor potsherd, patch, matchwood, immortal diamond,
> Is immortal diamond.[23]

The perfect, crystalline order into which Babbitt sets this poem does indeed take on the aspect of an alchemical transformation of the potential chaos of atonality (the 'poor potsherds' of a once integral art?). In the same year (1955) Strawinsky was using the simile of 'dazzling diamonds'[24] to describe the serial music of Webern, with its multi-faceted and reflecting qualities, its miniature scale, its flawless beauty, its inaccessibility to the masses.

In the heady atmosphere of the postwar avant-garde, centered on the summer courses at Darmstadt in the 1950s, the partisans of total serialism (who then included Pierre Boulez and Karlheinz Stockhausen) were challenged by a view diametrically opposed to their desire for rigour and control: that of John Cage (born 1912). For years, Cage's music had not only allowed the performer to make spontaneous choices, but left things to chance, by throwing dice and other methods that deliberately excluded the composer's preference. While for some this boded an irreconcilable conflict of philosophies, Boulez and Stockhausen were canny enough to incorpo-rate both the contraries into their own works, allowing spontaneous choice and chance to affect the eventual sounds of the work but not admitting for a minute that they had abandoned the principle of total control. Cage's motives, however, were quite different from theirs at the time. Influenced by Oriental and Gnostic philosophies and especially by Zen Buddhism, he deliberately withdrew the function of attachment, of preference for one sound over another, in favour of an openness to whatever sounds might occur. In the same way, Buddhism teaches that all suffering comes from the desire for one thing over another, and that liberation from it is reached through non-attachment. If a note is 'ugly' – if it is a noise, even – then so be it. Gautama Buddha could see beauty in the white teeth of a putrefying dog! For this philosophy, the sounds that surround us in everyday life – whether in civilization or in nature – have as much to offer as a symphony to the person in search of enlightenment: perhaps more, for they are more likely to still the mind and the desires. Cage's musical philosophy leads, in the end, beyond any necessity for music. Once he had composed (proposed?) his famous silent piece, *4' 33"*, his work was done. But just as a tree continues to flower year after year, perhaps just out of habit, Cage still composes music. After all, the Zen master after enlightenment still lives in his body, still enjoys his tea, though he is no longer subject to the illusion that these have any special value.

The common ground on which the postwar avant-garde met, transcending all their ideological differences, was tone. Call it also timbre, tone-quality, pure sound: it was that dimension of music which had been comparatively neglected during several centuries of harmonic, melodic and rhythmic exploration. This is why avant-garde music, to the great distress of the conventionally trained ear, seems to have no coherent melody, no harmonic language, no steady rhythm: it is just one sound after another. The very strangeness of its sounds – new combinations of instruments, weird sounds produced from them, electronic noises – draws attention to this dimension. While much of it simply disguises the predicament of composers who would otherwise have nothing to say, its broader effect is to focus on the very stuff of music, taken for granted in the past. (At the same time, artists take for their subject the actual substance of paint on canvas, and poets write poems in which they wonder what words really are.) When Wagner first analysed a tone in the Prelude to *Rheingold*, showing over eight minutes how it is made from the series of overtones in increasing density and rapidity of vibration, the first step had been taken towards a penetration by the listener of the single tone, as a microcosm to be explored in its own right, irrespective of its neighbours. The composers of the 1950s, in turn, present not melodies and harmonies but 'sonorous objects' for contemplation.

Stockhausen describes in his many writings how his early music moved from organization with reference to the note or single musical point ('punktuelle Musik') – the standpoint of Webern – through composition with 'groups' of notes (exemplified in *Gruppen for three Orchestras*, 1955–57), to the idea of the musical 'moment' ('Momentform', *Momente*, 1962–64). This no doubt reflects his own development in meditative listening, and it goes much further in his later works. But in the idea of the Moment we have what I called the sonorous object of contemplation: the musical entity which is a whole, and which can be perceived as a whole (momentarily) without awareness of the passage of time. Each moment is a glimpse of the sound-world, where time takes on a far different nature from its inexorable and irreversible flow down here. In contemplating these timeless moments, these musical creatures, one may enter a different state of consciousness. It is a state in which judgment is suspended – for everything that has being, in this case sound, has an equal right to be. One does not expect to go anywhere, unless it be deeper into the state. So connections between the moments, climaxes, formal architecture, all these are irrelevant.

Eventually one feels the need – and Stockhausen's work shows that he himself felt it – to expand the moment to the dimensions of the entire piece. So instead of the rather choppy, ever-changing parade of sound-objects characteristic of the 1950s and 1960s, we find a tendency in more recent years towards constancy, repetition, quasi-motionlessness, and a longer time-scale. And with this comes a rediscovery of the natural harmonic qualities of tone. Stockhausen turned the corner with *Stimmung for six vocalists* (1968), which is based on the phenomenon of the harmonic series. Hence our old friends the fifths, fourths and triads make their reappearance after their period of exile from the totalitarian rule of atonality.

No one who works with electronic or computer-generated music can remain indifferent to the phenomenon of tone, so fascinating and inexhaustible, so much its own world. The harmonic series itself, heard in isolation, has a strange power over the human soul. (Why else did the Romantics love the sound of the Aeolian harp, if not that it was the only way they had of hearing the harmonic series?) It is far from being exhausted, holding as it does the key to much more than music. Stockhausen's *Stimmung* showed the West what Mongolian and Tibetan singers have long known: that the human voice does not simply produce notes, but a whole spectrum of harmonics that can be isolated and articulated through the use of vowels (which, after all, have no other cause). David Hykes, founder of the Harmonic Choir and the Harmonic Research Society, has developed the principle much further, using the acoustics of the medieval abbey church of

Le Thoronet to enhance this bouquet of harmonics that floats over everything we sing or say.[25] Thus he makes a link with those Cluniac monks who built their church according to musical proportions, in order to enrich their plainchant and to bring them into contact with the hidden dimensions of tone.

Just as melody, harmony and rhythm, while still indispensable to music, have taken second place to tone in recent decades, so a new partner has come forward to join the trio of theorist, composer and performer. It is the listener who now becomes an indispensable participant, and whose activity is perhaps the main goal, rather than the expression of the composer's emotions or of the performer's virtuosity. We may have seen the end of the epoch of Great Composers, which will after all only have lasted about 500 years. Music can do without them, as it does almost everywhere else in the world. The listener or singer can reach the ultimate states that music can offer just as well through plainchant or folk music as through the grandiose apparatus of Bayreuth or the Ninth Symphony.

The new emphasis on the listener and on the act of listening invites everyone without exception to participate in music to the utmost, just as the outpouring of formerly guarded knowledge enables individuals to pursue their spiritual quests independently of church dogmas and authority. That seems to be the peculiar quality of our time. As each person takes up this challenge, so the mass of humanity, presently seething in the crucible of its possible transmutation, changes atom by atom into the Tincture. And in the little world of music with which this book has been concerned, as each person is led by it to a clearer understanding of what they are, so the Harmony of the World (which is the will of God) may sound forth on Earth, as it does in Heaven.

PART III

THE MUSIC OF THE SPHERES

1. The Cosmological Framework

Since modern rationalism has untuned the sky, the Music of the Spheres is still mentioned but seldom heard. One reason is that the spheres in question are no longer believed in. We must begin by reconstructing the cosmology which allows them being, and that means the geocentric system as it was accepted before the Scientific Revolution. According to this view, the Earth remains unmoving at the centre of all things, while around it spin eight concentric spheres which bear the heavenly bodies. These spheres may be visualized as solid shells of crystalline ether, harder than adamant yet more translucent than air;[1] or they may be purely mathematical loci for the orbits of the planets. The outermost sphere which bounds the entire universe perceptible to mortal sense is the Star-bearer. It is 'thick inlaid with patines of bright gold'[2] – the Fixed Stars – and hurtles round the Earth from East to West every twenty-four hours. It carries with it the entire planetary system, as anyone can see by watching the Sun's journey by day or the Moon's by night. At the same time, the spheres of the seven Wandering Stars – the planets Moon, Mercury, Venus, Sun, Mars, Jupiter, and Saturn – revolve more slowly in the opposite direction, creeping around the Zodiac from West to East. Each planet moves at its own speed: the Moon completes the zodiacal circuit in a month, the Sun in a year, Saturn in about thirty years.

For the ancient astronomers who studied the planetary motions carefully, the task of saving the appearances by devising a reasonable explanation was an increasingly complex and challenging one. As observations became more accurate, there were more and more irregularities to be explained away. (The scientists' predicament has not changed today.) Late Antiquity, Islamic civilization, and the European and Byzantine Middle Ages accepted the Aristotelian idea that everything in the heavens must move in perfect circles: a dogma that required a system of ever more numerous epicycles, like wheels within wheels, in order to account for these apparent retrogradations, adnutations, and so on. It was partly in order to clear the field for a less cumbersome means of calculating positions that Copernicus suggested that the Sun be placed hypothetically at the centre. But these complications belong to the history of observational astronomy. The musical cosmos, in contrast, is astronomically simple and philosophically ideal, as befits its function as the model for things below; it is a kind of geometry of the musical language. Yet as soon as it crystallizes into sound, complexity reigns.

We must now unravel the threads of this vexed subject. As in the book as a whole, the way to understanding lies through finding the appropriate standpoint from which to consider every theory. Without that readiness to shift attitudes and to keep one's mind open to several different and sometimes contradictory levels of being, any study of planet-tone or zodiac-tone theories is limited to an academic approach which regards its subject as historically instructive but devoid of intrinsic truth.

2. Planet-Scales, Type A

As soon as the idea of the Music of the Spheres occurs, the question arises of how it can be related to earthly music. The simplest answer is that just as the spheres are ranked like the rungs of a ladder set up to Heaven from Earth, so each should correspond to one pitch, the totality making a musical scale (from Latin *scala* = ladder; cf. German *Tonleiter*). Plato describes them thus in the 'Myth of Er' (*Republic*, X, 617b) as eight whorls or rings rotating around the earth, on each of which stands a Siren who sings her own note, all together making a harmony.

The idea behind the scales of Example 1,[3] and Type A scales in general, is attributed to the School of Pythagoras: it is that the planetary spheres are spaced at intervals comparable to those stoppings of a string that produce a scale. According to the Greek writers, Pythagoras reckoned the distance from the Earth to the Moon's sphere to be 126,000 stades,[4] which he represented by the interval of a whole-tone. The rest of the scale, with its tones, semitones, etc., then shows the relative distances of the other spheres from one another. The scale as the elder Pliny gives it is in the chromatic form (genus) of the Greek Dorian mode. It consists of two disjunct chromatic tetrachords (the separate four-note groups marked by square brackets), plus one added note at the bottom.

Censorinus and Theon of Smyrna, however, lower the note of the Fixed Stars, making it exactly an octave from that of the Earth. Theodore Reinach[5] proposed an ingenious explanation for this anomaly. He found in the treatise of Aristeides Quintilianus[6] (*c.* AD 300) two 'ancient' scale-forms, not actually associated with planets, which Aristeides called the enharmonic genus of the Dorian and the Phrygian modes:

'Dorian'	D	E	E+	F	A	B	B+	C	E
'Phrygian'	D	E	E+	F	A	B	B+	C	D

(+ = quarter-tone sharp)

Reinach points out that since in Greek notation there is no way of distinguishing the chromatic from the enharmonic genus, the later writers who are our only sources may have mistakenly transferred these ancient scales into the chromatic genus by replacing the inner notes of each

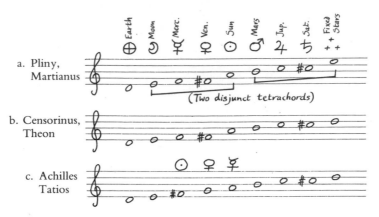

Example 1: Planet-scales, Type A

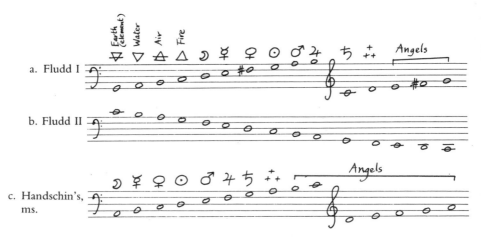

Example 2: Two-octave planet-scales, Type A

tetrachord with their chromatic forms. This would give the two scales
D E F F♯ A B C C♯ E and D E F F♯ A B C C♯ D, which
are exactly the same as the scales of Pliny and Censorinus, respectively. To
explain why this change occurred, Reinach makes the point that in ancient
Greece the enharmonic genus was the most highly regarded by theorists,
but that by the time of these Latin writers its excessive difficulty had led to
its replacement by the simpler chromatic genus.

Whether or not one accepts this theory, type A is fundamentally a
projection into the heavens of a scale system based on the nine-stringed
Greek lyre, which could have been tuned in any of these ways. It is an
attempt to make the heavens accord with a system of earthly music, while
asserting on the contrary that the earthly system is a result of the heavenly

order. Therefore it will change from age to age, as the musical system changes.

The longer scales of Example 2[7] add tones above and below the planets, representing the lower spheres of the four elements (Earth, Water, Air, Fire) and the higher world of the Angelic Intelligences, which we will consider in Section 11 along with some more scales of this kind. To illustrate and explain these scales, both the twelfth-century anonymous writer published by Jacques Handschin[8] and the seventeenth-century Hermeticist Robert Fludd[9] showed the tones along the string of a monochord. This is a one-stringed instrument used for demonstrating harmonic theory. The open string gives its fundamental, lowest tone; stopping the string at the half-way point and then plucking it gives the tone an octave higher; stopping it a third of the way along gives the perfect fifth, and so on. All tones are calculable as the various fractions of the whole string. The monochord string can equally well symbolize a celestial measuring-rod that determines the distances between the spheres. Therefore it can serve as a means for translating distances directly into pitch relationships. But Fludd, at least, certainly did not consider it as astronomically correct. He uses it as a symbol for the harmonious relationships between the different spheres or levels of being.

3. Modern Schemes: Titius-Bode and Goldschmidt

It seemed that there was, after all, a rational mathematical pattern behind the planetary distances when in 1772 the astronomers Johann Daniel Titius and Johann Elert Bode discovered what is now generally known as Bode's Law:[10] that by taking 4 as Mercury's mean distance from the sun and adding the series 3×1, 3×2, 3×4, 3×8, etc., one obtains figures very close to the actual mean distances of the planets from the Sun, reckoned in astronomical units. (An astronomical unit is the mean distance of the Earth from the Sun.)

Planet	Titius-Bode Distance	Actual Mean Distance	Approximate Tone
Mercury	4 + 0 = 4	0.387	c'''''
Venus	4 + 3 = 7	0.723	db''''
Earth	4 + 6 = 10	1.000	g'''
Mars	4 + 12 = 16	1.524	c'''
*Ceres (asteroid)	4 + 24 = 28	2.77	db''
Jupiter	4 + 48 = 52	5.203	eb'
Saturn	4 + 96 = 100	9.539	e♮
*Uranus	4 + 192 = 196	19.182	E+
*Neptune	4 + 384 = 388	30.055	A,
*Pluto	4 + 768 = 772	39.5	E,,

* not known in 1772

When Uranus and the asteroids were discovered in the predicted places, much attention was given to this law. The pattern seemed to break down with Neptune, but then Pluto turned out to occupy the next predicted distance after Uranus. Whether it is a natural law or merely a curiosity remains undecided by astronomers. Translated into musical terms (with Mercury here assigned to the top note of the piano) the Bode numbers represent the progressive approximation of a perfect octave. But the Divine Monochord is not exactly harmonious from this point of view.

At the beginning of the twentieth century another attempt was made to discover a harmony in the planetary distances. Victor Goldschmidt was an eminent crystallographer who wrote an encyclopedia of crystal forms in thirteen volumes. In his search for the law governing crystal formation, he had found a principle which seemed to hold good: in mathematical terms, it related the stage-by-stage growth of crystals to a series of nodal points comparable to those which sound the harmonics of a string or pipe. He was to find in this same 'principle of complication' the answer to the question: Why did the planets and their moons, on emerging from the incandescent gas-ball of the young Sun, take up the positions they now hold?

Goldschmidt's procedure[11] is to take as the nodal points of the Solar System the mean distances of the planets from the Sun, and to express them as simple proportions. As his 'astronomical unit' of 1 he takes not the Earth's distance but Jupiter's. His values are not exact so much as 'ideal' (compare those in the Titius-Bode table above). He was looking for the norm that lies behind phenomena but which is never exactly manifested,[12] just as the perfectly average human being is never to be found, or as one overlooks slight mistunings in the interests of temperament.

Because of the great differences between the inner and outer planets, Goldschmidt classed them as two separate systems, condensed at different times.

1. *Five large, light, rapidly-rotating outer planets*

Sun	Jupiter	Saturn	Uranus	Neptune	Pluto	Universe
0	1	2	4	6	8	∞

2. *Four small, dense, slower-rotating inner planets*

Sun	Mercury	Venus	Earth	Mars	Jupiter
0	1/13	1/7	1/5	1/3	1

The goal of Goldschmidt's method is to reduce such sets of numbers to a section of the harmonic and subharmonic series which proceeds from 1 in both directions towards the infinitely great and the infinitely small. Here the numbers are interpreted as vibration-ratios and given pitch equivalents:

$$\frac{1}{\infty}\,(=0)\ldots\frac{1}{4}\quad\frac{1}{3}\quad\frac{1}{2}\quad 1\quad 2\quad 3\quad 4\quad \ldots\infty$$

$$\text{C}\quad\text{F}\quad\text{c}\quad\text{c}^{\text{I}}\quad\text{c}^{\text{II}}\quad\text{g}^{\text{II}}\quad\text{c}^{\text{III}}$$

Goldschmidt's values for the outer planets simply need to be halved in order to fit neatly into this series:

Sun	Jupiter	Saturn	Uranus	Neptune	Pluto	Universe
0	$\frac{1}{2}$	1	2	3	4	∞
	c	c^{I}	c^{II}	g^{II}	c^{III}	

But the values for the inner planets, given above, must first be transformed to a series between the limits of 0 and ∞. Goldschmidt uses for this a formula which he developed in his work on crystals, called the Formula of Transformation.[13] The result is a new series of values which needs only to be multiplied by 6 in order to become another section of the harmonic and subharmonic series:

Sun	Mercury	Venus	Earth	Mars	Jupiter
0	1/12	1/6	1/4	1/2	∞
0	1/2	1	3/2	3	∞
	c	c^{I}	g^{I}	g^{II}	

By a simple set of arithmetical operations, Goldschmidt has succeeded in turning the planetary distances into a series of harmonious octaves and fifths.

Is this merely a clever mathematical juggling act? One might suspect so, were it not that something similar emerges whenever the astronomical data are investigated with a Pythagorean attitude: cosmic harmony never fails to manifest. We will see a detailed example of this in the section on Kepler, below. There is no room here to do more than mention the comparable systems of Thomas Michael Schmidt, who derives significant harmonies from the time-periods of the planets' rotations; of Rodney Collin, who does so based on conjunctions; of W. Kaiser, based on mean distances from the sun; of 'Azbel' (Emile Chizat), who makes the Titius–Bode numbers yield a perfect concord; or of Alexandre Dénéréaz, working from the Golden Sections of planetary distances.[14] As one tries to comprehend this strange phenomenon, certain associations spring to mind. First, there is C.G. Jung's discovery, while doing research in astrology, that those of his assistants who already believed in astrology obtained more supportive data than those who did not, although the two groups were working with the same, absolutely 'objective' material, and were making no interpretations of it.[15] Second, there is the situation in modern physics in which the outcome of an experiment is dependent on the expectations of the experimenter, the ambiguous nature of light as wave and particle being the classic example. Third, there is the mentalistic doctrine briefly explained in Chapter One, according to which we each project our own universe, subject of course to certain common laws. For those who are open to the possibility of cosmic harmony, their cosmos will be demonstrably harmonious. The number of different ways in which this has happened is simply an indication that the essential harmony of the solar system – the thing-in-itself, as it were – is of a scope and a harmonic complexity that no single approach can exhaust. The nearest one can come to understanding it as a whole is to consider some great musical work, and think of the variety of analytical approaches that could be made to it, none of them embracing anything like the whole.

4. Planet-Scales, Type B

Planetary scales of Type B, unlike Type A, are never associated with astronomical distances. Their tones are caused instead by the motions of the planets, their differences in pitch being due to the different rates of revolution. Cicero makes this clear in the *Dream of Scipio*:

The outermost sphere, the star-bearer, with its swifter motion gives forth a higher-pitched tone, whereas the lunar sphere, the lowest, has the deepest tone. Of course the earth, the ninth and stationary sphere, always clings to the same position in the middle of the universe. The other eight spheres, two of which, Mercury and Venus, move at the same speed, produce seven different tones, this number being, one might almost say, the key to the universe.[16]

The Earth is silent in all scales of this type because it is stationary, and there is no sound without motion. Macrobius, who wrote the *Commentary on the Dream of Scipio* that was a mainstay of medieval education, refrained from translating Cicero's words into actual pitches, but Boethius suggested notes for most of them (see Example 3).[17] In using a diatonic scale for this, Boethius, like all other theorists of Type B, obviously did not have any illusion that astronomical quantities were being translated into music (as is sometimes assumed in Type A). Whereas the planetary distances have been the subject of debate for centuries, there has never been any doubt about how long it takes them to go around the Zodiac. It is plain that their periods, ranging from the Moon's 28 days to Saturn's 30 years, do not fit a simple diatonic scale. So the scales of Type B are all symbolic.

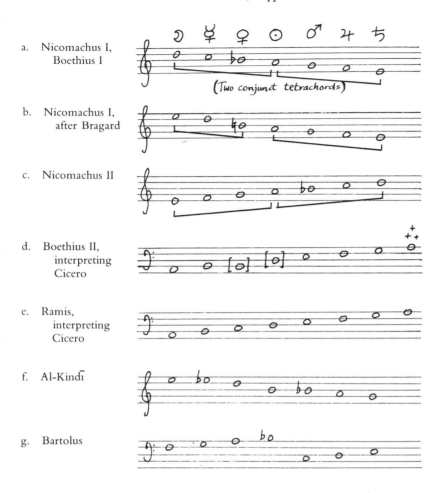

a. Nicomachus I,
   Boethius I

b. Nicomachus I,
   after Bragard

c. Nicomachus II

d. Boethius II,
   interpreting
   Cicero

e. Ramis,
   interpreting
   Cicero

f. Al-Kindī

g. Bartolus

Example 3: Planet-scales, Type B

Certainly the hierarchy of speeds is behind the Type B arrangements, but even this is ambiguous and can be regarded in at least two ways. For Cicero, the question is one of speed relative to the Earth. The Fixed Stars, with their daily rotation, are therefore the fastest, while all the planets lag behind to a lesser or greater extent. The Moon is the slowest, because in only 28 days it lags a whole cycle behind the Zodiac, Saturn the fastest. Alternatively, one can compute the planetary speeds relative to the Zodiac itself, and the scale will then run the other way, as we find in the Arabic sources of Al-Kindī and the Ikhwān al-Ṣafāʾ.[18] This view is particularly indicated if, like Anaximander and some other early Greek astronomers, one believes that

131

the Earth rotates and that the Fixed Stars are at rest. The fastest planet is then the Moon, Saturn is the slowest, and the Fixed Stars are immobile, hence have no note at all.

Nicomachus of Gerasa[19] gives planet scales of Type B running in both directions. (He actually gives three, but one of them simply reverses Venus and Mercury.) The scales consist of a pair of conjunct tetrachords spanning a seventh (marked by square brackets). Roger Bragard[20] suggested an emendation on the grounds that by Pythagoras' time (and Nicomachus is also reporting Pythagorean doctrines) the two conjunct tetrachords had already been made disjunct in Greek musical theory. Nicomachus in fact loyally misattributes this innovation to Pythagoras himself.[21] Bragard prefers to interpret Nicomachus' words as requiring a pair of disjunct tetrachords, one of them defective (Example 3b). But this impairs the symbolism which is only present when the planets are assigned the seven different notes of the scale, without any octave reduplication; and this alone is a good reason to doubt the emendation.[22] For if these scales have no symbolic value, they are worthless, and one cannot imagine the wise men of Antiquity having bothered with them.

An important symbolic element common to Types A and B alike is that the *mese* (a'), the central note of the Greek system, is usually assigned to the Sun, notwithstanding the geocentric model which is presupposed, at least exoterically, by all these authors. Robert Fludd's two-octave scales also express the special function of the Sun in his philosophy as God's Tabernacle in the cosmos, by placing it at the crucial midpoint of his monochord string, sounding an octave on either side (see Example 2). Fludd's many cosmic scales[23] can run up or down, cover one, two, or three octaves, but the Sun is always placed in the middle, and the scale is always in the major mode which was the norm for his time, as its inversion, the Greek Dorian, was formerly.

5. Planets, Tones, and the Days of the Week

The diatonic sequence of notes from which both Dorian and major modes are drawn is founded on the perfect fifth and fourth, the most basic of intervals excepting the octave, which generates no new pitch. A series of six perfect fifths or fourths in either direction produces the seven different tones of a diatonic scale:

B E A D G C F (4ths up or 5ths down)

F C G D A E B (5ths up or 4ths down)

The ancient Egyptians, according to Dio Cassius[24] (second–third century AD) used this sequence of fifths or fourths to relate the scale of the seven planets to the order of days in the week. Dio is usually interpreted as intending the scale of Example 4a (identical in form to Example 3a), when he instructs us to begin with Saturn and take every fourth planet (returning on the right when we overshoot on the left). The days of the week and their planetary rulers then appear with the following notes:

Saturday	Sunday	Monday	Tuesday	Wednesday	Thursday	Friday
♄	☉	☽	♂	☿	♃	♀
B	E	A	D	G	C	F

Thus, at least, Dio Cassius is understood by most of those (and they are not many) who have concerned themselves with this passage, such as the Abbé Roussier, Fabre d'Olivet, Edmond Bailly, Ernest Britt and the Henschels.[25]

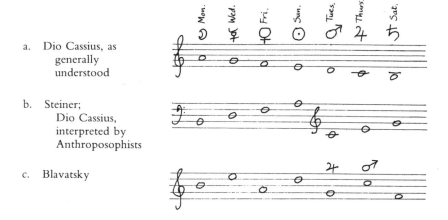

a.   Dio Cassius, as
     generally
     understood

b.   Steiner;
     Dio Cassius,
     interpreted by
     Anthroposophists

c.   Blavatsky

Example 4: Type B scales associated with days of the week

Britt uses these tones to deduce the planetary rulerships for each of the Greek modes (*tonoi*). He uses the earlier versions of the modes made from two conjunct tetrachords meeting on a central note, the latter being the 'final' or tonic. The Dorian mode thus well earns its place of honour in Greek theory and in Plato's philosophy, for it is the only mode whose scale exactly reproduces the cosmic order, centered on the Sun. Here is Britt's table:[26]

1. Dorian = Sun

♄ ♃ ♂ ☉ ♀ ☿ ☽

B C D E F G A

2. Aeolian = Moon

☉ ♀ ☿ ☽ ♄ ♃ ♂

E F G A B C D

3. Phrygian = Mars

☽ ♄ ♃ ♂ ☉ ♀ ☿

A B C D E F G

4. Ionian = Mercury

♂ ☉ ♀ ☿ ☽ ♄ ♃

D E F G A B C

5. Lydian = Jupiter

☿ ☽ ♄ ♃ ♂ ☉ ♀

G A B C D E F

6. Hypolydian = Venus

♃ ♂ ☉ ♀ ☿ ☽ ♄

C D E F G A B

7. Mixolydian = Saturn

♀ ☿ ☽ ♄ ♃ ♂ ☉

F G A B C D E

Britt, though he declares himself only as a follower of the Polish philosopher Hoëné Wronski (1776–1853), is also apparently a Theosophist, concerned with bringing about a rapprochement between the newly discovered doctrines of Eastern religions and the ancient traditions of the West. Therefore he goes further, correlating the tones and planets with the sevenfold constitution of Man 'as taught by Hindu theosophy'.[27] This causes the notes to be arranged in an equally significant sequence, that of three conjunct triads:

D	Ātmā	Soul	} of the spiritual body
B	Buddhi	Life	
G	Manas	Matter	
E	Kāma Rūpa	Life	} of the astral body
C	Linga Sharira	Soul	Matter
A	Prāna	Life	} of the physical body
F	Sthula Sharira	Matter	

Whoever Britt was following in his theosophy, it was not H.P. Blavatsky (1831–91), the great synthesizer of Eastern and Western esotericism and founder of the Theosophical Society, for a very different arrangement is attributed to her in the notes and papers published posthumously as 'Vol. III' of *The Secret Doctrine*.[28] In interpreting Dio, she begins by reversing Mars and Jupiter, to place the seven planets, as she says, in 'their correct sequence as determined by the order of the colours in the solar spectrum and the corresponding colours of their ruling planets'.[29] The musical scale thus follows that of the visible spectrum, the lowest tone C corresponding to the slowest light vibrations, those of red:

Red	Orange	Yellow	Green	Blue	Indigo	Violet
♂	☉	☿	♄	♃	♀	☽
Tuesday	Sunday	Wednesday	Saturday	Thursday	Friday	Monday
C	D	E	F	G	A	B

When Blavatsky gives the correspondences to the human constitution (admitting that this is only an 'exoteric' view), she assigns no note to Ātmā, saying that as the Supreme Spirit it includes all the other principles. At the other end of the scale, she omits the physical body (Sthula Sharira). Here is Blavatsky's system:

	Ātmā
B	Linga Sharira or Chhāyā (shadow or double)
A	Manas (higher mind or human soul)
G	Auric envelope
F	Kāma Manas (lower mind or animal soul)
E	Buddhi (spiritual soul; vehicle of Atma)
D	Prāna or Jīva (life-principle)
C	Kāma Rūpa (seat of animal life)

Rudolf Steiner, speaking when he was still leader of the German section of the Theosophical Society, gave yet another order as being that of the 'Cosmic Scale' in an unpublished question-answering of 17 March 1908.[30] This makes the days of the week a scale, the planets (see Example 4b) a sequence of thirds:

Sunday	Monday	Tuesday	Wednesday	Thursday	Friday	Saturday
☉	☽	♂	☿	♃	♀	♄
A	B	C	D	E	F	G

The Anthroposophical writers naturally use this arrangement. Hermann Pfrogner[31] has ingeniously reinterpreted Dio Cassius to yield the same result, while Anny von Lange[32] has described in great detail the ways in which the seven modes, and their inversions, reflect these planetary rulers in the feelings they invoke and in their occult implications. The seven modes and their rulerships are now distinguished largely by the placement of the two cesuras which von Lange perceives between F/G and B/C:

Mars mode	Mercury mode
CDEF GAB C	DEF GAB CD

Jupiter mode	Venus mode
EF GAB CDE	F GAB CDEF

Saturn mode	Sun mode
GAB CDEF G	AB CDEF GA

Moon mode
B CDEF GAB

Anny von Lange's discussion is long, intricate, and consistent within the world of her own beliefs. She says of these modes that:

It is of the highest importance for every study and every field of musical practice always to begin the day's work with the appropriate mode. One thereby connects oneself and one's music directly with the energy-streams of the Cosmos. One opens a door to them, so to speak, in the body, soul, and spirit.[33]

This suggestion, so radical in the twentieth century, is no different in intention from the musical magic of a Ficino, who summoned the planetary energies to his aid by surrounding himself with their symbols and singing hymns of the appropriate kind:[34] nor from the Pythagorean practice of sanctifying the beginning of each day with a song. But the difference is that those people had music of many modes available – the Greeks, moreover, having all of them in the three genera, diatonic, chromatic, and enharmonic – whereas music since 1600 has overwhelmingly favoured only two of them, the minor mode on A and the major on C. How is one to find a Mixolydian song with which to start Monday morning? Apparently one must create one's own.

In the Renaissance, before the eight Church modes had finally been reduced to the modern major and minor, there were some last-ditch efforts to recapture the ethos and the marvellous effects claimed for the modes in Classical times. But while keeping their Greek names, the modes had changed their natures. The Dorian octave species, which in Greece had been alternatively E D C B A G F E (diatonic), E C♯ C♮ B A F♯ F♮ E (chromatic), or E C B+ B A F E+ E (enharmonic), was now simply D E F G A B C D. Ramis de Pareja attached the Church modes to the eight notes of the planetary scale derived from Cicero (Example 3e), and described their ethos in a few words:[35]

I	Dorian D—D	Sun 'dispels sleep'
II	Hypodorian A—A (final D)	Moon 'induces sleep'
III	Phrygian E—E	Mars 'choleric and irascible'
IV	Hypophrygian B—B (final E)	Mercury 'the mode of flatterers'
V	Lydian F—F	Jupiter 'always denotes joy'
VI	Hypolydian C—C (final F)	Venus 'beneficient, yet also feminine'
VII	Mixolydian G—G	Saturn 'tends to melancholy'
VIII	Hypermixolydian A—A (final A)	Starry heaven 'an innate beauty and loveliness, free from all qualities and suitable for every use'

Abraham Bartolus,[36] an obscure early seventeenth-century theorist, was clearly thinking about keys, not modes, when he made his list of planet-scales (Example 3g), because he includes B♭ as a planetary note and the basis of a scale. He gives the pitches in lute tabulature; I do not know how he chose them. He observes that Mars' mode of C is the military key (this was the key of trumpets in his day) but is puzzled that so few composers have chosen to write in B♭, the key of the Sun: he says that he knows of only two examples of music in this key. But he believed in the efficacy of his system sufficiently to claim that one could deduce which were the ruling planets in someone's horoscope, by observing the keys of music they preferred.

Cicero's remark that the number seven seems to be the 'key to the universe' is the key to understanding all these seven-note planetary scales of the B type. It would be out of place to insert here, as Macrobius does in his *Commentary on the Dream of Scipio*, a dozen-page encomium of the Septenary.[37] Suffice it to say that this number holds pride of place in every department of esoteric study. Whether it be the system of seven Chaldaean Planets which is still the mainstay of philosophical astrology, the seven metals of Alchemy, the seven Chakras (subtle centres of the body) in Yoga, the seven Heavens of Islam, or the seven Rays, Globes, Rounds, and Root-races of Theosophy, the Septenary is sure to appear whenever the human being traverses a hidden structure of time or space.

Now it so happens that there are seven independently moving bodies (Greek *planētes*, 'wanderers') in the visible heavens, and it is equally the case that the progression of seven fifths, and seven only, completes the diatonic scale without introducing notes of a foreign, chromatic order. The mind attuned to symbolic thought sees nothing coincidental in this. Still less is it inclined to treat the Septenary as the invention of archaic peoples so awed by the seven planets that they applied the number to everything else. No: both musical scale and visible planets are understood to manifest in their respective domains a more primal, archetypal Septenary. There would only be cause for surprise if this were not the case, for instance if the musical scales in use all round the world tended to have eight or eleven notes to the octave. Therefore those who assign planetary qualities to the notes of the scale are acknowledging this seven-ness as a fundamental law of the universe: a law that must manifest in all self-contained systems such as those mentioned in the preceding paragraph. Yet there is something naïve about the further conclusions that are sometimes drawn from this correspondence, such as the emotional qualities claimed for a certain mode on the strength of the planet believed to rule it. Quite apart from disagreement among the authorities as to which note belongs to which planet, there is the solid evidence of three hundred years of Western music which has somehow managed to express every 'planetary' emotion while using only two modes, the major and the minor. We will return to this problem of correspondences in connection with the signs of the Zodiac and the twelve notes of the chromatic scale.

6. Planet-Scales, Type C

Planetary scales of Type C (Example 5) are not scales in the usual sense, but the frameworks upon which scales are built. The Greek system (5h) has certain fixed tones that remain invariable no matter whether the notes that fill the gaps of a fourth are in the diatonic, chromatic, or enharmonic genus. In Plato's Pythagorean dialogue *Timaeus*, the creation of the World–Soul is described in several stages, one of which[38] gives a set of intervals (5j) whose resemblance to the fixed tones could not be ignored. It is probably correct to assume a Pythagorean or at least Neopythagorean source for Type C. According to Plutarch's treatise *On the Procreation of the Soul in the Timaeus*, the notes which bound the five tetrachords are in the same proportion as the intervals between the planets.[39] The fragmentary last chapter of Ptolemy's *Harmonics*[40] give a similar system, while an inscription at Canobus in Egypt,[41] recording the mathematical principles of Ptolemy, adds to these the low note *proslambanomenos* ('added note') for the elements of Earth and Water, and the high note *hyperhyperbolaeon* ('above the highest') for the Fixed Stars, giving the intervals in proportional numbers. The same scale is copied in several medieval manuscripts. The philologist Carl von Jan[42] emended this Canobus scale by interpreting the numbers as string-lengths, regarding 8 as merely a theoretical base, and eliminating the untidy fraction 21 1/3. Anatolius[43] (third century) also read the numbers as string-lengths, but rather than reversing them he inverted the scale itself.

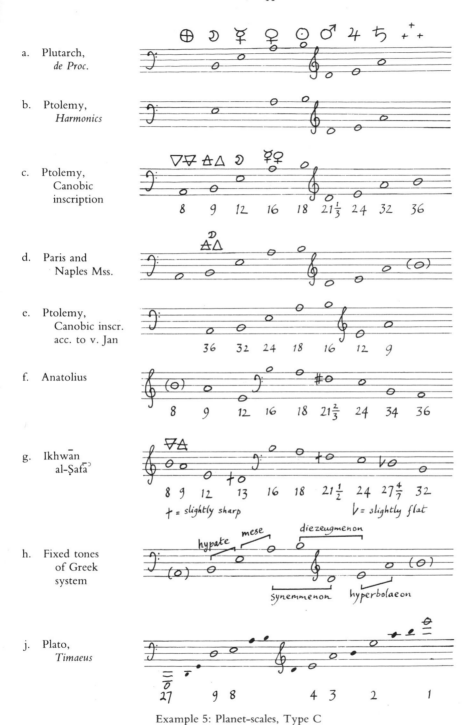

Example 5: Planet-scales, Type C

There is much deviation in these Type C scales, just as there is in the other types, necessitating a formidable grasp of Greek musical, astronomical and mathematical theory if every detail is to be accounted for. But the overriding symbolic intention is that the heavens should correspond not to a single octave-species but to the entire range of notes used in music. In Type C no one mode, nor any of the three genera, is preferred above any other: these are the bare bones of music, to be clothed in multifarious ways.

This expansion of range opens up a new symbolic dimension: that of the harmonies of the spheres relative to each other. The exposition in Ptolemy's *Harmonics*, brief and corrupt as it is, indicates a correspondence between the musical consonances and the compatibilities between planets in astrology. Saturn and Mars, for instance, are assumed to have influences inimical to that of the Sun, whereas Jupiter's is compatible with the Sun's. So here Saturn's note A is a dissonant seventh away from the Sun's note B; Mars' note D is a minor third away (regarded as a dissonance by the Greeks), while Jupiter's note E makes a concordant perfect fourth.

Anatolius' interpretation of the numbers as representing string lengths brings us back to the thought behind Type A: that the musical proportions encode planetary distances. A tenth-century Islamic work which owes much to Classical sources is explicit on this point. The *Treatise on Music* of the Ikhwān al-Ṣafā'[44] (Brethren of Purity) introduces a complete set of tone-numbers for ten spheres (giving separate ones to Earth and Air) in the following words:

On the subject of the virtue of the number 8, the mathematician philosophers have advanced the theory that a harmonious proportion exists between the diameters of the celestial spheres and those of earth and air. The proof of this is that if we express the diameter of the earth by 8, that of the sphere of air by 9, then the diameter of the sphere of the moon by 12 [the other figures are given] . . . the diameter of the earth and that of the moon will be in the proportion of 3:2 . . . [all the other consonant proportions given]. As for Mercury, Mars and Saturn, they do not have a [harmonic] proportion. That is why these heavenly bodies are called maleficent.[45]

So the malefic quality has a physical explanation in the unharmonic distances at which the planets are placed.

7. Systems with Movable Tones: Eriugena, Anselmi

We are entering a new realm of the subject. There is a certain rigidity in the thinking that produces scales of Types A, B, and even C, in which the phenomena are made to fit a preconceived notion of musical order. Another approach asks the phenomena themselves to reveal their order. To pose this question is to admit that one does not already know the answer to the structure of the universe; but it expresses the faith that such an order exists, since the cosmos is the work of the Divine Reason. One is therefore ready to adapt one's musical preconceptions and to shift one's point of view as may be necessary, for instance from consideration of speeds to that of distances. What is most astonishing is that those who have approached the subject in this spirit have received confirmation of those very musical principles that the more simplistic but no less intuitive mind desires to see in the heavens: only now these principles do not merely save the appearances, they fit them to perfection. Here we see encapsulated the entire purpose of theoretical science, as yet unfulfilled in the wider world, which is to reveal the universe as the work of an intelligent Mind.

There was one man in the Middle Ages who understood the problem in this way, although he was prevented by lack of astronomical data from developing his theories very far. John Scotus Eriugena, an Irish monk of the ninth century, was bold enough to develop a cosmology of his own which released the planets from identification with concentric spheres around the

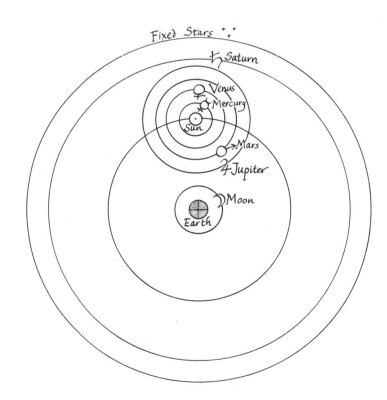

The Cosmos, according to John Scotus Eriugena

Earth (see diagram). At the same time he was imbued with the belief in concord and discord as the real motive forces in the universe. In seeking possible harmonies within his own cosmology, he took in the considerations of both Types A and B (though it is not clear that he always knew when he was changing viewpoints). Eriugena returned to the question of the planetary distances and of their harmony several times,[46] but his most fully developed theory occurs in a little-known commentary on Martianus Capella, and that only in one of the manuscript copies of this commentary.[47]

Eriugena first considers the planetary harmony in terms of speed. His scale of speeds is idiosyncratic: a compromise between the two varieties (Moon-fast and Moon-slow) explained above in connection with Type B. Ignoring the distinction between rotation relative to the Earth and relative to the Fixed Stars, he considers the Starry Sphere the fastest, the next fastest being the Moon, then Mercury, etc., up to the slowest, Saturn. The Sun, as ever, is at the midpoint, and the system spans two octaves.

The sound of the sphere hence concords with the sound of Saturn in quadruple ratio, and they produce a double octave which, as in the organ or on strings, is the principle of principles and the highest of excellencies. The sound of the Sun is between Saturn and the sphere, like the *mese* between the aforesaid two strings.[48]

A few lines later he has shifted to consideration of the relative distances, not speeds. And since he is looking at the wandering planets themselves, not at their immutable spheres, he sees that their distances must vary widely.

As you see, the sounds do not always relate by the same intervals, but according to the altitude of their orbits. No wonder, then, that the Sun sounds an octave with Saturn when it is running at the greatest distance from it; but when it begins to approach it, it will sound a fifth, and when it gets closest, a fourth. Considered in this manner, I think it will not disturb you when we say that Mars is distant from the Sun sometimes by a tone, sometimes by a semitone. . ... Hence it is to be believed that all the musical consonances can be made by the eight celestial sounds. I do not mean just in the three genera (diatonic, chromatic, and enharmonic), but even in others beyond the conception of mortals.[49]

Eriugena approaches the harmony of the spheres with an originality and flexibility of mind extraordinary for his time. His last sentence is the epitome of the attitude to which I referred above: the readiness to discover things that do not fit neatly into the packages prepared by human system-builders. Another such free and original vision would not appear for six hundred years, by which time the evolution of earthly music had made yet other possibilities thinkable, notably that of counterpoint and multiple harmonies. Writing in 1434, at the height of the polyphonic era, Giorgio

Anselmi of Parma was able to envision the planets no longer tied to dreary monotones but each singing its own song in counterpoint with the others. Anselmi was an astrologer and physician as well as amateur music theorist. His work on music, which remained in manuscript until 1961, gives a picture of the planetary cycles and epicycles, each watched over by angelic spirits, as participants in the cosmic game which is without purpose or ulterior motive beyond the pure joy of Being. Perhaps the 'playing' of music is the closest we can get to imagining and emulating this. Anselmi writes:

A single sphere does not always produce the same harmony, but manifold *phthongoi, limmata, dieses* and *commata* [the smaller intervals of Greek theory]; so that the Blessed Spirits must be imagined not only with the sound of their own spheres, but also with those situated nearby: now leading in song, now following, now pursuing, now accompanying, and playing in wonderful harmony in an ever more graceful game.[50]

He bases the relative intervals of the planets – to be regarded as approximate loci modified by epicycles, etc. – as follows:

Moon (highest pitch)

Mercury, Venus, Sun } 3 octaves

} twelfth

Mars

} 2 octaves

Jupiter

} twelfth

Saturn

Fixed Stars (lowest pitch)

These proportions are derived from the periods of their rotation around the Earth: Saturn's 30 years to Jupiter's 12 give the proportion 5:2, which is an octave plus a fifth, and so forth. This early Renaissance system, like those of modern researchers, is therefore an empirical one, taking the results of physical observation first and then looking for the harmony inherent in them. What one must then be prepared to accept is that one's finding may break the bounds of current musical practice, as Anselmi's 8-octave range did in an era when all music lay within a 3-octave limit.

8. Kepler's Planetary Music

The full application of these principles could only by made by someone endowed with the unique combination of visual imagination, mathematical skill, and philosophical understanding, living at a time when astronomic observation had reached the highest degree of precision obtainable with the naked eye. Such a man was Johannes Kepler (1571–1630). By the end of his career he had solved both the problem of our Type A scales (what law governs the planetary distances?) and that of Type B (what governs their velocities?) His solution of the first was geometrical, that of the second musical, and his Third Law of Planetary Motion (that the squares of the periodic times are to each other as the cubes of the mean distances from the Sun) provided the link between them. An early and fervent convert to the Copernican system, he was only twenty-three when, pondering the question of why there should be only six planets (instead of the canonical seven), and what governed their distances from the Sun, he was visited by a mystical intuition that the secret of the solar system lies in the five regular or Platonic solids.[51] In between the six orbits of Mercury, Venus, Earth, Mars, Jupiter, and Saturn he then inscribed the five solids in the order octahedron, icosahedron, dodecahedron, tetrahedron, and cube; and behold, not only was the number of six planets accounted for, but their proportional distances were closely in accord with Copernicus' figures. As Max Caspar relates it,[52] 'The experience loosed a flood of tears. He was amazed that precisely he, although he was a sinful person, had received this revelation, especially as he had not intended to enter the whole matter as an astronomer, but rather had undertaken the investigation purely for his intellectual diversion.'

His calling was determined as he worked day and night to justify his vision through calculation, and he saw his whole life's work in the context of this revelation of the Divine Reason at work in Creation. Yet the figures from Tycho Brahé's observations, as Kepler worked on them year after year, stubbornly refused to fit the regular solids with the precision of which Divine Reason was surely capable. Some other factor must be at work. It was the difficulties of calculating the orbit of Mars that led to the answer and to the overwhelming realization that the orbits of the planets are not perfect circles, nor even the elaborate combinations of pseudo-circles which astronomers from Ptolemy to Copernicus had used to keep the circularity of the heavens inviolate, but ellipses with the Sun at one of their foci. Regarded from the point of view of space, these ellipses (requiring greater and lesser distances from the Sun) provided a sort of cushion between each pair of Platonic solids. From the point of view of time, they explain the variable speeds of the planets, which move faster as they approach the Sun. It remained to find a rationale for the ellipses being just so, and it was to musical harmony that Kepler turned for this. He compared each planet's angular velocities at perihelion (nearest to the Sun) and aphelion (furthest from the Sun), and expressed this ratio as a musical interval. Example 6

144

shows the planet-songs as he conceived them.[53] Owing to the limitations of seventeenth-century notation he was not able to notate glissandos, nor show the full range (closely equivalent to that of the piano keyboard), as we have done. But his verbal explanation makes both points clear.

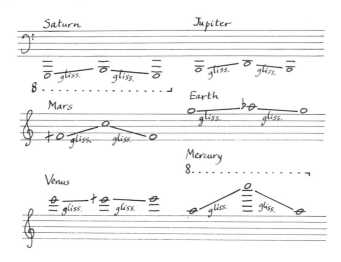

Example 6: Kepler's Planetary Songs

This was not all. Kepler had broken new ground in listening to the Music of the Spheres not from the point of view of Earth, like all his predecessors, but from the Sun. Henceforth it is no longer a harmony made for the benefit of our own planet, but the song which the cosmos sings to its lord and centre, the Solar Logos. Like Eriugena's planets, each of Kepler's has a variety of notes: there is no question here of a simple planet-tone scale of any type. Unlike Eriugena, however, Kepler lived in an age when musical polyphony was the norm. The planetary music, in no wise inferior to that of Man, must therefore be polyphonic, too.

As Eriugena had already pointed out, the musical possibilities of these sliding scales are almost inexhaustible. Most of the chords they make together are dissonant to one degree or another, but once in many years a five- or six-part consonance will occur. The time-scale exceeds human imagination, even human life: a single journey of Saturn up and down a major third takes 30 years! These harmonies have fortunately been made accessible to the ear in an electronic recording by Willie Ruff and John Rodgers,[54] suitably accelerated so that one can actually hear them

Harmonies of the Planets' angular velocities, as seen from the Sun

		Harmonic Number							
		1	9	5	3	25	27	15	2
Pluto aphelion *a* / perihelion *b*	$a:b = 9:25$		D			G♯			
	$a:c = 5:24$			E	G				
	$a:d = 8:18$	C	D						
	$b:c$ [not given]								
Neptune aphelion *c* / perihelion *d*	$b:d = 8:9$	C	D						
	$c:d = 80:81$			EE^{+1}					
	$c:e = 5:9$		D	E					
	$c:f = 9:20$		D	E					
	$d:e = 5:9$		D	E					
Uranus aphelion *e* / perihelion *f*	$d:f = 15:32$							B	C'
	$e:f = 5:6$			E	G				
	$e:g$ [not given]								
	$e:h = 3:5$			E	G				
Saturn aphelion *g* / perihelion *h*	$f:g = 5:6$			E	G				
	$f:h$ [not given]								
	★$g:h = 4:5$	C		E					
	$g:i = 2:5$	C		E					
	★$g:k = 1:3$	C			G				
	★$h:i = 1:2$	C							C'
Jupiter aphelion *i* / perihelion *k*	$h:k = 5:12$			E	G				
	★$i:k = 5:6$			E	G				
	$i:l = 9:50$		D			G♯			
	★★$i:m = 12:25$				G	G♯			
	★$k:l = 5:24$			E	G				
	$k:m = 4:27$	C					A		
Mars aphelion *l* / perihelion *m*	★$l:m = 2:3$	C			G				
	$l:n = 9:20$		D	E					
	★$l:o = 5:12$			E	G				
	★$m:n = 2:3$	C		E	G				
	$m:o = 3:5$			E	G				
Earth aphelion *n* / perihelion *o*	★$n:o = 15:16$							B	C'
	$n:p = 3:5$			E	G				
	★$n:q = 3:5$			E	G				
	★$o:p = 5:8$			E					C'
	$o:q = 5:8$			E					C'
Venus aphelion *p* / perihelion *q*	★$p:q = 24:25$				G	G♯			
	$p:r = 5:9$		D	E					
	★$p:s = 1:4$	C							C'
Mercury aphelion *r* / perihelion *s*	★★$q:r = 16:27$	C					A		
	$q:s = 81:320$			EE^{+1}					
	★★$r:s = 9:20$		D	E					

★Ratios originally discovered by Kepler
★★Ratios originally discovered by Kepler but wrongly estimated

changing. Particularly audible on the recording is the interval between Earth and Venus, whose relationship Kepler (always fond of sexual metaphors) describes as a marital one, oscillating from the 'masculine' sixth G♯-E to the 'feminine' one G♮-E; also the gradually changing drone which Saturn gives to the whole symphony.

Max Caspar, who devoted his life to Kepler scholarship, points out that one cannot judge Kepler's *Harmonia Mundi*, any more than one judges Plato's *Timaeus*, by whether or not it is 'true' in the terms of positivist science. His words are worth quoting at length:

> In truth, if a work presents science with such a valuable contribution as the third planet law (not to mention the mathematical and musical fruits), then a critic must seek the lack in himself if he does not achieve an understanding of the manner of contemplating nature out of which the work has arisen. This lack consists in the thinking being stuck fast in a rut of a one-sided contemplation of nature. It has been forgotten that that which is visible is a symbol of that which is invisible. Therefore, the poet, the artist, brings us closer to nature and can convey more and profounder and better things about it. Someone who has once been plunged in the cosmos of Platonic philosophy lives from this truth. That was the case with Kepler.[55]

At the same time it is important to recognize that Kepler's astronomical data were so nearly accurate that his planetary harmonies are no less valid today than they were in his time. The ratios (hence intervals) which he gives for the extreme angular velocities of each planet require only two corrections in order for them to accord fully with modern measurements.[56] What is more, the newly discovered planets Uranus, Neptune, and Pluto also exhibit harmonic ratios of the same kind. Francis Warrain, in an exhaustive study of the *Harmonia Mundi*, assembled the data in the table opposite as a correction and completion of Kepler's harmonies (which are marked in the table with an asterisk).[57]

The ratios compare the velocities of the planets at their fastest (perihelion) and slowest (aphelion), by calculating how far they go in 24 hours, measured in minutes and seconds of arc as viewed from the Sun. These ratios are then simplified by octave reduction to give an interval between C and C'. For example, the ratio between Jupiter's maximum and Mars' minimum speed (ratio $k:l$) is as 5:24. That is equivalent to the interval of two octaves plus a minor third. The two octaves are eliminated by dividing 24 by 4, which gives the ratio 5:6, a minor third. The placement in the scale on the right of the table is determined by where each interval occurs in the harmonic series on C. The minor third first occurs between the fifth and sixth harmonics, which are E and G.

A glance at the notes on the right is enough to show that the law of chance is out of the question here. Of 74 tones, 58 belong to the major triad CEG. There is not a single fourth or major seventh. Besides the diatonic harmonics and the chromatic G♯, there is the syntonic comma 80:81, which gives the two valid tunings for E[58] (ratios $c:d$, $q:s$). All beliefs in cosmic harmony are justified by this table alone, which is based entirely on empirical measurement.

9. Intervals and the Astrological Aspects

Kepler was an astrologer as well as an astronomer: sometimes an astrologer *malgré lui*, as when his job required him to compile an annual almanac of predictions for the coming year, but never a doubter as to the influence of the planets on earthly existence. In the early *Mysterium Cosmographicum*, besides revealing his intuition of the five solids, he tried to set astrology on a rational and harmonic basis. From empirical evidence he believed that the most plausible element of the science was the function of planetary aspects. Already possessed by a vision of world harmony, he explained them by analogy with the regular plane figures of geometry and with the consonances of music.[59] Omitting the geometrical matter, his observation is basically that one can regard the zodiacal circle as a length to be divided as one would stop a monochord string. Comparison of the whole length to the greater portion remaining will then give the interval corresponding to each aspect. Here are the three primary divisions:

☍   Opposition (planets 180° apart)
Ratio of whole circle to half 360:180 = 2:1
Interval: Octave

△   Trine (planets 120° apart)
Ratio of whole to greater part 360:240 = 3:2
Interval: Perfect Fifth

□   Square (planets 90° apart)
Ratio of whole to greater part 360:270 = 4:3
Interval: Perfect Fourth

Kepler was impressed, as Ptolemy had been before him, by the fact that these three most powerful aspects are expressed by the same ratios as the three perfect consonances of music. One can amplify this to make a complete table of the aspects in modern astrological use and find the intervals corresponding to them (Figure 1, p. 150).

Rudolf Haase, who more than anyone else today carries on the Keplerian ideal of harmonic research, saw something unsatisfactory about this system. Perfectly correct from the quantitative point of view, it falls short in view of the astrological qualities traditionally assigned to the aspects. To take the most obvious example, the opposition, which here makes a harmonious octave, is actually the most tension-producing of all aspects. Haase suggests an alternative scheme which assigns 30°, or one astrological sign, to each semitone (Figure 2, p. 151).[60]

The opposition is now a dissonant tritone, the unison and octave coincide, the major and minor third fit respectively with the positive trine and negative square. Haase also mentions that in recent music even the semitone and major seventh are treated as consonant, just as their aspects, the semisextile and sextile, are valid in astrology.[61] But he does not mention that they are astrologically far more harmonious than the square, so the correlation remains an imperfect one.

The basic difference between these two systems is that the first regards the Zodiac as a hypothetical monochord string, hence a logarithmic scale, whereas the second uses the circle to represent a closed system of arithmetically equal intervals. In Figure 1, the first 90° quadrant contains a perfect fourth (five semitones); the second a perfect fifth (seven semitones); the third, if used, would contain another whole octave, for it would mark the division of the string in the ratio 1:4 (double octave), and the intervals of the fourth would be theoretically indefinite, as they are on the monochord. What we face here is the incompatibility of musical and astronomical distance; the incommensurability of the logarithmic scale of the monochord, on which equal divisions produce increasing intervals, with the geometry of a circle divided into 360 equal degrees. In Figure 1 the monochord wins, in Figure 2 the circle.

The astrological aspects naturally belong to the circular point of view, since they represent a combination of planetary energies meeting the earth at a definite and significant angle. Kepler's own interest in this was particularly in the effects of such aspects on the earth itself as manifested in the weather. For years he had kept daily weather diaries to help him research this matter, and he considered it empirically proven. In a beautiful analogy, he says:

It is the custom of some physicians to cure their patients by playing music. How can music work in the body of a person? Namely in such a way that the soul of the person, just as some animals do also, understands the harmony, is happy about it, is refreshed and becomes accordingly stronger in its body. Similarly the earth is affected by harmony and quiet music. Therefore there is in the earth not only

149

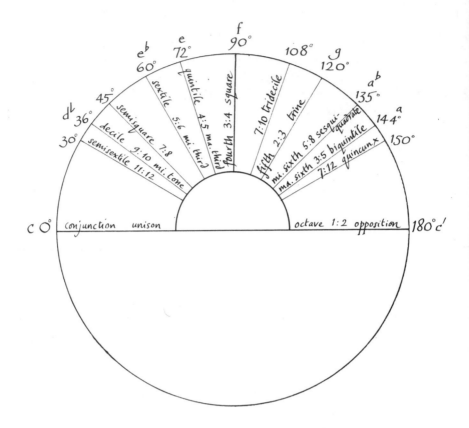

Figure 1: Aspect-interval correspondences, developed from Kepler's method

dumb, intelligent humidity, but also an intelligent soul, which begins to dance when the aspects pipe for it. If strong aspects last, it carries on its function more violently by pushing the vapours upwards, and thus causes all sorts of thunderstorms; while otherwise, when no aspects are present, it is still and develops no more exhalation than is necessary for the rivers.[62]

Students of astrology will be aware that aspects are most effective when exact, but that they possess an 'orb' of a few degrees each way within which their efficacy can still be felt. Beyond the orb there is a dead zone until the influence of the next aspect begins. One can regard the aspects, then, as marking a limited number of nodes of influence that activate the planets as they enter them. In the same way, one could call the intervals of music just such a limited series of nodes, also possessing a certain power even if not exact. Tempered tuning takes advantage of this tolerance to present the ear

150

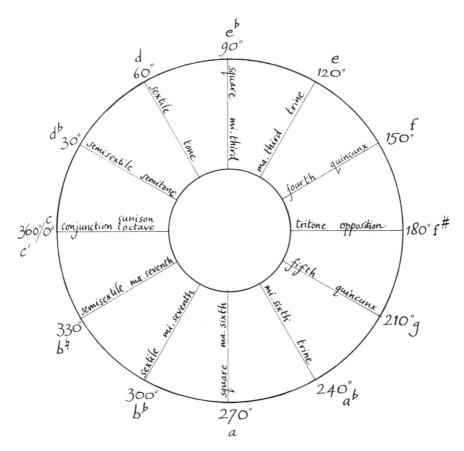

Figure 2: Aspect-interval correspondences as suggested by Haase

with slightly out-of-tune intervals, which are heard without distress as if they were true. The more extreme mistuning common in performance, especially by singers, demands and receives a wider orb still. Yet periodically there have been agitations for the use of pure intonation, in the belief that the full effects of music are lost when intervals are tempered.

The aspect-interval analogy is therefore a dynamic one; to reduce it to a static system is to misrepresent one or the other. To make this plainer, one need only try to apply the system of either Figure 1 or 2 to complexes of more than two planets or notes – which is usually the case in both astrology and practical harmony. Take the astrological Grand Trine, the most harmonious of all configurations, in which three planets make an equilateral triangle, each being in trine to the other two. In Figure 1, this would produce either a chord of two perfect fifths, c g d', or, if the logarithmic

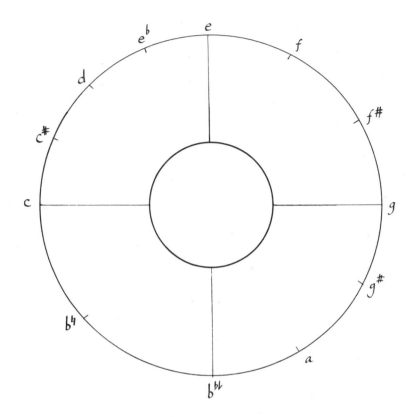

Figure 3: Kayser's tone-circle

progression were continued, the subharmonic series c g g'. In Figure 2 the result would be an augmented triad, c e g♯. What would best correspond with it is, I suppose, the triad c e g, but there is no way of obtaining this.

One attempt at a synthesis of these two incompatibilities is the tone-circle of Haase's teacher Hans Kayser (1891–1964).[63] This takes the circle as representing a single octave, but divides it harmonically, as in Figure 3.

Kayser makes no comment here on the astrological aspects, but says that one should think of this octave-circle as just one turn of a tone-spiral extending indefinitely in both directions like a helix. Each turn is another octave, and the four quadrants give the four primary nodal points: harmonics 1, 5, 3, and 7, transposed within the octave to become the notes C, E, G, and the flat B♭.

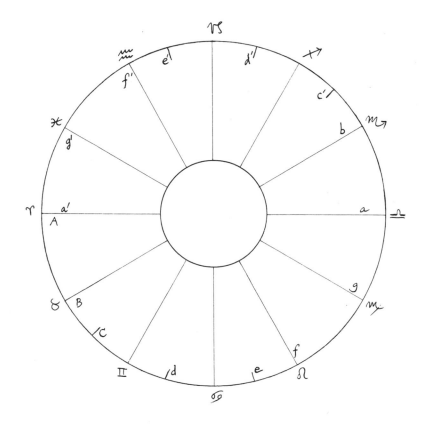

Figure 4: Ptolemy's Tone-Zodiac

10. *Tone-Zodiacs*

Just as some theorists make the planets span a single, others a double octave, so it is with the musical symbolism of the Zodiac. The oldest tone-zodiac is that of Ptolemy's *Harmonics*, [64] in which the circle corresponds to the Greek two-octave system; see Figure 4.

This is a compromise, too: the opposition falls on the octave, as in Figure 1, but the circle is equally divided and finite, as in Figure 2. (That Ptolemy could look at the problem from both angles is clear from his subsequent discussion of interval and aspect ratios.)

As Ernest McClain points out,[65] Ptolemy's zodiacal signs actually correlate not with any scale in Greek usage, but with a whole-tone scale in equal temperament. The third book of the *Harmonics* (possibly the last thing

153

Ptolemy wrote, for it is unfinished) is an astonishing work of synthesis between music, the psyche, and the cosmos. The tone-zodiac is just one of his many analogies, perhaps original with him but probably rooted, like much of his work, in the Babylonian tradition of astronomy and numerology. Unlike those theorists who have had one flash of intuition and then try to fit everything into a rational system based on it, Ptolemy has a versatile, Geminian mind. In this book he flits from one analogy to another, each suggestive but sometimes contradictory. To some readers (even to the otherwise sympathetic Kepler) this is annoying and Ptolemy's parallels rather absurd. But it is the sign of truly harmonic thought whose nature, as Hans Kayser wrote,[66] is not to be conclusive but to open up the possibility of perceiving harmony everywhere in the universe: a harmony that is no less really there because it is sometimes perceived as a picturesque or extravagant analogy, unassimilable by rational thinking.

Since music theory in more recent civilization uses not a two-octave but a single-octave base, modern tone-zodiacs always correlate the twelve signs of the Zodiac with the twelve notes of the equally tempered chromatic scale in which F♯ = G♭, G♯ = A♭, etc. In none of the cases that follow can I do full justice to the systems that have given them birth. Some of them, especially Anny von Lange's and Marius Schneider's, are very elaborate, and to understand them properly one must read the German and Spanish originals. But I will show how the various solutions of the tone-zodiac problem each spring from a different philosophical intention. This very diversity is characteristic of harmonic thought, and if some of what follows seems far-fetched, it does not impair the validity of the experiment in general.

The most obvious solution is the one proposed by the two Dutch authors of a weighty treatise on cosmic harmony from a broadly theosophical viewpoint, Joan and Mary Henschel.[67] They take both the signs of the Zodiac and the chromatic scale in ascending order, assigning C to the first sign, Aries, and so forth, bending the scale into a circle just as Ptolemy did. When it comes to expand the single tones into scales, they acknowledge the traditional division of the zodiacal signs into positive (the odd-numbered ones) and negative (even) by giving to the positive signs an upward major scale, to the negative ones a downward minor one, beginning from the assigned keynote. Their system is shown in Figure 5.

The Henschels use their tone-zodiac mainly to explain the relative compatibilities of people born 'under' (meaning when the Sun was in) the various signs. However, the assessment of character and compatibility through sun signs alone is poor astrology, since it ignores the other nine planets and the house positions which may represent conditions outweighing the solar influence. The note-for-note tone-zodiac also

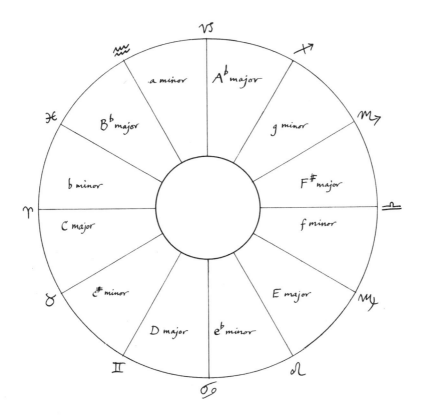

Figure 5: The Henschels' Tone-Zodiac

produces some dubious musical results. The Henschels actually call the perfect fifth and fourth 'dissonant'[68] intervals because they represent the relationships of inharmonious signs such as Aries-Virgo and Aries-Scorpio (signs which differ both by element and quality: Aries = cardinal fire, Virgo = mutable earth, Scorpio = fixed water). The intervals they call 'absolutely consonant', on the other hand, are the major third and augmented fifth, which join signs of the same element (e.g. the three fiery signs Aries C, Leo E, Sagittarius G♯).

A far more convincing chromatic zodiac sequence is proposed in an *Astrological Journal* article[69] by the Irish musicologist Michael McMullin. This couples each major key with its relative minor, thus avoiding the Henschels' omission of several keys, and proceeds in the opposite direction, making Pisces the musical starting point.

McMullin supports this ordering with examples of many well-known works, taking into account especially the planetary rulerships of the zodiac

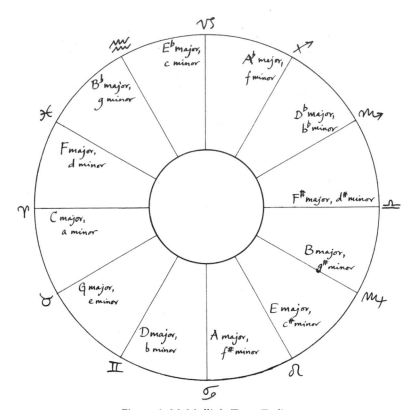

Figure 6: McMullin's Tone-Zodiac

signs. The examples are striking, and certainly worth consideration. For Sagittarius, which is ruled by Jupiter and corresponds to the three-flat keys of E♭ and C minor, he cites Beethoven's 'Eroica' and the Promethean Fifth Symphony; Sibelius' Fifth Symphony with its finale depicting Thor (the Norse Jupiter) wielding his hammer; and the noble melody of 'Jupiter' in Holst's *The Planets*. But when he comes to consider the aspect-interval correspondences, which are naturally identical to those which the Henschels tried to explain, McMullin admits that they are not altogether convincing.

These chromatic zodiacs are based on the very plausible equation of the zodiacal circle with the octave-space, each divided into twelve exactly equal parts. Just as the zodiac is the matrix for all possible astrological configurations, so is the octave-space for all musical proportions. But most of the other theorists rearrange this simple chromatic order of tones.

One way is to separate the seven diatonic from the five chromatic ones, as they are distinguished in black and white on the piano keyboard. This is the arrangement found in the works of Max Heindel and Corinne Heline. Heindel (1865–1919) was the founder of one of the three American 'Rosicrucian' orders still active today;[70] his philosophy is largely a digest of Blavatsky's and Steiner's teachings. The anonymous student who compiled a book of Heindel's musical theories explains the twelve signs of the Zodiac as reflecting 'twelve great life waves evolving in our scheme of evolution, five of which have completed their work and withdrawn from manifestation'.[71] These five are represented by the first five signs of the Zodiac and by the five chromatic tones. The other seven life-waves, 'active during the Earth period', correspond to the seven diatonic tones. To each note a major key is assigned.

The philosophical vision behind this, familiar to esotericists, is of a grand movement of universal evolution of successive waves of souls each manifesting for a cosmic period, then progressing in the next period to a higher degree of the cosmic or spiritual hierarchy. As the Persian poet Rūmī put it:

> I died as mineral and became a plant,
> I died as plant and rose to animal,
> I died as animal and I was Man.[72]

According to the Rosicrucian author, today's humanity is Piscean, but is ruled by the preceding hierarchies. The angelic orders of Scorpios, 'Lords of Form', and Sagittarians, 'Lords of Mind', are in charge of our particular development, which is that of the mind.[73] But his musical conclusions are of devastating banality:

The keynote of the Lords of Mind (Sagittarians) is F major. Its scale has one flat, namely B♭. Any music written in the key of one flat will tend both to influence and to develop man's mental powers. Examples: *America; Work, For the Night Is Coming; Where He Leads Me I Will Follow*.[74]

This unfortunate writer gets into the same trouble as Abraham Bartolus did three centuries earlier: the paucity of music in theoretically desirable keys. For B major, the Key of Humanity itself, he can only think of *The Star-Spangled Banner*. And he never attacks the issue of transposition, let alone that of the changes of absolute pitch in historical times.

Another eclectically theosophical writer, Corinne Heline, adopts the same tone–zodiac, but considers the keys more from a therapeutic angle:

The keynote of Sagittarius is F major and the keynote of the earth is also F major. Many of nature's sounds, therefore, are set to this key. This is the reason why compositions in F major are especially relaxing to tired nerves; also effective in restoring a fatigued body and in calming a distracted mind.[75]

157

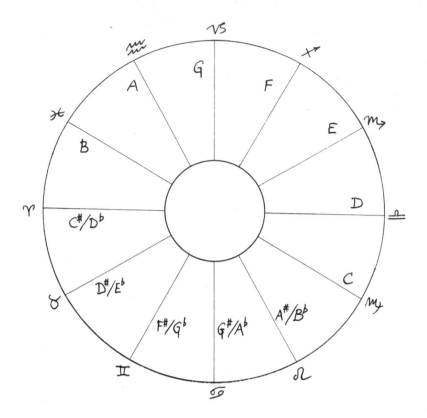

Figure 7: The Heindel Tone-Zodiac

Some of her recommendations evoke a beautiful atmosphere of healing through the combined influences of music, colour, and the stars. For the over-nervous Gemini, for instance,

a harp is recommended as the best instrument and compositions in F sharp, with minor notes played almost as an undertone. If the patient can be in a room decorated in pastel shades of spring green or mauve, and the environment of peace and freedom from any sudden or startling noise, such music should produce complete release from nerve tension followed by a long period of restful, restorative sleep.[76]

If that were my complaint, I would far rather commit myself to Ms. Heline's hands than to a mental hospital, but alas, there is not much of intellectual worth to be gained from this sort of musical astrologizing.

Quite the contrary is the case with the Anthroposophical version, in which the circle of the Zodiac is the circle of fifths. I have compiled this table of correspondences, resembling the ones in Renaissance magic books, from Ernst Hagemann's edition of Steiner's musical lectures:[77]

Anthroposophical Table of Correspondences

Sign	Power	Sense	Part of Body	Consonant	Keys
Aries	Balance	word, speech	head	V	C major, A minor
Taurus	Tone imagination	thinking	larynx	R	G major, E minor
Gemini	Symmetry	ego	lower arms	H	D major, B minor
Cancer	Separation	touch	rib cage	F	A major, F♯ minor
Leo	Self-isolation	life	[heart]	D,T	E major, C♯ minor
Virgo	Being in the body	movement	body organs	B,P	B major, G♯ minor
Libra	Stasis	balance	pelvis	C,Ch	F♯ major, D♯ minor
Scorpio		smell	reproductive organs	S,Z	D♭ major, B♭ minor
Sagittarius		taste	upper arms, thighs	G,K	A♭ major, F minor
Capricorn		sight	elbows, knees	L	E♭ major, C minor
Aquarius		warmth	shins	M	B♭ major, G minor
Pisces		hearing	hands, feet	N	F major, D minor

As Hagemann, reporting and interpreting Rudolf Steiner, explains it, the Zodiac is our symbol for the twelve creative figurations of the Seraphim and Cherubim. These angelic beings work on the human race to endow us with the powers, senses, and consciousness impulses given in the table above. Regarding the musical analogies, Hagemann says that there are archangels, spirits of music, who carry these influences down, but that the major and minor keys are only dead receptacles for them.[78] Nevertheless, what is behind the colours and tones that we perceive is not merely vibration but spiritual being: each tone exists in the twofold mode of (1) the vibrating air and the ear, and (2) an inner experience on the etheric and astral levels. He calls the latter a sort of sucking-in process, 'fetching the tone from the spaceless'.[79] The twelve tones and their keys are therefore vehicles for the impulses of the angelic hierarchy under whose care the human race develops.

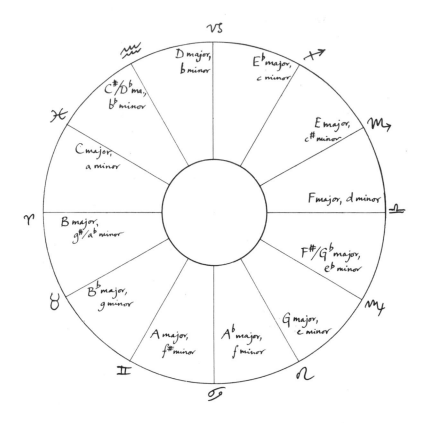

Figure 8. Anthroposophical Tone-Zodiac

Owing to the nature of the circle of fifths, the seven diatonic and five chromatic tones are separated here, as they are in the Heindel system, only they are in an entirely different order and refer to different signs. Hagemann mentions how the sector from C to A becomes 'brighter and higher', that from E to F♯ 'inwardly higher, spiritualized', while the descending fifths are 'darkened and made inward'.[80] These may be the characteristics with which the keys have been invested since the time of J.S. Bach. But how can one claim cosmic correspondences on the strength of the last two centuries of music? Were the influences on humanity of the chromatic tones and their angels missing in former epochs?

Apparently Anthroposophists believe that they were. For Steiner said that only since the fifteenth century, in what he calls the epoch of the Consciousness Soul, is it becoming possible for man to grasp his whole Ego-being and work consciously with all his twelve senses. Anny von Lange calls the twelve-tone circle an image of the Ego-being[81] and a representation of formative laws which reveal themselves step by step to the spiritual seeker.[82] It may therefore be appropriate that the same evolutionary epoch should have witnessed the first efforts of composers to range around the whole circle of fifths.

Our final tone-zodiacs are taken from the work of Marius Schneider (1903–82), the eminent Alsatian musicologist and ethnomusicologist who has created an entirely original system of symbology that traces its origins to the world-wide spiritual culture of the Megalithic era.[83] It is constructed with a mass of circumstantial detail, charts, tables, and quotations, periodically interspersed with visions of real poetic beauty descriptive of cosmic geography or of man's journey through life. When one searches for the first principles of this epic structure, one finds that it all began from a scale of animal-tone correspondences given by the Indian theorist Śārṅgadeva in the thirteenth century:[84]

D	E	F	G	A	B	C
peacock	bull	goat	crane	songbird	horse, fish	elephant

In the English edition of R.K. Shringy, Śārṅgadeva's text actually reads as follows:[85]

The seven notes commencing with *ṣaḍja* are produced respectively by the peacock, *cātaka* [a mythological bird], goat [or, in another edition, ram], heron, cuckoo, frog and the elephant.

Schneider nevertheless expands the scale to include alternative animals: tiger or lion for F, goose for C, peacock also for G and A.[86] As his other source for constructing a tone–zodiac, he cites a 'Chinese and Vedic' scale of elements:[87]

F	G	A	B
fire	air	earth	water

OR:

F	C	G	D	A
air	fire	metal	water	earth

I suppose that the animals named do suggest notes for the signs of Taurus (bull–E), Leo (lion or Tiger–F), and Pisces (fish–B), while the Vedic element-tone scheme implies an air sign for G (eventually Aquarius) and an earth sign for A (eventually Virgo). But one wonders at the assurance with which the other notes are assigned to make a neat chromatic scale, of which each four-

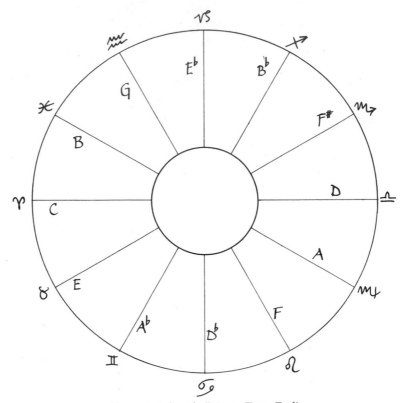

Figure 9: Schneider's Later Tone-Zodiac

note group comprises the signs, in astrological sequence, belonging to each of the qualities: Cardinal, Fixed, and Mutable:[88]

Cardinal Signs		Fixed Signs		Mutable Signs	
Aries (fire)	C	Taurus (earth)	E	Gemini (air)	Ab
Cancer (water)	Db	Leo (fire)	F	Virgo (earth)	A
Libra (air)	D	Scorpio (water)	F#	Sagittarius (fire)	Bb
Capricorn (earth)	Eb	Aquarius (air)	G	Pisces (water)	B

By giving each zodiacal sign its traditional planetary rulership, Schneider then constructs a 'tree':

F	♌	Sun/Moon	♋	Db
A	♍	Mercury	♊	Ab
D	♎	Venus	♉	E
F#	♏	Mars	♈	C
Bb	♐	Jupiter	♓	B
Eb	♑	Saturn	♒	G

— and shows how this 'irrational' scale is actually derived from an overtone series beginning on D♭, corresponding to the many levels of his Megalithic cosmology:

20	f'''	Sun
19	e'''	Morning Star ⎱ Venus
17	d'''	Evening Star ⎰
16	d♭'''	Moon (= Earth)
15	c'''	Mars
13	a∧/b∨♭''	Jupiter
11	g∨''	Saturn
10	f''	Sun
9	e♭''	Fixed Stars (= Saturn)
8	d♭''	Moon of Sacrifice
7	c∨♭''	Fixed Stars (= Jupiter)
6	a♭'	'Stars' (Venus, Mercury)
5	f'	Primal Sun (*Ursonne*)
4	d♭'	Primal Moon (*Urmond*)
3	a♭	Mercury; Primal Venus, Primal Mars
2	d♭	Lunar World-Substance
1	D♭	Primal Spirit (*Urgeist*)

I cannot give the reader more than a glimpse of the vast musico-symbolic complex into which all of this fits: it is an extraordinary blend of traditional esoteric doctrines with Schneider's personal intuitions and inventions. At one moment one feels in the presence of genuine metaphysical insight; at another, his schemes seem mere prestidigitation. Witness the original tone-zodiac which he developed, in an earlier book,[89] from the same animal- and element-notes. The musical framework there was not the chromatic scale but the circle of fifths. By placing the fifths on a spiral (aptly called the 'form of cosmic evolution'), any note can be made to fall on the radius of almost any sign.

The arrangement which Schneider decided upon is quite similar to his later one (given above), only the signs are no longer in order within each quality:

Cardinal		*Fixed*		*Mutable*	
Cancer	C	Taurus	E	Sagittarius	G♯
Capricorn	C♯	Leo	F	Virgo	A
Libra	D	Aquarius	F♯	Gemini	B♭
Aries	E♭	Scorpio	G	Pisces	B

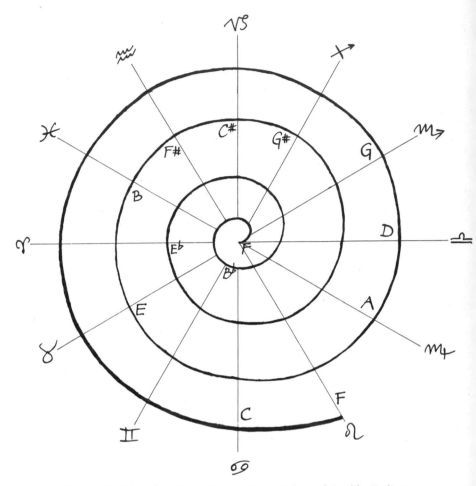

Figure 10: Schneider's Tone Spiral, Giving Solar and Earthly Zodiacs

When this zodiac, with its tones, is set out with the signs in their conventional order, from Aries to Pisces, Schneider calls it the 'normal' or Earthly Zodiac. When the signs are put in the order of the circle of fifths, beginning with Pisces and Aquarius and ending with Taurus, he calls it the Solar Zodiac. But as if this were not enough, he also develops a Lunar Zodiac, in the following way.[90] In traditional astrology, the twelve signs rule the parts of the body, from Aries at the head to Pisces at the feet. Schneider says that although it is not documented, there 'must exist' another mystical and lunar ordering that refers not to the physical but to the mystical body. He proposes an order which he superimposes on the traditional (but backward-reading) zodiacal circle, so that Leo, for example, now rules the feet, Libra the heart.

164

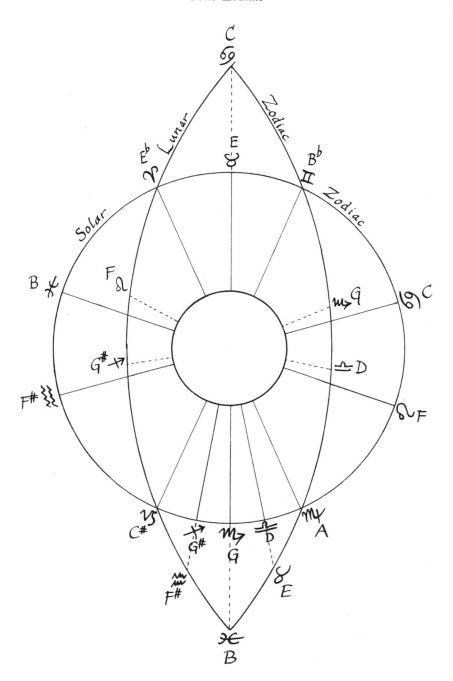

Figure 11: Schneider's Lunar and Solar Zodiacs Superimposed

Finally, he correlates all three zodiacs, with their tones:[91]

	Solar		Normal or Earthly		Lunar	
12	♉	E	♈	E♭	♉	E
11	♍	A	♉	E	♍	A
10	♎	D	♊	B♭	♎	D
9	♏	G	♋	C	♏	G
8	♋	C	♌	F	♊	B♭
7	♌	F	♍	A	♋	C
6	♊	B♭	♎	D	♈	E♭
5	♈	E♭	♏	G	♌	F
4	♐	G♯	♐	G♯	♐	G♯
3	♑	C♯	♑	C♯	♑	C♯
2	♒	F♯	♒	F♯	♒	F♯
1	♓	B	♓	B	♓	B

This coordination seems, he says, to be symbolized by the Tree of Life and the Caduceus, for the Zodiacs all begin alike, then branch out symmetrically from the centre. Of course he does not leave it at that, as we must: the Lunar Zodiac is shown to illustrate the initiatic way of the Shaman; a fourth zodiac (Solar no. 2) is developed; a mystic landscape and a figure of the Anthropos appear superimposed on the diagrams; the marriage of Heaven and Earth takes place in the mandorla where the celestial and terrestrial zodiacs intersect; all musical instrument forms are related to the zodiac-tones . . . and much more.

Puzzling as it may be in its tangled and idiosyncratic detail, Schneider's work is awesome in its cultural breadth and spiritual depth. His intuition about animals and tones as the key to archaic symbolism may be right or it may be wrong. If someone were definitely to discredit it, it would not matter greatly, any more than it matters that Kepler's system of the Platonic Solids has been discredited. For it was Kepler's erroneous insight that set him on the path that was to make him the founder of modern astronomy. Such occurrences are not uncommon in science, where, as the great physicist Max Planck has said, 'We find that the importance of a scientific idea depends, frequently enough, upon its value rather than on its truth.'[92] In this respect, science, at its highest, approaches the condition of the arts, in which nothing is merely true or false.

So far Schneider has not attracted visible disciples or commentators, with the exception of Juan-Eduardo Cirlot, whose *Dictionary of Symbols*[93] shows much appreciation for him. But neither does this matter unduly: Schneider's work is the image of his own soul and as such it has its own integrity. Only a few individuals this side of lunacy have succeeded, as he has done, in building complete and independent cosmologies of their own. Most people whose goal is esoteric understanding are content to work within one of the systems already revealed by such prime movers as Blavatsky, Steiner, Mathers, Jung, Gurdjieff, Ouspensky, and a handful of others. Another great original, Fabre d'Olivet, made a statement about his own work that serves as the verdict on each and every personal system of this kind:

If I am in error, I am in error; and that, after all, is a slight misfortune. . . . It matters little whether one imagines the world to be created out of nothing or out of something, nor whether one makes the sun go round the earth, or the earth around the sun . . . the only pernicious errors are those which insinuate themselves into morals or politics.[94]

From the disparity of cosmological opinions, even among the wise, it is obvious that the truth which shines, however dimly, through every system is in itself paradoxical and incapable of being grasped by the brain or expressed in the language of reason. Yet this should be no cause for dismay, still less for a feeling of existential impotence in the face of the Incomprehensible. It is said that before his death in 1947, P.D. Ouspensky spoke to some of the close friends who had spent twenty years listening to him expound his system and living by it. He told them: 'You must start again. You must make a new beginning. You must reconstruct everything for yourselves – from the very beginning.' As Rodney Collin, who tells this,[95] remarks, 'Every system of truth must be abandoned, in order that it may grow again.' Otherwise it will harden into dogma. Eventually, then, we must all create our own systems of universal understanding, though our present life may not be the time for this. Metaphysically speaking, this will be the gift of knowledge that we return to the Mind who made us and who knows its own universe through the unique knowledge of every being.

11. Angelic Orders and Muses: the Great Chain of Being

In the Renaissance it was recognized that the hierarchy of existence, the 'Great Chain of Being', has a subtle inner construction which, if one were to stretch the analogy, would appear as a series of loops or folds. Visually, the picture of such a chain becomes impossible; but music now fits the metaphor to perfection. The notes of music also form a hierarchy, from the lowest pitch to the highest, but within this scale there is an organizing factor at work that makes every eighth pitch the same, yet not the same: it is a repetition at a different octave.

An anonymous twelfth-century poet was perhaps the first to anticipate this doctrine as applied to the planetary and angelic orders. In his poem, which he sets to a kind of plainchant, he tells of how 'there is a concord of planets similar to that of notes,' illustrating it with a diagram in which the scale of planets is continued upwards for a further octave to include seven of the traditional Nine Orders of Angels, as given by St Gregory the Great (*Hom.* 36,7). We have already shown the planetary part of his scale in Example 2 (p. 126). Here it is complete:[96]

a	Seraphim
g	Cherubim
f	Thrones
e	Dominations
d	Principalities
c	Powers
b	Virtues
a	Fixed Stars
g	Saturn
f	Jupiter
e	Mars
d	Sun
c	Venus
B	Mercury
A	Moon

Two centuries later, Dante in the *Convivio* (*c.* 1305)[97] was to make explicit the correspondence of the lowest three spheres with the Angels, Archangels, and Thrones (following the peculiar ordering only found in this work), from which one can deduce a complete matching of spheres with their angelic governors:

Primum Mobile	Seraphim
Fixed Stars	Cherubim
Saturn	Powers
Jupiter	Principalities
Mars	Virtues
Sun	Dominations
Venus	Thrones
Mercury	Archangels
Moon	Angels

Giorgio Anselmi, the early Renaissance astrologer and physician mentioned on pp. 142–43, returned in his *De musica* of 1434 to the Gregorian order and omitted the Primum Mobile (which might, after all, be thought to correspond to God, as it does in Aristotle) in order to include the four elements at the lower end.[98]

Fixed Stars	Seraphim
Saturn	Cherubim
Jupiter	Thrones
Mars	Dominations
Sun	Principalities
Venus	Powers
Mercury	Virtues
Moon	Archangels
Elements	Angels

In his *Musica practica* of 1482 Ramis de Pareja, an important Spanish theorist, again assigned notes to the hierarchy, but he gave them not as Angels but as the Nine Muses whom Martianus Capella had already distributed across the spheres.[99] Ramis, moreover, continued his diagram to cover a second octave to a', though without any additional correspondences beyond indicating with a kind of spiral the octave equivalences.[100]

a'			
g'			
f'			
e'	}	*not assigned*	
d'			
c'			
b			
a		Fixed Stars	Urania
g		Saturn	Polyhymnia
f		Jupiter	Euterpe
e		Mars	Erato
d		Sun	Melpomene
c		Venus	Terpsichore
B		Mercury	Calliope
A		Moon	Clio
(silent)		Earth	Thalia

This threefold scheme of notes, planets and Muses became a favourite. It was repeated by Franchinus Gaffurius (*De Harmonia Musicorum Instrumentorum Opus*, 1518), Henry Cornelius Agrippa (Book II of *De Occulta Philosophia*, 1533), Heinrich Glarean (*Dodecachordon*, 1547), and others. The Angels, it might seem, were usurped by the Muses in the humanistic enthusiasm of the time. But it is clear from their very first description in the *Theogony* of Hesiod[101] (8th–7th cent. BC) that the Nine Muses are the very same beings as the Angels of monotheism. All that one has to understand – and for many it is unthinkable, admittedly – is that these beings actually exist and that they are knowable. To Hesiod they appear as messengers who accost chosen human beings such as poets, charging them with a divine mission (Gk. *angeloi* = messengers), at the same time leading their own life a little below the summit of Olympus, i.e. just below the hierarchy of the Gods. The implication of the Muses' patronage of the arts, a theme so beloved in the Renaissance, is that the Arts in their essence are no human invention but a gift of superhuman origin and inspiration, reflecting some form of universal knowledge and wisdom; and that the route to this wisdom lies through mediation by a feminine principle. At the other extreme of Greek Antiquity, the Neoplatonist Proclus (AD 410–485) distinguishes the Muses from those other heavenly musicians, the Sirens,[102] by explaining that the gift bestowed by the Muses is an intellectual harmony, that of the Sirens a corporeal one – 'which is why the Muses are said to prevail over the Sirens and to be crowned with Sirens' feathers'. To the Christian division of the planetary from the angelic realms, then, we can equate the Classical distinction of Sirens from Muses.

The Angels return again in the fullest scheme of all, described in a verse epic on the history and destiny of France: *La Galliade* (1578) by Guy Lefèvre de La Boderie. La Boderie was a student and translator of two of the most subtle and erudite of Renaissance philosophers, Pico della Mirandola and Francesco Giorgi. In the latter's *Harmonia Mundi* (1525), which he translated into French, La Boderie had immersed himself in a world-view governed by Platonic harmonies and Kabbalistic correspondences. Giorgi himself had never assigned pitches to the entities which he brought into relationship, but he had gone much further than most authors in giving correspondences to the planets and angels for the Sephiroth (Divine Emanations or aspects) and the Hebrew Names of God. The scheme developed by La Boderie (with some unaccountable variations from Giorgi) is as follows, embracing tones, Jesus and the Angelic Orders, the Names of God, the Sephiroth, the planets, elements, and the faculties of creatures. The Angelic Orders now appear in the ordering of Dionysius the Areopagite.[103]

a'	Jesus	Ehieh	Kether	Primum mobile	
g'	Seraphim	Iah	Binah	Ninth sphere	
f'	Cherubim	Iehovah	Chokhmah	Fixed Stars	
e'	Thrones	El	Chesed	Saturn	
d'	Dominations	Iehovah	Geburah	Jupiter	
c'	Virtues	Elohim	Tiphereth	Mars	
b	Powers	Iehovah zevaoth	Netzach	Sun	
a	Principalities	Elohim zevaoth	Hod	Venus	Knowledge
g	Archangels	El sadai	Yesod	Mercury	Honour of King
f	Angels		Malkuth	Moon	Fear of God
e				Fire	Intellect
d				Air	Reason
c				Water	Sense
B				Earth	Life
A				Earth's Centre	Being

Ambitious as this scheme is, La Boderie does not exploit to the full the possibilities of musical symbolism. It was the English Hermeticist Robert Fludd (1574–1637), another close reader of Giorgi, who took the necessary step of extending the musical matrix beyond the two-octave gamut of Greek and medieval theory. Fludd's cosmological system contained three worlds: the elemental, comprising Earth, Water, Air and Fire; the Ethereal, comprising the spheres of the planets and Fixed Stars; and the Supercelestial, imagined as a further series of spheres containing the Angelic Hierarchy. Therefore in its full development his musical gamut covers three octaves, assigning one to each world and thereby symbolizing the correspondences between them as of one octave to another. In one of his several schemata,[104] designed to illustrate the Incarnation of God through the form of Universal Man, each octave has seven notes, as one would expect, but this requires some compromise. Clearly the ninefold Angelic Hierarchy will not fit, so Fludd devotes the highest octave instead to the Holy Trinity and man's higher faculties. The Fixed Stars are omitted, and the four Elements are stretched to fill seven steps:

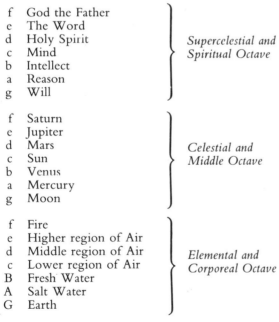

f	God the Father	
e	The Word	
d	Holy Spirit	*Supercelestial and*
c	Mind	*Spiritual Octave*
b	Intellect	
a	Reason	
g	Will	
f	Saturn	
e	Jupiter	
d	Mars	*Celestial and*
c	Sun	*Middle Octave*
b	Venus	
a	Mercury	
g	Moon	
f	Fire	
e	Higher region of Air	
d	Middle region of Air	*Elemental and*
c	Lower region of Air	*Corporeal Octave*
B	Fresh Water	
A	Salt Water	
G	Earth	

In another chart[105] which correlates man's Spirit and Soul with the spheres of the Universe, Fludd abandons the diatonic scale but retains the perfect intervals of octaves, fourths and fifths. He is therefore free to use all Nine Orders of Angels, to increase the number of celestial spheres to nine, and to reduce the elements to their proper four:

171

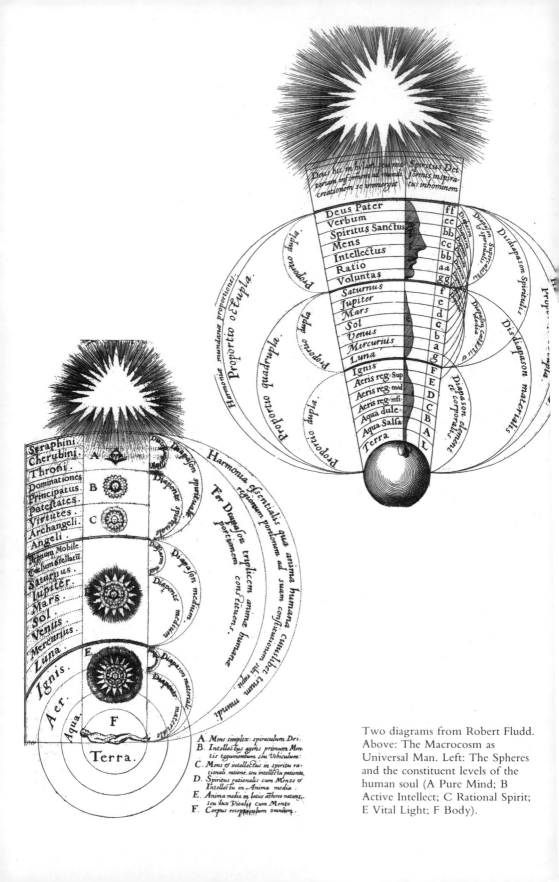

Two diagrams from Robert Fludd.
Above: The Macrocosm as
Universal Man. Left: The Spheres
and the constituent levels of the
human soul (A Pure Mind; B
Active Intellect; C Rational Spirit;
E Vital Light; F Body).

Seraphim Cherubim Thrones	} *Spiritual 4th*	
Dominations Principalities Powers Virtues Archangels Angels	} *Spiritual 5th*	} SPIRITUAL OCTAVE
Primum Mobile Fixed Stars Saturn	} *Middle 4th*	
Jupiter Mars Sun Venus Mercury Moon	} *Middle 5th*	} MIDDLE OCTAVE
Fire Air	} *Material 4th*	
Water Earth	} *Material 5th*	} MATERIAL OCTAVE

With these and the several other charts that appear in his books,[106] Fludd makes it clear that there is no one fixed way of looking at things. This capacity to shift viewpoints is a virtue he shares with other Hermeticists, such as Agrippa, whose widely-read book on *Occult Philosophy* had proposed schemes of cosmic correspondences based on all the numbers from one to ten, and twelve.

Only with this ambiguity in mind can one unravel the beautiful but at first sight baffling engraving of the Cosmic Monochord that occupies two pages of Fludd's *Anatomiae Amphitheatrum* (written 1621, published 1623). At the head stand four statements expressive of Fludd's essential monism:

The Monad generates a monad and reflects its ardour in itself.
The One is all things and all things are the One.
GOD is all that there is; from him all things proceed and to him all things return again.
The infinite dimension of the TETRAGRAMMATON: in and between all things.

Next comes the dimension of duality, essential to cosmic manifestation. At the left-hand end, where the tuning-peg governs the whole monochord, is Alpha in a triangle, symbol of God as beginning: 'The central principle or Dark Aleph.' To this corresponds, on the right, the Omega, symbol of God as 'end and circumference'. Towards the upper corners are parallel

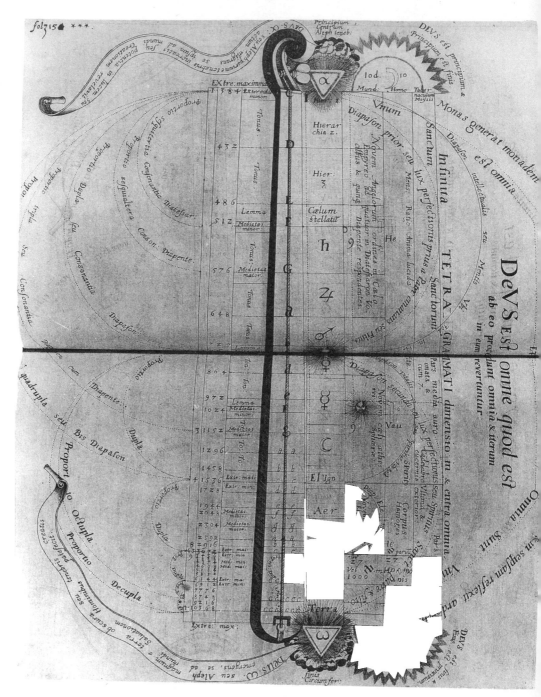

Robert Fludd's Cosmic
Monochord.

statements: 'God is the beginning, and the beginning is the end'; 'God is the end, and the end is the beginning'. Another symbol of this reciprocity is the Tetragrammaton, spelled out in palindromic form: Iod, He, Vau, He, Iod. The scrolls read as follows:

God (alpha), or the Lesser Aleph of the uncreated darkness, or potency, reveals itself
    for the world's creation by changing to light, or act.
God (omega), or the Greater Aleph, emerging from dark earth or the created
    darkness, reveals itself to men for the world's salvation.

The language of these statements must be understood in the context of Fludd's Kabbalistically derived doctrine of God's twin powers of non-acting and acting. The Lesser or Dark Aleph is the first emergence of a universe from non-manifestation; the Greater or Light Aleph is the completion of that universe, whether viewed as the end of time, as the final expansion of space (the circumference), or as the lowest point of the created hierarchy.

Three different musical systems are overlaid in the chart. First, on the monochord itself are the notes of the diatonic scale for three octaves from C to c^3, and thereafter the octaves alone up to c^6. This is musically correct, as are the proportions of string-length and the intervals marked on the lower arcs. Between c^6 and the bridge at the Omega end, there is theoretically an indefinite series of higher octaves. Similarly, the numerals in the lowest column, which give the proportions of string-length for each scale-tone in the lowest possible whole numbers, could be continued up to infinity if space allowed. The intervals are named in the adjacent column. At the right-hand end of the uppermost section, some of these octaves are assigned to classes in the cosmic hierarchy: to the Minerals, Vegetables, Animals, and to Man. As far as the notes and numbers in the bottom section are concerned, this scheme illustrates the division of the World-Soul as described in Plato's *Timaeus* by means of the numbers 1, 2, 3, 4, 8, 9, 27, here given on the lowest line of all.[107]

Second, there is a system of three octaves similar to those diagrams of Fludd's previously described, each assigned to one of the three worlds. The words immediately above the planetary symbols read:

Nine orders of Angels in the Empyrean Heaven, corresponding to the four notes of
    the diatessaron [4th] and five of the diapente [5th].
Nine spheres of the Ethereal Heaven.
Nine regions of the Elemental World.

Corresponding to these in the Microcosm is the series of three octaves shown by the three diminishing unbroken arcs. These are the 'intellectual or mental', 'vital or spiritual', and 'elemental or corporeal' octaves, i.e. the three major divisions of Man into Intellect or Spirit (in the higher sense), Soul, and Body.

Thirdly, there is a two-octave system, shown by the two equal arcs drawn in dotted lines:

First octave or light of perfection first emanating from the Father, viz. the Son.
Second octave or light of perfection, viz. the Holy Spirit, from the Father and the Son.

The monochord thus becomes in its highest respect the symbol of divine emanation in the Holy Trinity, the equality of Persons being aptly reflected in the identical pitch of the two halves of a string when stopped in the middle.

To the reader who has preferred not to follow these labyrinthine schemes, I owe a word of explanation as to why Robert Fludd, I, or anyone else considers them worthwhile. Fludd's deep and extensive learning had acquainted him with a number of disparate doctrines, each of which his natural ecumenicism recognized as containing a true insight into the nature of things. To name some of them: there was the mathematical description of Plato's *Timaeus*; the spatial system of the Ptolemaic cosmos, expanded by the addition of the Angelic Hierarchies; the Hermetic doctrine that Man the Microcosm reflects the structure of that Macrocosm; the evident hierarchy of states of consciousness, from the God-knowing Intellect down to the mineral realm. Finally, there was the inner organization of the Godhead itself into the three Persons of the Holy Trinity, into the fourfold Tetragrammaton I H V H, or into the duality of action and non-action. How is one to bring all these together? It is difficult to conceive of a more powerful application of *musica speculativa* – of music as mirror of reality – than Fludd's attempt to unify all these disparate truths through the symbol of the monochord and its scale.

12. The Three Means

As Dionysius expounds it, the way in which 'superessential harmony' is established in the Angelic Choirs is by threes, and therein by further triple divisions into 'first, middle and last'. The Nine Orders are the result of the second threefold division, a division that continues throughout the cosmos wherever it is a question of Intellect. (By Intellect I mean the Platonic *Nous* or 'higher mind', not the modern meaning of the rational understanding.) Division on the physical plane takes place, by contrast, in twos, as for example in the growth of cells. Dionysius recognized that it is only with the number 3 that the possibility of harmony, as distinct from mere proliferation and reproduction, begins.

One can express this search for the harmonizing third entity mathematically by taking two quantities *a* and *b*, between which we are to locate a mean quantity *m*:

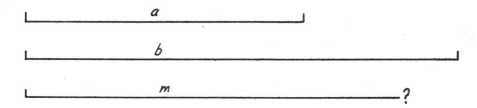

Is the best place for *m* exactly halfway between them? This will produce two arithmetically equal units, following the formula for the *arithmetic mean*, $mA = (a + b)/2$. Extension of such units will give an *arithmetical series*, shown by the equal arcs in the following diagram:

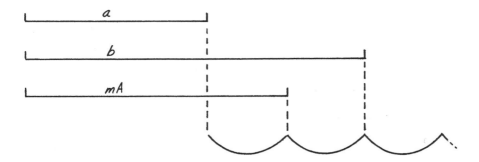

There is a kind of perfection here, certainly, but perhaps this is not the best kind of proportion to represent a hierarchy such as the angelic one, still less the Great Chain of Being whose innumerable members surely are not of equal importance. On paper, at any rate, arithmetical progression is the method of pure quantity: it can count the heads of men or of mice, but it cannot differentiate between them. Yet we will see that when interpreted musically this progression gives the Undertone or subharmonic series, something entirely different in symbolic value (see Section 15, below).

We turn next to the *geometric mean*, which is given by the formula $mG = \sqrt{ab}$. Many square roots cannot be expressed in the integral fractions that are all traditional arithmetic uses, but they can be constructed geometrically as easily as one draws the diagonal to a square. A *geometric series* progresses by multiplying each term by a constant:

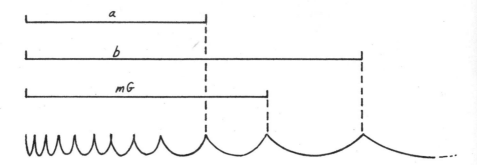

In one direction it expands to infinity; in the other it contracts to zero. Its musical expression is a sequence of identical intervals up or down. The series of octaves, for example, is produced by multiplying a string-length or a vibration ratio by successive factors of 2; the series of fifths by the constant 2/3. Symbolically this series represents a single symbol as it traverses the levels of being. In descriptions of the physical world it is useful as the logarithmic scale that facilitates the comparison of objects' relative, not absolute, sizes, or their rates of vibration. Geometry is of course the field of mathematics in which similar objects are recognizable as such, no matter how disparate their actual sizes.

The third mean is the *harmonic*, found by the formula $mH = 2ab/(a+b)$, and it generates the *harmonic series*. If one imagines the greater length b as a monochord string, the other two lengths a and mH as sounding portions of it, the three terms will always be found related as if they were adjacent terms in a harmonic series, or terms separated by equal numbers of intervening harmonics, such as $\frac{1}{2}$, $\frac{1}{3}$, $\frac{1}{4}$, or $\frac{1}{3}$, $\frac{1}{5}$, $\frac{1}{7}$, limited by 1 and ∞.

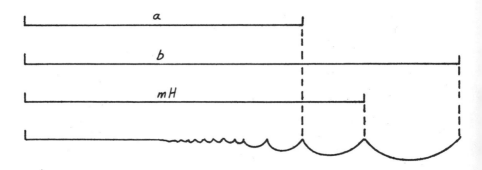

As simple musical examples of the three means, let us imagine b to be a monochord string 2 feet long, giving the note c and the length a to be exactly half of the string, giving the note c' an octave higher. The three means will then fall on different pitches as follows:

Arithmetical mean: $\quad mA = \dfrac{a+b}{2} = \dfrac{1+2}{2} = \dfrac{3}{2}$

which is the ratio of the perfect fifth. Thus the three terms of the arithmetic series are 2 : 3/2 : 1, or c f c'.

Geometrical mean: $\quad mG = \sqrt{ab} = \sqrt{1 \times 2} = \sqrt{2}$

$\sqrt{2}$ gives an equally tempered f♯ unobtainable in any traditional tuning system, thus dividing the octave at the tritone: c f♯ c'.

Harmonic mean: $\quad mH = \dfrac{2ab}{a+b} = \dfrac{2 \times 1 \times 2}{1+2} = \dfrac{4}{3}$

the ratio of a perfect fourth. Thus the three terms of the harmonic series are c g c'.

In the sections that follow we shall see some of the applications of these means and the series developed from them in musical symbolism. Perhaps the most familiar is the diatonic scale which, as explained briefly on p. 132, is formed from any seven adjacent terms of a geometric series ruled by the constant 3/2 or 2/3, the proportion of the perfect fifth.

Progression of seven fifths

Transposed to fit within a single octave and then placed in ascending order, these seven notes furnish the diatonic scale, here pitched for the sake of simplicity in the major mode on C:

Formation of the diatonic scale

But the seven–note scale is not complete until it has reached the octave (here in parentheses) and made its transition to a new 'plane', just as the seven planets of the Ptolemaic cosmos lead up to the eighth sphere of the Fixed Stars. The extended diatonic scale then becomes a perfect image of a universe whose key lies (as we read in the *Dream of Scipio*) in the number 7. Each octave-space contains a manifestation of the septenary on a different plane, and the ascent of the scale symbolizes the ascent of the soul through not one but many sevenfold regions.

13. Gurdjieff's Law of Octaves

George Gurdjieff (1872 or 1877–1949), founder of the Institute for the Harmonious Development of Man, is reported by his sometime pupil P.D. Ouspensky as teaching that 'The seven-tone scale is the formula of a cosmic law which was worked out by ancient schools and applied to music.'[108] In Gurdjieff's own system the diatonic scale does not serve merely as an image of the septenary: its inner organization becomes of paramount importance. The scale he chooses from the many possible ones is the modern major, characterized by its sequence of two whole-tone intervals (C-D-E), a semitone (E-F), three whole tones (F-G-A-B), and, if transition to the next octave is included, a final semitone (B-C'). In exactly the same way, Gurdjieff explains, all human and natural developments take place not by an even progression but with two discontinuities in every phase or cycle. These occur in the scale as the two semitones mi-fa (E-F) and si-do (B-C'). (Compare Anny von Lange's two cesurae, pp. 135–36.) Progress through the whole-tones is plain sailing, but when the semitones are reached the whole development can be knocked off course, even reversed, unless extra energy is brought to bear. Gurdjieff calls this necessary energy the 'additional shock' that may. be supplied from the resources of the developing thing or person, or may come deliberately or accidentally from outside. Ouspensky quotes the following explanation:[109]

In an ascending octave the first [semitone] 'interval' comes between mi and fa. If corresponding additional energy enters at this point the octave will develop without hindrance to si, but between si and do it needs a *much stronger additional* shock for its right development than between mi and fa, because the vibrations of the octave at this point are of a considerably higher pitch.

In Gurdjieff's system of work on oneself, the ascending scale is the model for one's deliberate growth, as one watches for the points which require an additional shock. But he also uses the scale as a symbol for the opposite process of emanation from above. Taken in the downward direction, it is the model for the descending levels of manifestation. God's work is not so difficult as our own, for (the quotation goes on) 'a descending octave develops much more easily than an ascending octave'. The first semitone occurs right away, between do and si, and the 'material for filling it in is often found either in the do itself or in the lateral vibrations evoked by do.' The fa is now reached without incident, and the second semitone fa-mi crossed with a '*considerably* less strong' shock than the first.

One cannot help wondering whether Gurdjieff would have invented a different scheme, had he lived in a culture and era when a different form of seven-note scale was the norm. For the semitones do not necessarily fall between the 3rd and 4th and the 7th and 8th steps. In the scale on D, for instance, they fall between steps 2 and 3, 6 and 7, whether one takes the scale up or down: D E F G A B C D' or D' C B A G F E D. As the Dorian or First Mode of the Middle Ages, and the diatonic Phrygian Mode of Ancient Greece, this D-mode with its perfect intervallic symmetry has a good claim for primacy. The modern major, however, is the inversion of the Greek diatonic Dorian (E D C B A G F E,), the mode preferred by the Demiurge of Plato's *Timaeus* for the construction of the world; so, allowing for a reversal of up and down, it is also a strong contender. Such matters could be argued *ad nauseam*: every speculative musician has a favourite scale.

We will not enter the intricacies of Gurdjieff's 'cosmic octaves', which puzzled even his closest followers. But Ouspensky transmits a simplified scheme[110] that is of great interest, covering as it does all the principal levels of being within the tones of a single octave. Like all earth-centered schemes, it gives the superficial impression that all of Creation is aimed towards our little world. But it is also true to our experience, as we have explained of geocentricity in general. We look through the pinhole of earthly, sensible existence to the ever expanding levels above us. And what is beneath the pinhole? Infinite contraction, according to this scheme, ending in a Nothingness that is paradoxically also the Absolute:

C'	The Absolute as All	} semitone requiring 'shock', supplied
B	All created worlds	} by the Will of the Absolute
A	Our galaxy, the Milky Way	
G	Our solar system; the Sun	
F	The planetary world	} semitone filled by organic life on
E	The Earth	} earth, receiving planetary influences
D	The Moon	
C	The Absolute as Nothing	

Herbert Whone suggests that these very meanings are concealed in the names given to the notes of the scale by Guido d'Arezzo in the tenth century: Ut, Re, Mi, Fa, Sol, La. In the sixteenth century, with the change from hexachordal to heptachordal theory, the leading-tone B was also given a name, Si, and in some countries the Ut was renamed the more singable Do. Whone gives the following table (some Latin words corrected):[111]

DO	(Dominus)	God as creator
SI	(Sider)	Star systems
LA	(Lactea)	The Milky Way, Man's particular galaxy
SOL	(Sol)	The Sun
FA	(Fata)	Planets – the spoken word – a man's fate
MI	(Microcosmos)	The Earth – Man's role upon the earth
RE	(Regina Coeli)	The Moon [Queen of Heaven]

We can add that the original Latin word Ut was a better name, being a word that embraces a whole range of meanings referring to cause: the English 'thus', 'since', 'as', 'in order that', 'how', 'like', etc., and also linking etymologically with Thoth, Egyptian god of creative intelligence, and the Sanskrit *tat*, the indefinable 'that'.

Gurdjieff's scale has more than a casual resemblance to the Great Monochord of Robert Fludd, described above, which is strung between the Light and Dark Alephs as twin faces of the Absolute. The late James Webb, friend of my youth and impartial student of Gurdjieff and Ouspensky, saw a similar connection between the Enneagram, another fundamental Gurdjieffian symbol, and a ninefold diagram in Athanasius Kircher's *Arithmologia*. Webb believed that 'in the *Arithmologia* Kircher was expressing a final synthesis of Renaissance mysticism and that Gurdjieff's cosmology somehow derives from it'.[112] The coincidences are striking, certainly, but not surprising when one remembers that all three philosophers were working (here, at any rate) within the same perennial tradition of Hermetic wisdom, with its significant numbers and its law of correspondence between the Above and the Below.

Gurdjieff uses the seven-note scale to symbolize evolution on the one hand and hierarchy on the other. But the septenary is not bound to the hierarchical dimension which has been our authors' almost exclusive concern. The octave-space can be conceived equally well not as a ladder

(Latin *scala*) but as a Pleroma: the fullness of manifestation on any or all levels into which flow the seven primal differentiations of God's power. In Theosophy (especially that of H.P. Blavatsky and Alice A. Bailey) much is taught about these 'Seven Rays'. A diagram will illustrate the essential difference between the two views of the septenary or of the seven notes.

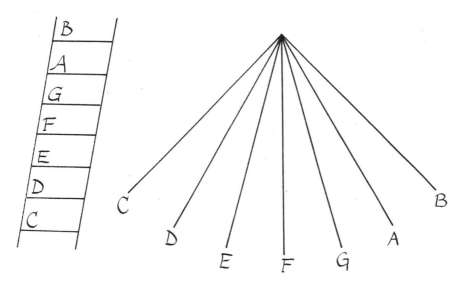

The Scale as ladder   The Scale as the Seven Rays

The second diagram answers to the fact that the notes of the scale are qualitatively different from one another, but such that a higher (or lower) pitch is not 'superior' to its neighbour, as the Seraphim may be to the Cherubim. Each has its own character and its part to play in the unfoldment of the musical Pleroma. Using a symbol in which there is even less suggestion of hierarchy, the ancient Gnostics made the seven tones of the Scale correspond to the seven Ionian vowels *A E H I O ΥΩ*.[113] These in turn matched the seven planetary powers, which on their own level are not so much a hierarchy as a reflection, in appropriate mode, of the Seven Rays. In an anonymous Gnostic text, [114] the Godhead is made to say:

The seven vowels celebrate me, who am the imperishable God; indefatigable Father of all beings, I am the indestructible lyre of the Universe; it is I who found out the harmonious concord of the heavenly whirlwind.

We will meet again this Creator, with his power to harmonize the rays that proceed from the Absolute. But in order to comprehend him, we must first turn to the symbolism of the harmonic series.

14. The Harmonic Series and its Symbolism

In the early modern era it was not widely known that the harmonic series corresponds to the vibrations into which any musically resonant body tends to fall. But the sequence of intervals was familiar as the series of integral divisions of a string (1/2, 1/3, 1/4, 1/5 . . .). Moreover, it was readily audible as the notes of the natural trumpet, the valveless instrument for which Bach and Handel wrote. The notes available on a natural trumpet in C are the first sixteen or so harmonics of its fundamental:

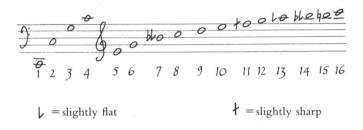

$\flat$ = slightly flat $\sharp$ = slightly sharp

The first 16 harmonics of the Overtone Series

This series of intervals is inexhaustible in its multifaceted symbolism. If the Angels' song is indeed one of knowledge, they could not choose a better theme on which to descant. Two simple interpretations of it were made by Andreas Werckmeister (1645–1706), a German provincial organist and theorist, who knew it as the 'trumpet scale'. The first of his schemes refers it to the Six Days of Creation, the second to the progressive revelation of God.

In Werckmeister's creation scheme,[115] the first note or fundamental corresponds to the creation of light, first awakener of the senses. On the second day, the waters were separated from the dry land, and this is represented by the first differentiation of an octave (1-2) with a 'formless void' within it. On the third day, this space was filled with herbs and trees, like the 3 which appears in the next octave 2–4. On the fourth day, with the creation of the Sun and Moon, we enter the third octave of 4, 5, 6, 7, 8: 'a light by which we can glimpse a complete harmony' with the greater and lesser lights represented by the major and minor thirds (4–5, 5–6). The problematic seventh harmonic, an out-of-tune B-flat, 'shows how times are not always good, but sometimes a dissonance must be mingled in with this life'. The fifth day and fourth octave sees the creation of the animals in all their variety, including both good and bad sounding notes: hence there are animals both clean and unclean. Finally on the sixth day Man is created to rule over the whole earth, just as the musician must rule over and control all these numbers or notes.

Werckmeister's second scheme[116] arises from the symbolism of the triad. He would have read in the older German theorists of the likeness of the Holy Trinity in the common chord or major triad (harmonics 4, 5, 6). Johannes Lippius, for example, had praised it in 1612 as the 'true and unitrisonic root of all the most perfect and most complete harmonies that can exist in the world . . . the image of that great mystery, the divine and solely adorable Unitrinity'.[117] Now Werckmeister applies the four octaves of the trumpet's harmonics to the four successive periods of divine revelation. Octave I (harmonics 1, 2) now symbolizes God the Father as He was before Creation; II (harmonics 2, 3, 4) the time of the Old Testament, when the Trinity was concealed; III (harmonics 4, 5, 6, 8) the time of the New Testament, in which the Trinity was revealed; IV (harmonics 8, 9, 10, 12, 15, 16) the melody of the Christian life, in earth and heaven. With good symbolic reason, he here excludes the dissonant harmonics 7, 11, 13, 14, for they would represent sin.

These dissonant harmonics are a problem, and not only for trumpet-players. The B-flats (7, 14) and A (13) that are rather too flat, and the F (11) that is not quite sharp are ironed out in practical music (with the striking exception of the horn-calls in Benjamin Britten's *Serenade*). But in theory they are all too present, and in symbolism they often serve the purpose not merely of representing but of explaining the evil in the world.

A very explicit association of the first dissonant harmonic (the seventh) with evil comes in the first work of Louis-Claude de Saint-Martin (1743–1803). Published in 1775 under his pseudonym of 'The Unknown Philosopher', this large work, entitled *Des Erreurs et de la vérité*, summarizes what Saint-Martin had learnt from his master the theosopher Martinès de Pasqually (1710–1774). This symbolism may therefore originate with the latter. Saint-Martin first explains the symbolism of the common chord (meaning harmonics 4, 5, 6, with the addition of 8). The major triad, he says, is the foundation of all music and an image of the Unity that encloses everything – or nearly everything.[118] The two different thirds that for Werckmeister expressed the double nature, divine and human, of God the Son take on a similar role here: they show that every being is under a double law, that of its own unitary Principle and that of the separate body it inhabits. But this duality, being the rule of all manifestation, is not itself evil. Ideally it is crowned and brought to completion by the addition of a new octave (8) above the triad: an image of the First Principle (the root of the triad, 4) in perfect concord with its original.

Saint-Martin now transposes this symbol to the level of macrocosmic entities and to a time before the worlds began. In fact, he is describing the rebellion of Satan against God and the consequent origin of evil. But he does not use these names, speaking instead of First [God] and Second [Satan] Principles.[119] The 'image of the Principle', he says, *should* be a perfect octave, but before the beginning of time it diverged,[120] asserting its own will and separating itself from the First Principle to become the origin of all evil – which is likewise the forsaking of one's own Principle to run after an illusory separateness. He does not make it clear whether he understands this note to be the flattened seventh degree of the scale, or the over-flat seventh harmonic:

Flat seventh degree

Seventh harmonic

But he obviously has in mind the note which changes a perfect major chord into a 'dominant seventh', thereby disturbing its harmonic equilibrium and demanding a particular resolution:

Major chord changing to dominant seventh and resolving

Some theorists, attempting to explain the origin of this dominant seventh chord, which has been the mainspring of tonal harmony since the seventeenth century, have traced it directly to the harmonic series. They say that it is an image of the overtones, 4, 5, 6 and 7, and should ideally be tuned like these harmonics, with an over-flat seventh, whenever it occurs.[121] This has the symbolic advantage of making every note contain, in its 7th and other dissonant harmonics, its own dissatisfaction and yearning for resolution. To sound the seventh is simply to bring this tendency out into

186

the open. Yet even when it is resolved, the resolution can never be final, for the chord to which it resolves will also contain its own seventh harmonic, its own discontent, like the seed of evil and disharmony present in every being. If we were to sound that note in the above resolution, it would be to insert an E-flat into the chord on F, thereby requiring a further resolution to the chord a fifth lower, on B-flat. And so the process would continue indefinitely, spiralling without hope of redemption through an eternal geometric series of ever lower fifths, into a hellish realm of double flats where no musician likes to venture:

Endless progression of dominant sevenths

But lest one should think the equation of this dissonance with the principle of evil too conclusive, or too facile, I turn to a person who recorded an entirely contrary opinion of the dominant seventh, Bettina Brentano von Arnim (1785–1859). In her youth, this brilliant woman had a correspondence with Goethe in which she aired her stream of consciousness – sometimes profound, often beautiful, occasionally scatter-brained. (One of her letters[122] records the famous speech of Beethoven in which he says that 'music is a higher Revelation than all wisdom and philosophy', and much else on his art and mission.) On 24 July, 1808, she writes to Goethe, who has been studying thorough-bass and feels like rejecting the flat seventh for its failure to fit in with the laws of harmony:

But, heathen, thou must become a Christian! The flat seventh does not harmonize certainly, and is without sensible basis; it is the divine leader, – the Mediator between sensual and heavenly Nature; it has assumed flesh and bone, to free the spirit to tone, and if *it* were not, all tones would remain in limbo . . . the flat seventh by its resolution leads all tones, which pray to it for delivery, in a thousand different ways, to their source – divine spirit.[123]

15. The Subharmonic Series

In order to take the next step towards understanding how the musical system can be an intelligible symbol of the world of Ideas, our view of the harmonic series must expand to include its inverse reflection in a subharmonic series.[124] That is, we posit a series of undertones which are the exact inversion of the overtones, generated by an arithmetical progression if regarded as a series of string lengths. The first sixteen undertones of a given note (here c''') will form an interval-pattern identical to that of the trumpet-scale given above, only now proceeding downwards:

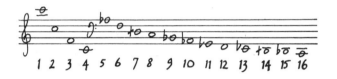

The first 16 harmonics of the Undertone Series

Do these undertones actually exist? Occasionally[125] it has been claimed that they have an objective and audible existence, but it is not necessary to believe this in order to appreciate their reality as symbols, which is for speculative musicians a higher and more 'real' reality than that of the audible harmonics. In fact, the undertones are probably better left in the realm of ideas as the unmanifested counterpart to the overtones. Something of their symbolic value will emerge if we consider that whereas the overtones correspond to successively faster vibrations and smaller vibrating particles (e.g. progressively shorter fractions of the monochord), the undertones represent slower and slower vibrations such as would be caused by increasingly large resonant bodies. The overtones lead to the 'microscopic' diminution of time and space, the undertones to 'astronomical' expansion. In just the same way, we know that every one of our actions (and, for a mentalist, our thoughts, too) must affect all the cells, molecules, and eventually the atomic particles within our body. But our actions also have an *exterior* result whose influence spreads out and eventually affects, however slightly, the entire universe. The latter is part of the *karma* (= action) that we create, often disbelieved by the unphilosophical because, like the undertones, it is imperceptible or delayed by long lapse of time, but none the less a metaphysical necessity. It is symbolically most apt that we can grasp the overtones with our senses, as we enclose our body's parts, but not the undertones, since they belong to the macrocosm outside us.

The twin rows of harmonics represent the universal forces of contraction (overtones) and expansion (undertones), which for many theosophers are at the very foundation of Being, and both necessary for Creation to emerge from Chaos.

Applying this to music, one may consider a single tone, say Middle C, surrounded by its overtones and undertones:

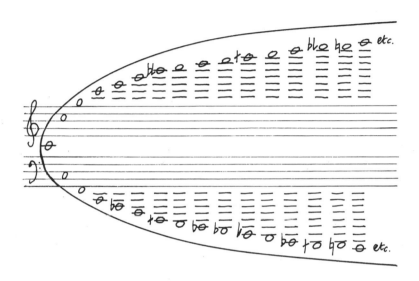

Middle C with its first 16 overtones and undertones

Its overtones fill all of microcosmic space; its undertones fill all of macrocosmic space. But the note itself, visible here at the cusp of a parabola, carries an emptiness around it. A little distance away there is the 'white noise' of innumerable harmonics extending in both directions. Only in the vicinity of the tone does this noise become resolved and clarified into intervals: holes in the undetermined chaos. Thus one could regard a tone not in the usual way, as a point radiating harmonics, but as a musical space created in chaos by the formative forces of harmony: forces that become more and more clearly focused as they proceed from complex to simple ratios, culminating in the perfect fourths, fifths, and octaves around the tone itself. In an analogous way, Rudolf Steiner had his students imagine flowers not as the result of interior, vegetative forces pushing the petals outward, but rather as moulded by exterior, cosmic forces pushing inwards. And here, too, the unimaginable complexity of forces in the environing cosmos resolves itself at the flower-head into the simple geometry of petals.

16. The Lambdoma and the Pythagorean Table

Albert von Thimus (1806–1878), a polymathic researcher into ancient harmonic theory, discovered in a treatise of Iamblichus[126] the hint that the Greeks had already discovered both the overtone and undertone series and expressed them in a diagram shaped like the letter lambda (Λ). He called this diagram the Lambdoma. Starting from unity (1/1), the overtones go down the right leg, the undertones down the left, marked both as numbers (fractions and multiples of unity) and as the corresponding tones, here named as if unity is the length of a monochord string sounding c. (For symmetry I retain the German pitch convention.)

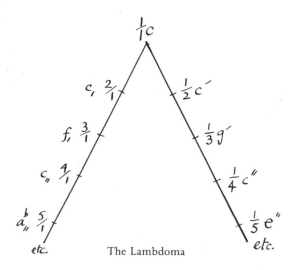

The Lambdoma

By filling in the enclosed space with a network of intermediate tones and expanding the angle to 90°, von Thimus developed the Lambdoma into a square diagram which he called the 'Pythagorean Table'.

Both von Thimus and his spiritual heir Hans Kayser believed that this was the fundamental diagram of the lost ancient science of Harmonics, hinted at by Plato in *Republic* VII, 530d–531c as the culmination of all learning, but never revealed publicly. Others say that von Thimus was mistakenly projecting on to the ancient Pythagoreans his own discovery of a scheme typical of early nineteenth-century mathematical theory.[127] We need not pursue the debate here, since the Pythagorean Table, whatever its origin, is an incomparable aid to speculative music, as a means toward symbolic explanation and possible illumination concerning cosmic and metaphysical realities.

The Pythagorean Table
(from Levarie and Levy, *Musical Morphology*, p. 230)

The Table is an image of the Universe. If extended to mathematical infinity it would contain every rational fraction and integer. Each one of these, expressed by a numerator and a denominator, is the product of an intersection between an overtone and an undertone row, i.e. every tone occurs as a member of one row of each type. If each is taken to represent one of the beings in the Universe, this dual origin emphasizes each being's dependence for manifested existence on a primordial duality, the initial split of the Lambdoma. One might say that whenever the two forces of contraction and expansion meet and are held in some proportional balance, a being arises – and a tone is sounded. Every being is both number and tone; both quantity and quality; both existence and value. All have the same root: the originating 1/1 tone that represents God the Creator.

The network of the Table also suggests the warp and weft of a loom and the symbolism of woven material, often used to represent the structure of the Universe. Here the vertical rows of 'macrocosmic' undertones are the fixed warp, the horizontal, 'microcosmic' overtones the weft. One can then apply to them the words of René Guénon on the symbolism of weaving:

The warp may be said to represent the principles that bind together all the worlds or all the states [of being], each of its threads forming the connection between corresponding points in these different states; and the weft, the chains of events that are produced in each of the worlds, each thread being the development of events in a given world. From a different viewpoint, it may also be said that the manifestation of a being in a certain state of existence, like any other event, is determined by the meeting of a thread of the warp with a thread of the weft.[128]

Guénon cites the individual human life as an example of such a meeting. However, these intersections do not exist in isolation. Apart from occupying a place on each row, all tone-values recur as it were in different 'reincarnations', e.g. 2/3 as 4/6, 6/9, etc., which all sound the same tone g. But, as Kayser comments,[129] the surroundings are different in every case. Now, if one connects any such series of equal tones, a remarkable thing happens: these lines meet at a point *outside* the Table, shown as 0/0 on the diagram.

17. Beyond manifestation: 1/1 and 0/0

To Hans Kayser, the single most important revelation of the Pythagorean Table was that outside and beyond it there lies this point 0/0 which sounds no tone but is the silence toward which all tones tend. If 1/1 is the Creator God, then 0/0 is what various traditions have called the Absolute, Beyond-Being, Nirvana, Parabrahman, the Thrice-Unknown Darkness, Mind in Itself; and its realm of mathematically impossible fractions (0/1, 1/0, etc., all equal either to zero or infinity) is the Unmanifest. Regarding the convergence of all the equal tone-lines on this point, Kayser observes that

herein lies, in the symbolism of harmonics, a consoling certainty. In spite of being torn by the strife between light and dark [= the twin rows], in spite of consonance and dissonance, each single existence-value with its reincarnations is directed toward the divine, whence it receives its true innermost value.[130].

, There is no musical equivalent for 0/0. In his beautiful poem on the Ascension, the Neoplatonic Bishop Synesius (*c.* 370–413) describes the music of the spheres as it greets the rising Christ, then concludes:

> But you, with spreading wings,
> Broke through the azure dome
> And rested in the spheres
> Of pure Intelligence:
> The source of all things good,
> The Heaven silence-filled.[131]

Though strictly speaking Synesius is describing a silent Heaven, not the Absolute, his intuition corresponds to that of metaphysicians like Kayser, Guénon and Brunton:[132] that all Being culminates in a Nothingness beyond Being that, unlike the *néant* of the Existentialists, is paradoxically its sole support and positive origin. Using the simile of silence, Guénon says that

as Non-Being, or the nonmanifested, comprehends or envelops Being, or the principle of manifestation, so silence contains within itself the principle of the word. In other words, just as Unity [1/1] is nothing but the metaphysical Zero [0/0] affirmed, the word is silence expressed. But inversely, metaphysical Zero, while being Unity unaffirmed, is also something more than that, and infinitely more.[133]

No wonder such a doctrine was kept secret in the past, because unless it is approached with a high degree of metaphysical sensitivity it can be parodied and inverted into a nihilism that undermines all religion and morality.

Our ascent can go no further. The Song the Angels sing is in its exoteric aspect a perpetual hymn of praise to the Creator (1/1), but esoterically it is nothing more nor less than the affirmation of their own emanation and their existence as 'tone-values'. They derive, as we do, from the Creator, but beyond that their being and ours – and His, too – are comprehended in the divine Non-Being (0/0) to which no prayer or praise can be addressed and from which no answer can ever be received. It can only be invoked in a silence and a darkness that, however feebly, imitate its own.

Notes

For full references see Bibliography.

PART I: ASCENDING PARNASSUS

1 *The Marvellous Effects of Music* (p. 11)

1 Adapted from the version in GRAVES, vol. I, p. 257.
2 VYSE, vol. II, pp. 321ff.
3 ROBINSON, p. 32.
4 SINNETT, p. 20.
5 BLAVATSKY, vol. II, p. 279. See also MICHELL 1967, pp. 41ff.
6 Cited in KIRCHER 1650, vol. II, p. 228.
7 RADHAKRISHNAN, vol. II, p. 271.
8 BBC Science Magazine interview with Don Robins, 1983. I am indebted to Todd Barton for the tape of this programme. See also ROBINS, passim.
9 NOVALIS, pp. 28f.
10 JENNY, passim, also summarized in HODSON, pp. 2–14.
11 MARTIANUS, sect. 907.
12 Ibid., sect. 11.
13 KIRCHER 1650, vol. II, pp. 411f.
14 Reported ibid., p. 229.
15 See Schneider's article in GODWIN 1987, on 'Sound Symbolism in Foreign Cultures'.
16 See GUÉNON 1958.
17 TOMPKINS & BIRD, pp. 145–62.
18 Ibid., summarizing RETALLACK.
19 *The Histories*, I. 23–4.
20 Classical sources summarized in LOCKLEY, pp. 18–43.
21 Ibid.
22 See SAVOLD.
23 LOCKLEY, p. 84.
24 *Homeric Hymn to Apollo*.
25 MARTIANUS, sects. 927–8. Included in Godwin 1986.
26 AL-GHAZĀLĪ, A. H., p. 219.
27 KIRCHER 1650, vol. II, pp. 227f.
28 THORNDIKE, vol. VII, p. 600.
29 Quoted in FLUDD 1617a, p. 177. Included in GODWIN 1986.
30 FLUDD 1617a, pp. 179f.
31 Ibid., p. 181.
32 THORNDIKE, vol. III, p. 448.
33 See WALKER, pp. 3–11.
34 Translated as FICINO. The musical chapter included in GODWIN 1986.
35 WALKER, p. 9.
36 STEFFANI, pp. 30f.
37 See WALKER, p. 231.
38 LEIBNIZ, vol. II, p. 698.
39 SCHMIDT J., p. 96.
40 BROWNE, p. 7.
41 Ibid., pp. 14ff.
42 Ibid., pp. 114ff.
43 Ibid., p. 121.
44 BROCKLESBURY, pp. 70ff.
45 Ibid., p. 19.
46 EULER.
47 ALBRECHT, pp. 108ff.
48 BROCKLESBURY, p. 45.
49 For whatever understanding I have of this subject, I am primarily indebted to the works of Paul Brunton, especially BRUNTON 1943, pp. 58ff.
50 IKHWĀN, p.12. Extracts included in GODWIN 1986b.
51 SCHOPENHAUER, vol. III, sect. 52.
52 Iamblichus, *Vit. Pyth.*, xxv. Included in GODWIN 1986.
53 Plutarch, *De Alex. Fort.*, 335.
54 Reported in KIRCHER 1650, vol. II, pp. 216f.
55 TYARD, fol. 103.
56 Reported in PODOLSKY, p. 5.
57 Ibid., p. 6.
58 Reported in COOMARASWAMY, p. 89.
59 *Vit. Pyth.*, xxv, trans. Thomas Taylor.
60 ALVIN, pp. 52ff.
61 CAGE, p. 93.
62 ROOLEY, pp. 212ff.
63 COOMARASWAMY, p. 52.
64 See SIGERIST; ROBLEDO.
65 By William de Marra; see THORNDIKE, vol. III, p. 534.
66 SCHNEIDER 1948, cited in ROBLEDO, p. 224.
67 ALVIN, p. 95.
68 SIGERIST, p. 113.
69 Article 'Tarantella' in MGG, vol. 13, cols. 117–19.
70 SCHNEIDER 1955, pp. 62f.

71 ROBLEDO, p. 232.
72 SIGERIST, p. 113, quoting 17th-century author Epiphanius Ferdinandus.
73 PRIESTLEY, pp. 50, 57–76.
74 Ibid., pp. 120ff.
75 See STREICH.
76 PONTVIK, p. 11.
77 E.g. CHASE; RISTAD.
78 On Anthroposophic music therapy, see STEBBING.
79 Cited in STEBBING, passim.
80 LI CHI, XVII, I, 29.
81 Ibid., XVII, III, 3.
82 Quoted in CENSORSHIP, p. 35, report on China by David Holm. The comparison with the ancient emperors is Holm's.
83 Ibid., p. 37.
84 On Damon, see ANDERSON, pp. 74ff.
85 LI CHI, XVII, I, 1.
86 See STOCKHAUSEN, vol. III, pp. 182–7.
87 FABRE 1915, p. 149.
88 FABRE 1928.
89 Ibid., pp. 7ff.
90 SCOTT, pp. 47ff.
91 Ibid., pp. 75ff.

2 *Hearing Secret Harmonies* (p. 46)

1 EVANS-WENTZ, p. 131.
2 Ibid., pp. 31f.
3 Ibid., p. 111.
4 Ibid., p. 103.
5 Ibid., p. 298, quoting *Silva Gadelica* ii.142–4.
6 MOAR, vol. IV, pp. 206f.
7 Ibid., vol. II, p. 211.
8 EVANS-WENTZ, p. 61.
9 STEINER 1974, pp. 117–26.
10 Ibid., pp. 161–3.
11 See HODSON for some illustrations of these.
12 STEINER 1974, p. 124.
13 See Introduction to his *Quatuor pour la fin du temps* (1944).
14 Communication from a friend, 1969.
15 *A Separate Reality: the Teachings of Don Juan.*
16 See HAMMERSTEIN 1974, pp. 94ff., on the musical hell of Hieronymus Bosch.
17 Cf. the lowest circle of Dante's Inferno.
18 SIEGEL, p. 212.
19 VAUGHAN, p. 5.
20 PATCH, p. 3.
21 ROLLESTON, p. 47
22 BRENDAN, p. 21.
23 EVANS-WENTZ, pp. 85, 105f., 115, 129f.
24 Ibid., p. 205.
25 Ibid., p. 154.
26 PATCH, p. 34.
27 Ibid., p. 107.
28 Ibid., p. 35.
29 SPENCE, p. 29; PATCH, p. 45.
30 LEAHY, p. 72.
31 PATCH, p. 30.
32 SPENCE, p. 29.
33 PATCH, p. 45; MOAR, vol. III, p. 121.
34 PATCH, p. 30.
35 BRENDAN, pp. 43–6.
36 Ibid., pp. 50–52.
37 PATCH, p. 32.
38 Ibid., p. 35.
39 See especially CORBIN, pp. 51ff. Included in GODWIN 1986.
40 Ibid., p. 131.
41 Loc. cit.
42 Ibid., p. 134.
43 JUNG 1961, pp. 289f.
44 *Republic*, X, 614b–621d. Included in GODWIN 1986.
45 Ibid., 617b.
46 *Somnium Scipionis*, V, 1; see MACROBIUS, p. 73. Included in GODWIN 1986.
47 MACROBIUS, p. 74.
48 *On the Sign of Socrates*, 590. Included in GODWIN 1986.
49 Loc. cit.
50 Treatise no. 1 of the *Corpus Hermeticum*.
51 Ibid., sect. 26; see HERMES, p. 16. Included in GODWIN 1986.
52 JUNG CW, vol. 14, para. 308.
53 Loc. cit.
54 Commentary on Aristotle's *De Caelis*, as quoted in TAYLOR 1824, note to Hymn 34. Included in GODWIN 1986.
55 On this distinction, see GUÉNON 1984, ch. 1.
56 Information from an unpublished paper of my colleague Gary Urton.
57 Strabo 3, 1.
58 SHILOAH 1978, pp. 64f.

59 Tal. Bab. *Yoma* 20b, cited in SENDRY, p. 163.
60 Cited in Grimm, *Deutsche Märchen*, 703.
61 See GOULD, pp. 26ff.
62 From *Ritter Gluck*. Included in GODWIN 1986.
63 See KIRCHER 1656.
64 See NOHM, vol. III, p. 412.
65 ALLEN, pp. 30–33. Included in GODWIN 1986.
66 Quoted in ALVIN, p. 152.
67 Communication from a friend, 1984.
68 Unpublished letter to 'Bertrand', 27 November 1873, quoted in William Salloch's catalogue, Ossinning, New York, 1983.
69 MESSIAEN, p. 3.
70 A story I have heard from David Hykes and others.
71 IDELSOHN, p. 414, citing V.M. Teitelbaum, *The Rabbi of Ljdai*.
72 SHILOAH 1978, p. 64.
73 ROTHMULLER, p. 175.
74 BUBER, pp. 79f; punctuation altered.
75 NOHM, vol. I, p. 333n., quoting Rabbi Shneor Zalman.
76 WERNER, p. 170.
77 Eric Werner in NOHM, vol. I, p. 333.
78 IDELSOHN, pp. 420, 431; the music on p. 422.
79 BUBER, pp. 106f.
80 SHILOAH 1978, p. 58.
81 AL-GHAZĀLĪ, A.H., pp. 229ff.
82 AL-GHAZĀLĪ, M.D., p. 104. Included in GODWIN 1986.
83 AL-GHAZĀLĪ, A.H., pp. 729f. Included in GODWIN 1986.
84 CORBIN, p. 132.
85 Ibid., p. 133.
86 SUHRAWARDĪ, p. 72.
87 MESSIAEN, p. 10.
88 HUJWĪRĪ, p. 405.
89 CUMONT, p. 262.
90 MATTHESON, p. 3.
91 Ibid., p. 19.
92 Ibid., p. 6.
93 Ibid., pp. 74, 118f.
94 Suhrawardī, quoted in CORBIN, p. 131.
95 HAMMERSTEIN 1962, pp. 53ff.

96 From HAMMERSTEIN 1962, p. 56.
97 Ibid., p. 58.
98 AURELIAN, ch. 20. Included in GODWIN 1986.
99 ROLLE, ch. 3. Included in GODWIN 1986.
100 See HAMMERSTEIN 1962, pp. 60f.
101 See especially Cantos X, lines 64–81; XII, 1–9; XIII, 1–30.
102 SUSO, ch. 7. Included in GODWIN 1986.
103 See SHILOAH 1978, p. 60.
104 ZOHAR, vol. III, sect. 18b.
105 Ibid., sect. 46a.
106 Quoted in AL-GHAZĀLĪ, A.H., ch. 6.
107 See GUÉNON 1984, ch. 3.
108 Ibid., ch. 13.
109 *Republic*, X, 617b–c.
110 CHATEAUBRIAND, pp. 491–3. Included in GODWIN 1986.
111 Ibid., p. 494.
112 STEINER 1974, pp. 22ff. Included in GODWIN 1986.
113 TEILHARD, pp. 26f.
114 *On the Celestial Hierarchies*, ch. 10. Included in GODWIN 1986.
115 TOLKIEN, p. 15.
116 Loc. cit.
117 LEWIS, pp. 87f.

PART II: THE GREAT WORK

3 *Musical Alchemy* (p. 81)

1 STEINER 1974, p. 25.
2 Ibid., p. 26.
3 Ibid., p. 28.
4 PROUST, pp. 362f.
5 Ibid., pp. 363f.
6 Ibid., pp. 365f.
7 MAUCLAIR, p. 114.
8 Ibid., p. 89.
9 ABELL, pp. 13f.
10 Ibid., p. 86.
11 Ibid., p. 138.
12 Ibid., p. 122.
13 Ibid., p. 144.
14 Ibid., p. 162.
15 HICKMANN, p. 24.
16 *Symposium*, 210d–e.
17 See references in NGD under 'Sams, Eric'.
18 See HOWAT.

19 MICHELL 1981.

20 See especially his essays in GODWIN 1987.

21 LI CHI, XVII, III, 23.

4 Music and the Currents of Time (p. 96)

1 This was the theme of Marius Schneider's doctoral dissertation, SCHNEIDER 1934/5.

2 Quoted in STRUNK, p. 185.

3 PALLIS, p. 106.

4 I owe this summary to a lecture by John Onians at Colgate University, December, 1984.

5 See DONINGTON, passim.

6 LEVARIE & LEVY 1983, pp. 191f.

7 See GOSSMAN, pp. 319–27, and STEFFEN, pp. 108–22.

8 RAMEAU, p. 61.

9 ROUSSEAU, p. 308.

10 Ibid., p. 304.

11 Ibid., p. 303.

12 Ibid., pp. 323f.

13 GOSSMAN, p. 321.

14 STEFFEN, p. 119.

15 Ibid., p. 120.

16 STEINER 1977, p. 47.

17 *Republic*, III, 401c.

18 GODWIN 1974.

19 STRAWINSKY & CRAFT, pp. 147f.

20 Quoted in the *Newsletter of the Institute for Studies in American Music*, vol. XIII, no. 2. Reproduced here by kind permission of Elliott Carter.

21 See HUSMAN, summarized by R. Haase in GODWIN 1987.

22 See ASHTON.

23 The second of *Two Sonnets for Baritone, Clarinet, Viola, and Cello*, 1955.

24 In *Die Reihe*, vol. 2 (June, 1955), p. 7.

25 In his recording, *Hearing Solar Winds*, Ocora 558 607 (distributor Harmonia Mundi).

PART THREE: THE MUSIC OF THE SPHERES (p. 123)

1 Cf. IKHWĀN, p. 36.

2 *The Merchant of Venice*, V, i, 59.

3 From Pliny, *Natural History*, II, 19–20; Martianus Capella II, 169–99; Censorinus, XIII, 3–4; Theon of Smyrna, III, 15;

Achilles Tatios, XVII.

4 The classical stade varies between about 500 and 600 feet. For its use in geodesy, see MICHELL 1981, pp. 31–3.

5 See REINACH, pp. 440ff.

6 See transcription in ARISTEIDES, 20.

7 From FLUDD 1617b, p. 90; FLUDD 1623, pp. 314f.; HANDSCHIN 1927b, p. 201.

8 Reproduction in HANDSCHIN 1927b, p. 201.

9 From FLUDD 1617b, p. 90.

10 See any general or scientific encyclopedia under 'Bode's Law', 'Titius-Bode Law', or 'Planets'.

11 GOLDSCHMIDT, pp. 56f., 66.

12 HAASE 1974, pp. 113f. This essay also translated in GODWIN 1987.

13 The formula is: $p = (z - z_1)/(z_2 - z)$ where p = harmonic number to be obtained, z = given value, and z_1, z_2 = the limits.

14 See SCHMIDT, T., pp. 174–185; COLLIN, pp. 78–87; W. Kaiser, reported (and criticized) in KAYSER 1950, pp. 214–16; AZBEL, passim; Dénéréaz, reported in ROUSTIT, pp. 44–6.

15 JUNG & PAULI, pp. 60–94.

16 In MACROBIUS, pp. 73f.

17 BOETHIUS, I, 27.

18 See SHILOAH 1974, p. 199; IKHWĀN, pp. 45f.

19 Nicomachus *Excerpta*, pp. 33–4; *Encheiridion*, p. 7 Jan.

20 BRAGARD, p. 211.

21 See LEVIN, pp. 75ff.

22 See also the discussion in HAAR, pp. 130–4.

23 See AMMAN, plates 25–7, and GODWIN 1979, pp. 42–53.

24 *Roman History*, XXXVII, 18.

25 ROUSSIER, pp. 73ff.; FABRE 1973, p. 71; BAILLY, p. 17; BRITT, pp. 5ff., HENSCHEL, p. 303.

26 BRITT, p. 21.

27 Ibid., plate opposite p. 46.

28 BLAVATSKY, vol. V, pp. 432ff., 453ff.

29 Ibid., p. 432.

30 See PFROGNER, p. 643.

31 Ibid., pp. 134–9.

32 LANGE, vol. II, pp. 123ff.

33 Ibid., p. 122.
34 See WALKER, pp. 12–24.
35 RAMIS, III, 3.
36 BARTOLUS, pp. 110ff.
37 MACROBIUS, pp. 99–117.
38 *Timaeus*, 35c–36a.
39 Plutarch, *De anim. proc.*, 1028–9, as interpreted by HAAR, pp. 144–6.
40 PTOLEMY, III, 16.
41 Ptolemy, *Opera omnia*, ed. Heiberg, pp. 149–55; see Pauly-Wissowa, vol. 64 (1959), cols. 1818–23.
42 JAN, pp. 32–7.
43 ANATOLIUS, pp. 56, 196f. See HAAR, pp. 149f.
44 On the Ikhwān-al-Ṣafāʾ and their doctrines, see NASR, pp. 25–104.
45 IKHWĀN, pp. 45f.
46 See HANDSCHIN 1927a; MÜNXELHAUS, passim.
47 See ERIUGENA.
48 Ibid., fol. 9r.
49 Ibid., fol. 12r.
50 ANSELMI, p. 150.
51 There are five possible solid figures which fulfil the conditions of having identical sides containing and related by identical angles.
52 CASPAR, p. 63
53 Adapted from KEPLER 1619, p. 322; original notation also in WERNER 1973, p. 878.
54 *Harmony of the World*, LP 1571, Yale University School of Music.
55 CASPAR, p. 289.
56 HAASE 1974, p. 104; translated in GODWIN 1987.
57 Adapted from WARRAIN in HAASE 1974, pp. 104f.
58 Derived alternatively by four fifths (C, G, D, A, E, = 81) or a major third (C, E, = 80).
59 KEPLER 1596, pp. 39–43; translated in GODWIN 1987.
60 Based on table in HAASE 1951, p. 513.
61 Loc. cit.
62 CASPAR, p. 95.
63 KAYSER 1950, pp. 148–153.
64 PTOLEMY, III, 8; pitches given there as Greek names.

65 MCLAIN, p. 151.
66 KAYSER 1950, p. 255.
67 HENSCHEL, pp. 271ff.
68 Ibid., pp. 275ff.
69 See MCMULLIN.
70 The Rosicrucian Fellowship; the others are H. Spencer Lewis' AMORC and R. Swinburne Clymer's Fraternitas Rosae Crucis.
71 HEINDEL, p. 36.
72 *Mathnawī*, III, 3901.
73 HEINDEL, p. 51.
74 Ibid., p. 67.
75 HELINE 1965, p. 36.
76 Ibid., pp. 105f.
77 STEINER 1974, pp. 93f.
78 Ibid., p. 95.
79 Ibid., pp. 110f.
80 Ibid., p. 104.
81 LANGE, vol. II, p. 15.
82 Ibid., vol. II, p. 4.
83 SCHNEIDER 1946, pp. 144ff.; 1955, pp. 52ff. The latter book contains an expanded, German version of pp. 57–104 of the earlier, Spanish work. Since it is more accessible, I refer to it by preference.
84 SCHNEIDER 1955, p. 18.
85 ŚĀRṄGADEVA, p. 147.
86 SCHNEIDER 1955, p. 18.
87 SCHNEIDER 1946, pp. 121ff., 372; 1955, pp. 16f.
88 What follows is taken from SCHNEIDER 1960.
89 SCHNEIDER 1946, pp. 189ff., fig. 21.
90 Ibid., pp. 193f., fig. 24.
91 Ibid., p.202, figs. 34–6.
92 PLANCK, p. 112.
93 CIRLOT, pp. xxxii ff. and passim.
94 Quoted from *Lettres à Sophie* in CELLIER, p. 77.
95 COLLIN, p. xxi.
96 From HANDSCHIN 1927b.
97 *Convivio*, II, 6, lines 105ff.
98 ANSELMI, I, sects. 157–168.
99 MARTIANUS, sects. 27–8.
100 RAMIS, Tractate 3, ch. 3.
101 *Theogony*, lines 75–9.
102 *Commentary on the Republic*, trans. A.-J. Festugière, vol. 3, pp. 193ff.
103 LA BODERIE, fols. 85v–87r.

104 *Utriusque cosmi historia*, II, a, 1, p. 254.
105 Ibid., p. 93.
106 See Godwin 1979 for illustrations of many of these.
107 See McClain, pp. 57ff.
108 Ouspensky, p. 124.
109 Ibid., p. 131.
110 Ibid., p. 132.
111 Whone, pp. 43f.
112 Webb, p. 518.
113 See Bailly; Wellesz.
114 Cited in Bailly, p. 8, from Eusebius, *Praeparatio evangelica*.
115 Werckmeister, pp. 142f.
116 Ibid., pp. 146ff.
117 Quoted in Rivera, pp. 146f.
118 St-Martin, p. 508.
119 Ibid., pp. 27ff.
120 Ibid., pp. 512ff.
121 E.g. Vogel, pp. 19ff., and in many of his other works.
122 See Brentano 1959, letter of 28 May 1810. Included in Godwin 1987.
123 Brentano 1839, vol. I, p. 282.
124 See Kayser 1950, pp. 26f.
125 E.g. in Cowell, pp. 21ff.
126 *Commentary on Nicomachus' Arithmetic*; see Thimus, vol. I, p. 3.
127 Personal communication from Ernest McClain.
128 Guénon 1958, p. 69.
129 Kayser 1970, p. 150.
130 Ibid., p. 151.
131 Hymn VIII. Included in Godwin 1986.
132 See Brunton 1984, pp. 378–92.
133 Guénon 1984, p. 48.

Bibliography of Works cited

Abell: Arthur M. Abell, *Talks with Great Composers*, New York, Philosophical Library, [1955]

Albrecht: Johann Wilhelm Albrecht, *Tractatus physicus de effectibus musices in corpus animatum*, Leipzig, 1734

Alvin: Juliette Alvin, *Music Therapy*, New York, Basic Books, 1975

Amman: Peter J. Amman, 'The musical theory and philosophy of Robert Fludd', in *Journal of the Warburg and Courtauld Institutes*, vol. 30 (1967), pp. 198–227

Anatolius: Anatolius, *Theologumena arithmetika*, ed. G. Ast, Leipzig, 1817

Anderson: Warren D. Anderson, *Ethos and Education in Greek Music*, Cambridge, Mass., Harvard Univ. Press, 1966

Anselmi: Giorgio Anselmi, *De musica*, ed. G. Massera, Florence, Olschki, 1961

Aristeides: Aristeides Quintilianus, *On Music*, trans. Thomas Mathiesen, New Haven, Yale Univ. Press, 1983

Ashton: Dore Ashton, *A Fable of Modern Art*, London, Thames and Hudson, 1980

Aurelian: Aurelian of Réôme, *Musica disciplina*, trans. J. Ponte, Colorado Springs, Colorado College Music Press, 1968

Azbel: Azbel (Emile Chizat), *Harmonie des mondes: Loi des distances et des harmonies planétaires*, Paris, Hugues-Robert, 1903

Bailly: Edmond Bailly, *Le Chant des voyelles*, Nice, Bélisane, 1976

Bartolus: Abraham Bartolus, *Musica mathematica*, Altenburg, 1614

Balzac: Honoré de Balzac, *Séraphîta*, trans. Bell & Scott, Philadelphia, Gebbie, 1899

Blavatsky: H.P. Blavatsky, *The Secret Doctrine*, Adyar Edition, 6 vols., Adyar, Theosophical Publishing House, 1971

Boethius: Boethius, *The Principles of Music*, trans. Calvin M. Bower, Ph.D. diss., George Peabody College, 1967

Bragard: Roger Bragard, 'L'Harmonie des Sphères selon Boèce', in *Speculum*, vol. 4 (1929), pp. 206–13

Brendan: *The Voyage of Saint Brendan*, trans. J. O'Meara, Dublin, Dolmen, 1978

Brentano 1839: Bettina Brentano von Arnim, *Goethe's Correspondence with a Child*, London, 1839

Brentano 1959: Bettina Brentano von Arnim, *Goethes Briefwechsel mit einem Kind*, in *Werke und Briefe*, Frechen, Bartmann, 1959, vol. II

BRITT: Ernest Britt, *Gamme sidérale et gamme musicale, etude paléosophique*, Paris, Aux Ecoutes, 1924

BROCKLESBURY: Richard Brocklesbury, *Reflections on Ancient and Modern Music*, London, 1749

BROWNE: Richard Browne, *Medicina musica*, London, 1729

BRUNTON 1943: Paul Brunton, *The Wisdom of the Overself*, New York, Dutton, 1943

BRUNTON 1984: *The Notebooks of Paul Brunton: Perspectives*, Burdett, New York, Larson, 1984

BUBER: Martin Buber, *Hasidism and Modern Man*, ed. and trans. Maurice Friedman, New York, Horizon Press, 1958

CAGE: John Cage, *Silence*, Cambridge, Mass., MIT Press, 1961

CASPAR: Max Caspar, *Kepler*, trans. C. Doris Hellman, London, Abelard-Schuman, 1959

CELLIER: Leon Cellier, *Fabre d'Olivet*, Paris, Nizet, 1953

CENSORINUS: Censorinus, *De die natali*, ed. Otto Jahn, Berlin, 1847

CENSORSHIP: *Index on Censorship*, vol. 12, no. 1 (1983), special issue on music entitled 'Music is Dangerous'

CHASE: Mildred Portnoy Chase, *Just Being at the Piano*, Culver City, Calif., Peace Press, 1981

CHATEAUBRIAND: François-René de Chateaubriand, *Les Natchez*, in *Oeuvres complètes*, vol. III, Paris, 1834

CIRLOT: J.E. Cirlot, *A Dictionary of Symbols*, trans. Jack Sage, New York, Philosophical Library, 1962

COLLIN: Rodney Collin, *The Theory of Celestial Influence*, London, Watkins, 1980

COOMARASWAMY: Ananda K. Coomaraswamy, *The Dance of Siva*, New York, Noonday Press, 1957

CORBIN: Henry Corbin, *Spiritual Body and Celestial Earth*, Princeton Univ. Press, 1977

COWELL: Henry Cowell, *New Musical Resources*, New York, Knopf, 1930, repr. Something Else Press, 1969

CUMONT: Franz Cumont, *Recherches sur le symbolisme funéraire des Romains*, Paris, 1942

DÉNÉRÉAZ: Alexandre Dénéréaz, *La Gamme, ce problème cosmique*, Zurich, Hug, n.d.

DIONYSIUS: Dionysius the Areopagite, *The Mystical Theology and The Celestial Hierarchies*, trans. Editors of The Shrine of Wisdom, Brook, Surrey, Shrine of Wisdom, 1965

DONINGTON: Robert Donington, *The Rise of Opera*, London, Faber, 1981.

ERIUGENA: John Scotus Eriugena, Ms. Commentary on Martianus Capella, in Bodleian Library Ms. Auct. T. II. 19

EULER: Leonhard Euler, *Lettres à une princesse*, St Petersburg, 1739

EVANS-WENTZ: W.Y. Evans-Wentz, *The Fairy-Faith in Celtic Countries*, New York, Lemma, 1973 (reprint of O.U.P., 1911)

FABRE 1896: Antoine Fabre d'Olivet, *La Musique expliquée comme science et comme art . . .*, ed. Jean Pinasseau, Paris, Dorbon Aîné, 1928

FABRE 1915: Antoine Fabre d'Olivet, *Hermeneutic Interpretation of the Origin of the Social State of Man* [= *Histoire philosophique du genre humain*, 1824], trans. Nayán Louise Redfield, New York, Putnam, 1915

FABRE 1973: Antoine Fabre d'Olivet, *La Vraie Maçonnerie et la céleste culture*, Lausanne, La Proue, 1973

FICINO: Marsilio Ficino, *The Book of Life*, trans. Charles Boer, Irving, Texas, Spring Publications, 1980

FLUDD 1617a: Robert Fludd, *Tractatus apologeticus*, Leiden, 1617

FLUDD 1617b: Robert Fludd, *Utriusque cosmi . . . historia*, Oppenheim, 1617–21

FLUDD 1623: Robert Fludd, *Anatomiae amphitheatrum*, Frankfurt, 1623 (includes *Monochordum mundi*, 1621, pp. 287–331)

AL-GHAZĀLĪ, A.H.: Abū Ḥāmid al-Ghazālī, *The Book of the Laws of Listening to Music*, trans. Duncan B. Macdonald, in *Journal of the Royal Asiatic Society*, vol. 22 (1901), pp. 195–252, 705–748; vol. 23 (1902), pp. 1–28

AL-GHAZĀLĪ, M.D.: Majd ad-Dīn al-

Ghazālī, *Bawariq al-Ilma* (Treatise on Sufi Music and Dance), trans. in James Robson, *Tracts on Listening to Music*, London, Royal Asiatic Society, 1938, pp. 97–104

GODWIN 1974: Joscelyn Godwin, 'Protest and Quest in Popular Songs', in *The Golden Blade*, no. 26 (1974), pp. 96–105

GODWIN 1979: Joscelyn Godwin, *Robert Fludd, Hermetic Philosopher and Surveyor of Two Worlds*, London, Thames & Hudson, 1979

GODWIN 1982: Joscelyn Godwin, 'The Revival of Speculative Music', in *Musical Quarterly*, vol. 68 (1982), pp. 373–389

GODWIN 1986: Joscelyn Godwin, ed., *Music, Mysticism and Magic: a Sourcebook*, London, Routledge & Kegan Paul, 1986

GODWIN 1987: Joscelyn Godwin, ed., *Cosmic Music: Three Musical Keys to the Interpretation of Reality*, trans. M. Radkai, West Stockbridge, Mass., Lindisfarne Press, 1987

GOLDSCHMIDT: Victor Goldschmidt, 'Über Harmonie im Weltraum', in *Annalen der Naturphilosophie*, vol. 9 (1910), pp. 51–110

GOSSMAN: Lionel Gossman, 'Time and History in Rousseau', in *Studies on Voltaire and the Eighteenth Century*, vol. 30 (1964), pp. 311–49

GOULD: Rupert Gould, *Enigmas*, New York, University Books, 1965

GRAVES: Robert Graves, *The Greek Myths*, 2 vols., Hardmondsworth, Penguin, 1955

GUÉNON 1958: René Guénon, *The Symbolism of the Cross*, trans. Angus Macnab, London, Luzac, 1958

GUÉNON 1984: René Guénon, *The Multiple States of Being*, trans. Joscelyn Godwin, Burdett, New York, Larson, 1984

HAAR: James Haar, *Musica Mundana: Variations on a Pythagorean theme*, Ph.D. diss., Harvard Univ., 1960

HAASE 1951: Rudolf Haase, 'Musik und Astrologie', in *Musica*, vol. 5 (1951), pp. 511–3

HAASE 1974: Rudolf Haase, *Aufsätze zur harmonikalen Naturphilosophie*, Graz, Akademische Druck- und Verlagsanstalt, 1974

HAMMERSTEIN 1962: Reinhold Hammerstein, *Die Musik der Engel: Untersuchungen zur Musikanschauung des Mittelalters*, Bern and Munich, Francke, 1962

HAMMERSTEIN 1974: Reinhold Hammerstein, *Diabolus in Musica*, Bern and Munich, Francke, 1974

HANDSCHIN 1927a: Jacques Handschin, 'Die Musikanschauung des Johannes Scotus (Erigena)', in *Deutsche Vierteljahrschrift für Literaturwissenschaft und Geisteswissenschaft*, vol. 5 (1927), pp. 316–41

HANDSCHIN 1927b: Jacques Handschin, 'Ein mittelalterlicher Beitrag zur Lehre von der Sphärenharmonie', in *Zeitschrift für Musikwissenschaft*, vol. 9 (1927), pp. 193–208

HEINDEL: *The Musical Scale and the Scheme of Evolution*, compiled by a Student of Max Heindel, Oceanside, California, Rosicrucian Fellowship, 1970

HELINE 1965: Corinne Heline, *Music: The Keynote of Human Evolution*, La Canada, California, New Age Press, 1965

HELINE 1969: Corinne Heline, *The Cosmic Harp*, La Canada, California, New Age Press, 1969

HENSCHEL: Joan and Mary Henschel, *Van Chaos tot Harmonie*, Amsterdam, Strengholt, 1954

HERMES: *Corpus Hermeticum*, ed. A.D. Nock, trans. (French) A.-J. Festugière, 4 vols., Paris, Les Belles Lettres, 1946–54

HERODOTUS: Herodotus, *The Histories*, trans. A.D. Godley, Cambridge, Mass., Loeb edn., 1950

HICKMANN: H. Hickmann and W. Stauder, *Orientalische Musik*, Leiden, Brill, 1970

HODSON: Geoffrey Hodson, *Music Forms: Superphysical Effects of Music Clairvoyantly Observed*, Adyar, Theosophical Publishing House, 1979

HOWAT: Roy Howat, *Debussy in Proportion, a Musical Analysis*, Cambridge Univ. Press, 1983

HUJWĪRĪ: Ali ibn Usman Hujwīrī, *Kashf al-Mahjub* (*The Unveiling of the Veiled*), trans. R.A. Nicholson, London, 1911

HUSMANN: H. Husmann, *Vom Wesen der Konsonanz*, Heidelberg, 1953

IAMBLICHUS: Iamblichus, *The Life of Pythagoras*, trans. Thomas Taylor, London, 1818

IDELSOHN: A.Z. Idelsohn, *Jewish Music in its historical development*, New York, Henry Holt, 1929

IKHWĀN: *The Epistle on Music of the Ikhwān al-Ṣafāʾ* trans. Amnon Shiloah, Tel-Aviv University, 1978

JAN: Carl von Jan, 'Die Harmonie der Sphären', in *Philologus*, N.F. vol. 6 (1894), pp. 13–37

JENNY: Hans Jenny, *Kymatik*, 2 vols., Basel, 1967, 1974

JUNG 1961: C.G. Jung, *Memories, Dreams, Reflections*, New York, Pantheon, 1961

JUNG CW: C.G. Jung, *Collected Works*, trans. R.F.C. Hull, 20 vols., Princeton University Press (Bollingen Series). Cited is vol. 14 (*Mysterium conjunctionis*)

JUNG & PAULI: C.G. Jung and Wolfgang Pauli, *The Interpretation of Nature and the Psyche*, New York, Pantheon Books, 1955

KAYSER 1950: Hans Kayser, *Lehrbuch der Harmonik*, Zürich, Occident, 1950

KAYSER 1970: Hans Kayser, *Akróasis*, trans. Robert Lilienfeld, Boston, Plowshare Press, 1970

KEPLER 1596: Johannes Kepler, *Mysterium cosmographicum*, in *Gesammelte Werke*, ed. Caspar, vol. I (Munich, 1938)

KEPLER 1619: Johannes Kepler, *Harmonice mundi*, in *Gesammelte Werke*, ed. Caspar, vol. VI (Munich, 1940)

KIRCHER 1650: Athanasius Kircher, *Musurgia universalis*, facsimile of Rome, 1650 edn., Hildesheim, Olms, 1970

KIRCHER 1656: Athanasius Kircher, *Itinerarium exstaticum*, Rome, 1656

LA BODERIE: Guy Lefèvre de La Boderie, *La Galliade*, Paris, 1578

LANGE: Anny von Lange, *Mensch, Musik und Kosmos*, 2 vols. Freiburg i.Br., Die Kommenden, 1956, 1968

LEAHY: A.H. Leahy, *Heroic Romances of Ireland*, New York, Lemma, n.d. (reprint of London, 1905–6)

LEIBNIZ: G.W. von Leibniz, *Philosophical Papers and Letters*, trans. Leroy E. Loemker, 2 vols., Univ. of Chicago Press, 1956

LEVARIE & LEVY 1974: Siegmund Levarie and Ernst Levy, 'The Pythagorean Table', in *Main Currents in Modern Thought*, vol. 30 (1973), pp. 117–29

LEVARIE & LEVY 1983: Siegmund Levarie and Ernst Levy, *Musical Morphology: A Discourse and a Dictionary*, Kent State U.P., 1983

LEVIN: Flora R. Levin, *The Harmonics of Nicomachus and the Pythagorean Tradition*, University Park, Pa., American Philological Association, 1975

LEWIS: C.S. Lewis, *The Magician's Nephew*, New York, Macmillan, 1955

LI CHI: *The Lî Kî or Book of Rites*, trans. James Legge, *Sacred Books of the East*, vol. 28, Oxford, Clarendon Press, 1885

LOCKLEY: Ronald M. Lockley, *Whales, Dolphins and Porpoises*, Newton Abbot, David & Charles, 1979

MACROBIUS: Macrobius, *Commentary on the Dream of Scipio*, trans. William Harris Stahl, New York, Columbia Univ. Press, 1952

MARTIANUS: Martianus Capella, *The Marriage of Mercury with Philosophy*, trans. William Harris Stahl and Richard Johnson, with E.L. Burge, as Vol. II of *Martianus Capella and the Seven Liberal Arts*, New York, Columbia Univ. Press, 1977

MATTHESON: J. Mattheson, *Behauptung der Himmlischen Kunst aus den Gründen der Vernunft, Kirchen-Lehre und heiligen Schrift*, Hamburg, 1747

MAUCLAIR: Camille Mauclair, *La Religion de la musique et les héros de l'orchestre*, Paris, Fischbacher, [1938]

McCLAIN: Ernest G. McClain, *The Pythagorean Plato*, New York, Nicholas-Hays, 1978

McMULLIN: Michael McMullin, 'The Zodiac and the Twelve Tones of the Musical Scale', in *The Astrological Journal*, Spring, 1984

MESSIAEN: Olivier Messiaen, *Recherches et expériences spirituelles*, Notre-Dame de Paris, 4 Dec. 1977, Paris, Leduc, 1977

Bibliography

MEYER-BAER: Kathi Meyer-Baer, *Music of the Spheres and the Dance of Death*, Princeton Univ. Press, 1970

MGG: *Die Musik in Geschichte und Gegenwart*, ed. F. Blume, Kassel, Bärenreiter, 1955–

MICHELL 1967: John Michell, *The Flying Saucer Vision*, London, Sidgwick and Jackson, 1967

MICHELL 1981: John Michell, *Ancient Metrology*, Bristol, Pentacle Books, 1981

MOAR: *The Mythology of All Races*, 10 vols., Boston, Archaeological Institute of America, 1916–32

MÜNXELHAUS: Barbara Münxelhaus, 'Aspekte der Musica Disciplina bei Eriugena', in *Jean Scot Erigène et l'histoire de la Philosophie*, Paris, CNRS, 1977, pp. 253–262

NASR: Seyyed Hossein Nasr: *An Introduction to Islamic Cosmological Doctrines*, Boulder, Shambhala, and London, Thames and Hudson, 1978

NGD: *The New Grove Dictionary of Music and Musicians*, ed. S. Sadie, London, Macmillan, 1980

NOHM: *The New Oxford History of Music*, Oxford University Press, 1957–

NOVALIS: Novalis (Friedrich von Hardenberg), *Heinrich von Ofterdingen*, Stuttgart, Reclam, 1976

OUSPENSKY: P.D. Ouspensky, *In Search of the Miraculous*, New York, Harcourt, Brace & World, 1949

PALLIS: Marco Pallis, 'The Metaphysics of Musical Polyphony', in *Studies in Comparative Religion*, vol. 10, no. 2 (1976), pp. 105–8

PATCH: Howard Rollin Patch, *The Other World, According to Descriptions in Medieval Literature*, Cambridge, Mass., Harvard Univ. Press, 1950

PFROGNER: Hermann Pfrogner, *Lebendige Tonwelt*, 2nd rev. ed., Munich and Vienna, Langen Müller, 1981

PLANCK: Max Planck, *The Philosophy of Physics*, New York, Norton, 1936

PLINY: Pliny the Elder, *Natural History*, trans. H. Rackham, Cambridge, Mass., Harvard Univ. Press (Loeb edn.), 1979

PODOLSKY: Edward Podolsky, ed., *Music Therapy*, New York, Philosophical Library, 1954

PONTVIK: Aleks Pontvik, *Grundgedanken zur psychischen Heilwirkung der Musik*, Zürich, Rascher, 1948

PRIESTLEY: Mary Priestley, *Music Therapy in Action*, London, Constable, 1975

PROUST: Marcel Proust, *Swann's Way*, trans. C.K. Scott Moncrieff, New York, Heritage Press, 1954

PTOLEMY, *Harmonics*: Ingemar Düring, *Ptolemaios und Porphyrios über die Musik*, New York, Garland, 1980 (reprint of Göteborg, 1934)

RADHAKRISHNAN: S. Radhakrishnan, *Indian Philosophy* (Indian edn.). 2 vols., London, Allen and Unwin, 1940

RAMEAU: Jean-Philippe Rameau, *Nouvelles réflexions sur sa démonstration du principe de l'harmonie*, Paris, 1742, modern reprint by Broude, New York, 1975

RAMIS: Bartolomeo Ramis de Pareja, *Musica Practica*, Bologna, 1482, ed. J. Wolf, Wiesbaden, 1968

REINACH: Théodore Reinach, 'La Musique des Sphères', in *Revue des études grecques*, vol. 13 (1900), pp. 432–449

RETALLACK: Dorothy Retallack, *The Sound of Music and Plants*, Santa Monica, Calif., De Vorss, 1973

RISTAD: Eloise Ristad, *A Soprano on her Head*, Moab, Utah, Real People Press, 1982

RIVERA: Benito Rivera, *German Music Theory in the Early 17th Century: The Treatises of Johannes Lippius*, Ann Arbor, UMI Research Press, 1980

ROBINS: Don Robins, *Circles of Silence*, London, Souvenir Press, 1985

ROBINSON: Lytle W. Robinson, *The Great Pyramid and Its Builders: A Study of the Edgar Cayce Readings*, Virginia Beach, A.R.E. Press, 1958

ROBLEDO: Luis Robledo, 'Poesía y música de la tarántula', in *Poesía* (Madrid), no. 5–6, (1979–80), pp. 224–32

ROLLE: Richard Rolle of Hampole, *The Fire of Love*, trans. Richard Misyn, London, Early English Text Society, 1896 (orig. ser., no. 106)

ROLLESTON: T.W. Rolleston, *The High Deeds of Finn and other Bardic Romances of Ancient Ireland*, New York, Lemma, 1973 (reprint of London, 1910)

ROOLEY: Anthony Rooley, ' "I Saw My Lady Weepe": The First Five Songs of John Dowland's "Second Book of Songs" ', in *Temenos*, No. 2 (1982), pp. 197–216

ROTHMULLER: Aron Marko Rothmuller, *The Music of the Jews: an Historical Appreciation*, trans. H.S. Stevens, South Brunswick, N.J. Thomas Yoseloff, 1967

ROUSSEAU: Jean-Jacques Rousseau, *Examen de deux principes avancés par M. Rameau*, in *Escrits sur la Musique*, Paris, 1825 (= vol. 13 of *Oeuvres*), pp. 297–324

ROUSSIER: Pierre Joseph Roussier, *Mémoire sur la musique des Anciens*, Paris, 1770, reprinted New York, Broude, 1966

ROUSTIT: Albert Roustit, *La Prophétie musicale dans l'histoire de l'humanité*, Paris, Horvath, 1970

ST-MARTIN: Louis-Claude de Saint-Martin, *Des Erreurs et de la Vérité*, Edinburgh, 1775, reprinted n.p., Le Lis, 1979

ŚĀRṄGADEVA: *Saṅgīta-Ratnākara* of Śārṅgadeva, trans. and comm. by R.K. Shringy, vol. I, Delhi, Motilal Banarsidass, 1978

SAVOLD: David Savold, 'How do whales catch their dinner?', in *Science* 85, vol. 6, no. 4 (May 1985), p. 26

SCHMIDT, J.: Johann-Michael Schmidt, *Musico-Theologia, oder erbauliche Anwendung musikalischer Wahrheiten*, Bayreuth, 1754

SCHMIDT, T.: Thomas Michael Schmidt, *Musik und Kosmos als Schöpfungswunder*, Frankfurt, Verlag Thomas Schmidt, 1974

SCHNEIDER 1934/5: Marius Schneider, *Geschichte der Mehrstimmigkeit*, 2 vols., Berlin, Borntraeger, 1934/5

SCHNEIDER 1946: Marius Schneider, *El origen musical de los animales-símbolos en la mitología y la escultura antiguas*, Barcelona, Instituto español de musicología, 1946

SCHNEIDER 1948: Marius Schneider, *La danza de espadas y la tarantela; ensayo musicológico, etnográfico y arqueológico sobre los ritos medicinales*, Barcelona, Instituto español de musicología, 1948

SCHNEIDER 1955: Marius Schneider, *Singende Steine: Rhythmus-Studien an drei katalanischen Kreuzgängen romanischen Stils*, Kassel, Bärenreiter, 1955

SCHNEIDER 1960: Marius Schneider, 'Die musikalischen Grundlagen der Sphärenharmonie', in *Acta musicologica*, vol. 32 (1960) pp. 136–51

SCHNEIDER 1979: Marius Schneider, *Klangsymbolik in fremden Kulturen*, Vienna, Lafite, 1979 (trans. as 'Sound-Symbolism in Foreign Cultures' in GODWIN 1987)

SCHOPENHAUER: Arthur Schopenhauer, *The World as Will and Idea*, trans. R.B. Haldane and J. Kemp, 3 vols., Boston, Osgood, 1883

SCHULLIAN & SCHOEN: Dorothy M. Schullian and Max Schoen, eds., *Music and Medicine*, New York, Henry Schuman, 1948

SCOTT: Cyril Scott, *Music, its Secret Influence Throughout the Ages*, New York, Weiser, 1969 (reprint of 1959 revised edition)

SENDREY: Alfred Sendrey, *Music in the Social and Religious Life of Antiquity*, Rutherford, Fairleigh Dickinson U.P., 1974

SHILOAH 1974: Amnon Shiloah, 'Un ancien traité sur le ʿūd d'Abū Yūsuf al Kindī; traduction et commentaire', in *Israel Oriental Studies*, vol. 4 (1974), pp. 179–205

SHILOAH 1978: Amnon Shiloah, 'The Symbolism of Music in the Kabbalistic Tradition', in *World of Music* (Mainz), vol. 22 (1978), pp. 56–69

SIEGEL: Linda Siegel, *Music in German Romantic Literature: a Collection of Essays, Reviews and Stories*, Novato, California, Elra Press, 1983

SIGERIST: Henry E. Sigerist, 'The Story of Tarantism', in SCHULLIAN & SCHOEN, pp. 96–116

SINNETT: A.P. Sinnett, *The Pyramids and Stonehenge* [lectures given in 1892–3], London, Theosophical Publishing House, 1958

SPENCE: Lewis Spence, *The Magic Arts in Celtic Britain*, London, Rider, n.d.

STEBBING: Lionel Stebbing, ed., *Music Therapy: a New Anthology*, Horsham, Sussex, New Knowledge Books, 1975

STEFFANI: Agostino Steffani, *Quanta certezza habbia da suoi principii la musica*, Amsterdam, 1695

STEFFEN: Albert Steffen, *Krisis, Katharsis, Therapie im Geistesleben der Gegenwart*, Dornach, Verlag für schöne Wissenschaft, 1944

STEINER 1974: Rudolf Steiner, *Vom Wesen des Musikalischen*, edited and annotated by Ernst Hagemann, Freiburg i. Br., Die Kommenden, 1974

STEINER 1977: Rudolf Steiner, *Eurhythmy as Visible Music*, trans. V. and J. Compton-Burnett, London, Rudolf Steiner Press, 1977

STOCKHAUSEN: Karlheinz Stockhausen, *Texte zur Musik*, 4 vols., Cologne, DuMont Schauberg, 1963–76

STRAWINSKY & CRAFT: I. Strawinsky and Robert Craft, *Expositions and Developments*, New York, Doubleday, 1962

STREICH: Hildemarie Streich, 'Musik im Traum', in *Musiktherapeutische Umschau*, vol. I (1980), pp. 9–19

STRUNK: Oliver Strunk, *Source Readings in Music History*, New York, Norton, 1950

SUHRAWARDĪ: Suhrawardī, *Epistle on the State of Childhood*, trans. S.H. Nasr, in *Temenos*, no. 4 (1984), pp. 53–76

SUSO: *The Life of Blessed H. Suso, by Himself*, trans. T.F. Knox, London, 1865

TAYLOR: Thomas Taylor, *The Mystical Hymns of Orpheus*, 2nd ed., London, 1824

TEILHARD: Pierre Teilhard de Chardin, *Hymn of the Universe*, trans. Simon Bartholomew, New York, Harper and Row, 1965

THEON: Theon of Smyrna, *Mathematics Useful for Understanding Plato*, trans. J. Dupuis and R. and D. Lawlor, San Diego, Wizard's Bookshelf, 1979

THIMUS: Albert von Thimus, *Die harmonikale Symbolik des Alterthums*, 2 vols., Cologne, 1868, 1876, repr. Hildesheim, Olms, 1972

THORNDIKE: Lynn Thorndike, *A History of Magic and Experimental Science*, 8 vols., New York, Columbia Univ. Press, 1923–58

TOLKIEN: J.R.R. Tolkien, *The Silmarillion*, London, Allen and Unwin, 1977

TOMPKINS & BIRD: Peter Tompkins and Christopher Bird, *The Secret Life of Plants*, New York, Harper and Row, 1973

TYARD: Pontus de Tyard, *Solitaire Seconde*, 1555, in his *Discours Philosophiques*, Paris, 1587

VAUGHAN: *The Magical Writings of Thomas Vaughan (Eugenius Philalethes)*, ed. A.E. Waite, London, 1888, reprinted Mokelumne Hill, California, Health Research, 1974

VOGEL: Martin Vogel, *Die Zukunft der Musik*, Düsseldorf, Ges. zur Förderung der systematischen Musikwissenschaft, 1968

VYSE: Howard Vyse, *Operations Carried On at the Pyramid of Gizeh in 1837 . . .*, 2 vols., London, 1840

WALKER: D.P. Walker, *Spiritual and Demonic Magic from Ficino to Campanella*, Notre Dame and London, Univ. of Notre Dame Press, 1975

WARRAIN: Francis Warrain, *Essai sur l'Harmonices Mundi ou Musique du Monde de Johann Kepler*, 2 vols., Paris, 1942

WEBB: James Webb, *The Harmonious Circle*, London, Thames and Hudson, 1980

WELLESZ: Egon Wellesz, 'Music in the Treatises of Greek Gnostics and Alchemists', in *Ambix*, vol. 4 (1951), pp. 145–158

WERCKMEISTER: Andreas Werckmeister, *Musicae mathematicae hodegus curiosus*, Frankfurt and Leipzig, 1687, reprinted Hildesheim, Olms, 1972

WERNER 1959: Eric Werner, *The Sacred Bridge*, New York, Columbia Univ. Press, 1959

WERNER 1973: Eric Werner, 'The Last Pythagorean Musician: Johannes Kepler', in *Aspects of Medieval and Renaissance Music: Essays presented to Gustave Reese*, New York, Norton, 1973

WHONE: Herbert Whone, *The Hidden Face of Music*, London, Gollancz, 1974

ZOHAR: *The Zohar*, trans. Harry Sperling and Maurice Simon, 5 vols., London and Bournemouth, Soncino Press, 1949

205

Index

Index

Grieg, Edvard 85
Guénon, René 74, 98, 192–3
Guido d'Arezzo 182
Gurdjieff, George I. 167, 180–2

Haase, Rudolf 7, 149–50, 152
Hagemann, Ernst 48–9, 158–60
Handschin, Jacques 126–7
harmonic series 146, 178, 184–92
harmonics, science of 190
Harmony 23; and hierarchy 41;
  as focus of listening 93; in
  Chinese philosophy 40; of
  Angelic Hierarchies 76–7; of
  highest world 76; term for the
  planetary spheres 58; universal
  41; versus melody 107–9
Heaven 71; and Earth 40, 122,
  166
Heindel, Max 156–8
Heline, Corinne 156–8
Heliocentricity 59–60
Hell, music of 51
Henschel, Joan & Mary 133,
  154–5
Herbert, George 18
Hermes 11, 16
Hermes Trismegistus,
  Hermeticism 18, 24, 57, 85, 96,
  105, 171, 176, 182
Herodotus 20
Hesiod 169
Hinduism 14, 69–70, 73, 92, 98,
  110, 134, 137, 161
Hoffmann, E.T.A. 61
Holst, Gustav 156
Hopkins, Gerard Manley 119
Hūrqalyā 56
Huxley, Aldous 50
Hykes, David 121–2

Iamblichus 31, 190
Ikhwān al-Ṣafā᾽, see Brethren of
  Purity
Imaginal World 56–7, 71
Imagination, World of the 56
India 31, 43–4, 100
insanity 51–2
inspiration: described by
  composers 84–5, 116; in
  modern age 110, 116; levels of
  85–7
Ireland, legends of 46–7, 52–5
Islam 23, 56, 67, 74, 137, 140

Jacques de Liège 101
Jan, Carl von 138, 139
jazz 113
Jenny, Hans 16
Judaism 60, 64, 65, 66, 73, 74
Jung, C.G., Jungian psychology
  56–8, 117, 129, 167

Kabbalah, Kabbalists, 64–6, 73–
  4, 170, 175
Kaiser, W. 129
Kayser, Hans 152, 154, 190–3
Kepler, Johannes 60, 143–9, 154,
  166
keys and zodiacal signs 157–60
al-Kindi 131
Kircher, Athanasius 16, 23–4, 61,
  182
Kleist, Heinrich von 51

Lambdoma 189–191
Landini, Francesco 101
Lange, Anny von 135–6, 154,
  180
Lauer, Hans Erhard 7
Le Jeune, Claude 31
Lefèvre de la Boderie, Guy 170
Leibniz, G.W. von 26
Leonardo da Vinci 81, 103–4
Leonin 100
Levarie, Siegmund 106, 191
Levy, Ernst 106, 191
Lewis, C.S. 77–8
Li Chi (Book of Rites) 40–2, 94
liberation 74, 95
Lippius, Johannes 185
listener, listening 87–92, 122
Logos 77, 145

Machaut, Guillaume de 91, 101
Macrobius 70, 130, 137
Mannerism 102
Mao Tse-tung 41
Martianus Capella 16, 23, 126,
  141, 169
Marx, Karl, Marxism 30, 112
Mass 55, 71, 83
Matheson, Johann 71
Mauclair, Camille 84
McClain, Ernest 153
McMullin, Michael 155–6
means 176–80
meditation 34, 92, 121
melancholy 25, 32–3, 37
melody 93, 107–9
Memnon, cry of 61
memory and inspiration 82, 87
Mersenne, Marin 13
Messiaen, Olivier 50, 63, 69,
  115, 117
metaphysical Zero (0/0) 192–3
Michael, Archangel 54
Michell, John 92
Microcosm 60, 74
mind-body connection 27–8
modes: church 136, 181; effects
  of 42; Greek 42, 125–6, 132–4,
  136, 181; planetary 125–6, 137
monochord 127, 178; cosmic
  173–6; zodiac as 148, 150

Moscato, Rabbi 60
Mozart, W.A. 50, 109
Muses 16, 82, 169–70
music: an aid to labour 88–9;
  and ceremonies 40; as
  psychopomp 61–2; avant-garde
  119–22; baroque 105–7; body-
  90; chance 119; classic period
  106–9; head- 90–91; heart- 90–
  91, 93; in politics 40–41;
  instrumental, purity of 106,
  112; medieval 99–102;
  perceived unconsciously 88;
  popular 113–15; Renaissance
  102–4; visceral 88
music therapy 34–40
Muzak 88–9
mystics, inner music of 72–3

Names of God 170
nationalism in music 113
New Age 43, 115
Nicomachus of Gerasa 131–2
Nordoff, Paul 40
Notre-Dame, School of 100
Nous (see also Spirit) 25, 176
Novalis (Friedrich von
  Hardenberg) 15–16, 19–20

Offices 30, 55, 63
opera 105–6, 111
Organum 100
Orpheus 11, 16, 18, 24, 104, 115
Otherworld, the 52–6
Ouspensky, P.D. 167, 180–2
overtones, see harmonics

Pallis, Marco 102–3
Paracelsus, Theophrastus, 17,
  47–8
Paradise 53, 55
Patch, Howard 52
performer, role of 83
Perotin 85, 100
Peruvian legends 60
Pfrogner, Hermann 135
Philip V 32–3
Philippe de Vitry 101
plainchant 62–4, 69, 86–7, 100–1
Planck, Max 166
planets 58, 125–48; and angels
  168–173; angular velocities of
  144–7; astrological properties of
  140; mean distances from sun
  127–8; movements of 124, 131,
  142–4; music on other 84;
  outer 146–7; polyphony of
  142–6; songs of 145
plants and music 16–19
Plato 43–4, 98, 133; Laws 42;
  Republic 42, 74–5, 113–114,
  125; Symposium 87; Timaeus 29,

207